Foxes in Love
Volume 1

by Toivo Kaartinen

FENRIS
™

FOXES IN LOVE: VOLUME 1

Published by Fenris Publishing
Flagstaff, Arizona
https://www.fenrispublishing.com

ISBN 978-0-9995916-4-2
Printed in the United States, United Kingdom, or Australia
First trade paperback edition: November 2020

Cover and interior art by Toivo Kaartinen

For my partner, my blue fox, the moon of my life.

TOIVO KAARTINEN

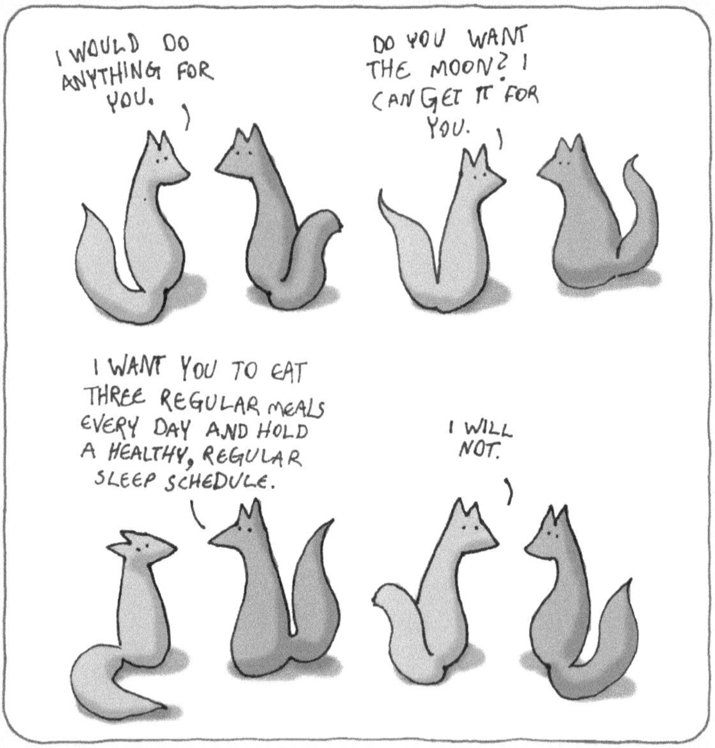
I WOULD DO ANYTHING FOR YOU.
DO YOU WANT THE MOON? I CAN GET IT FOR YOU.
I WANT YOU TO EAT THREE REGULAR MEALS EVERY DAY AND HOLD A HEALTHY, REGULAR SLEEP SCHEDULE.
I WILL NOT.

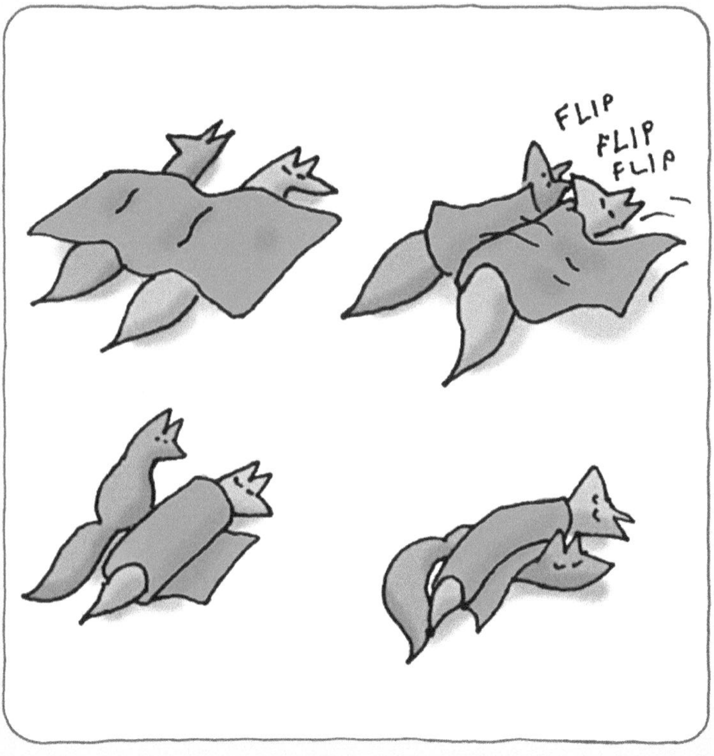
FLIP
FLIP
FLIP

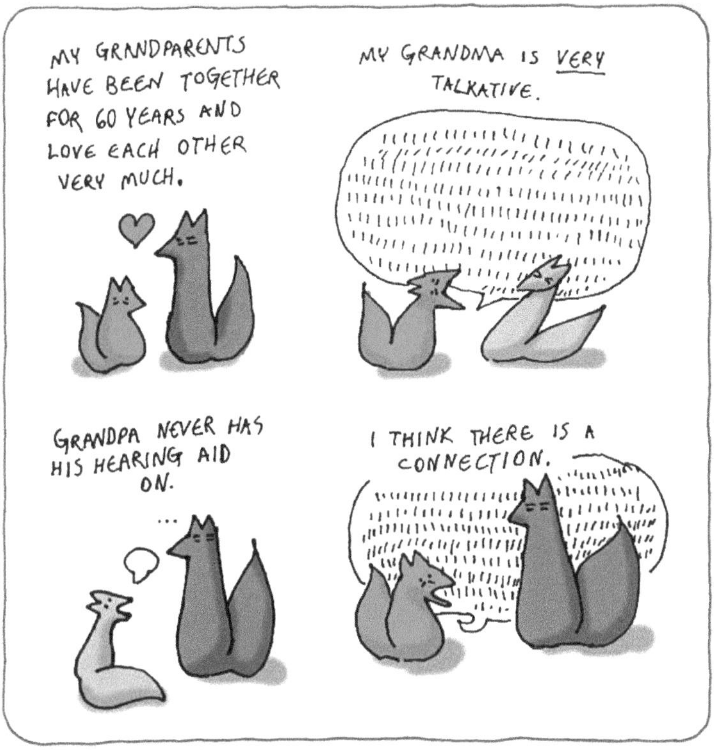
MY GRANDPARENTS HAVE BEEN TOGETHER FOR 60 YEARS AND LOVE EACH OTHER VERY MUCH.
MY GRANDMA IS VERY TALKATIVE.
GRANDPA NEVER HAS HIS HEARING AID ON.
...
I THINK THERE IS A CONNECTION.

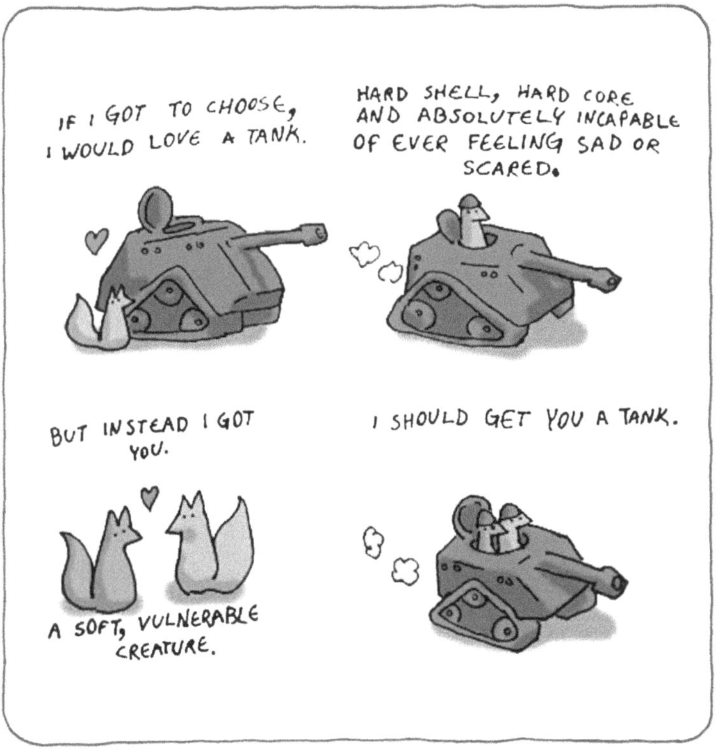
IF I GOT TO CHOOSE, I WOULD LOVE A TANK.
HARD SHELL, HARD CORE AND ABSOLUTELY INCAPABLE OF EVER FEELING SAD OR SCARED.
BUT INSTEAD I GOT YOU.
A SOFT, VULNERABLE CREATURE.
I SHOULD GET YOU A TANK.

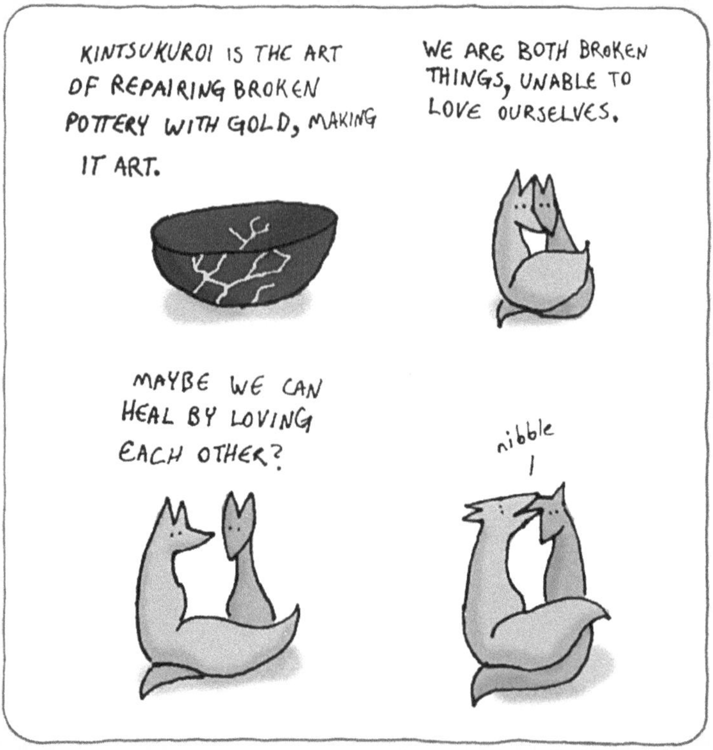
KINTSUKUROI IS THE ART OF REPAIRING BROKEN POTTERY WITH GOLD, MAKING IT ART.
WE ARE BOTH BROKEN THINGS, UNABLE TO LOVE OURSELVES.
MAYBE WE CAN HEAL BY LOVING EACH OTHER?
nibble

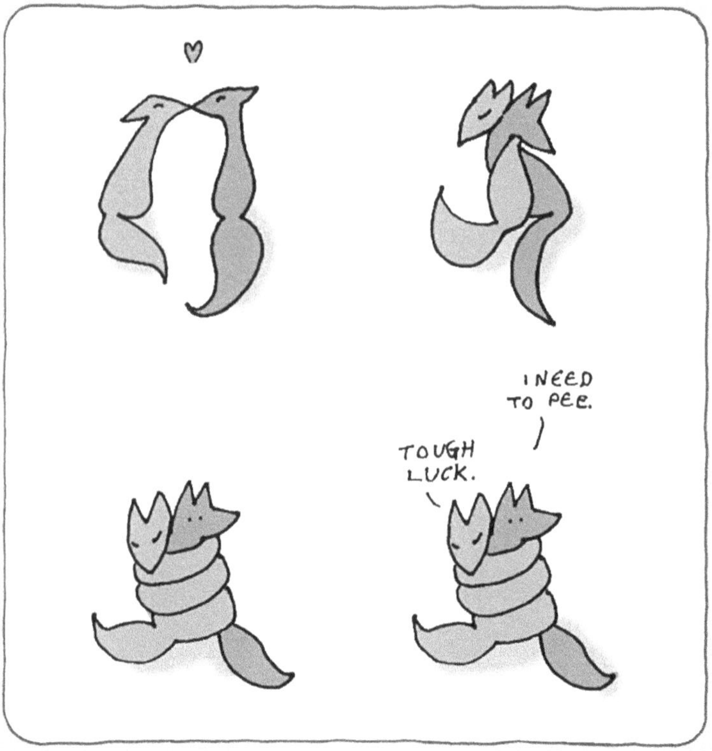
I NEED TO PEE.
TOUGH LUCK.

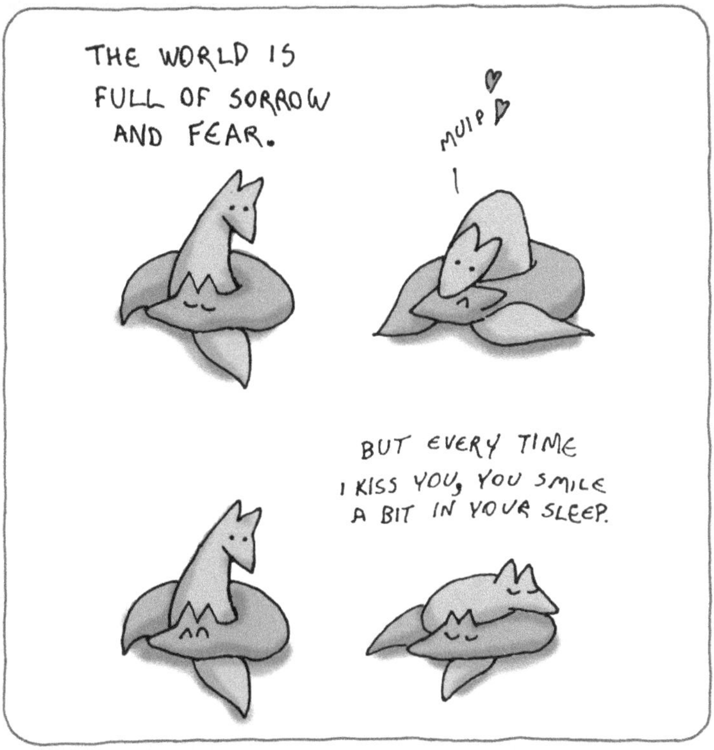
THE WORLD IS FULL OF SORROW AND FEAR.
MUIP
BUT EVERY TIME I KISS YOU, YOU SMILE A BIT IN YOUR SLEEP.

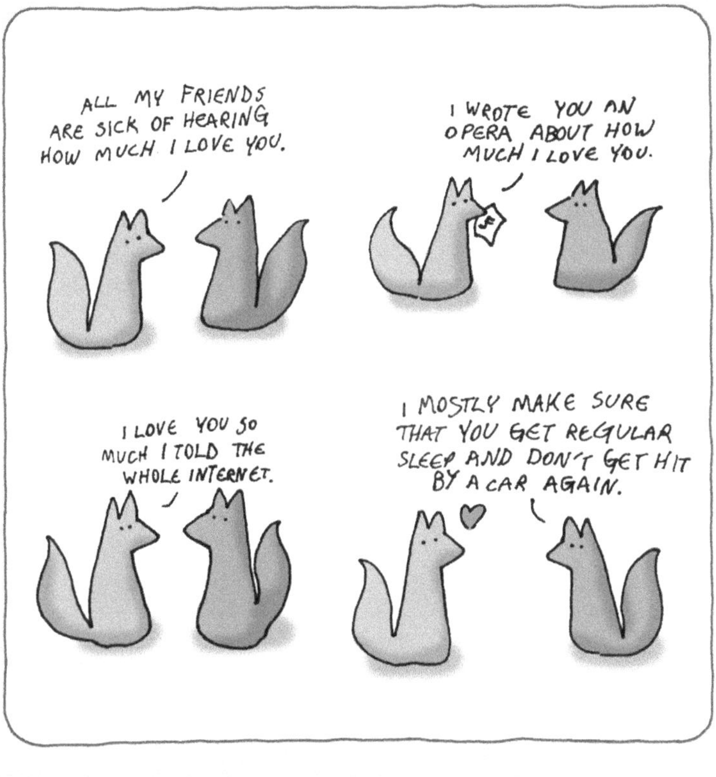
ALL MY FRIENDS ARE SICK OF HEARING HOW MUCH I LOVE YOU.
I WROTE YOU AN OPERA ABOUT HOW MUCH I LOVE YOU.
I LOVE YOU SO MUCH I TOLD THE WHOLE INTERNET.
I MOSTLY MAKE SURE THAT YOU GET REGULAR SLEEP AND DON'T GET HIT BY A CAR AGAIN.

TOIVO KAARTINEN

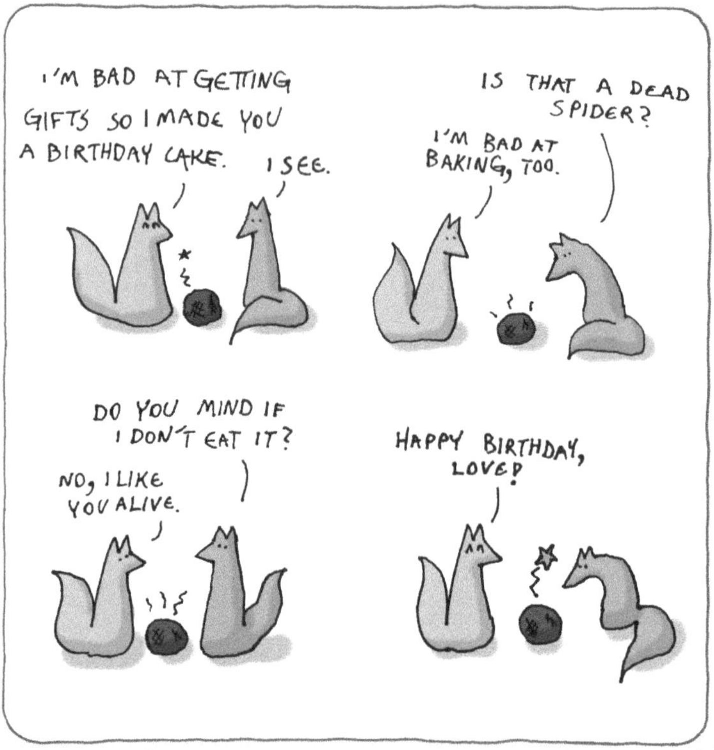
I'M BAD AT GETTING GIFTS SO I MADE YOU A BIRTHDAY CAKE.
I SEE.
I'M BAD AT BAKING, TOO.
IS THAT A DEAD SPIDER?
DO YOU MIND IF I DON'T EAT IT?
NO, I LIKE YOU ALIVE.
HAPPY BIRTHDAY, LOVE!

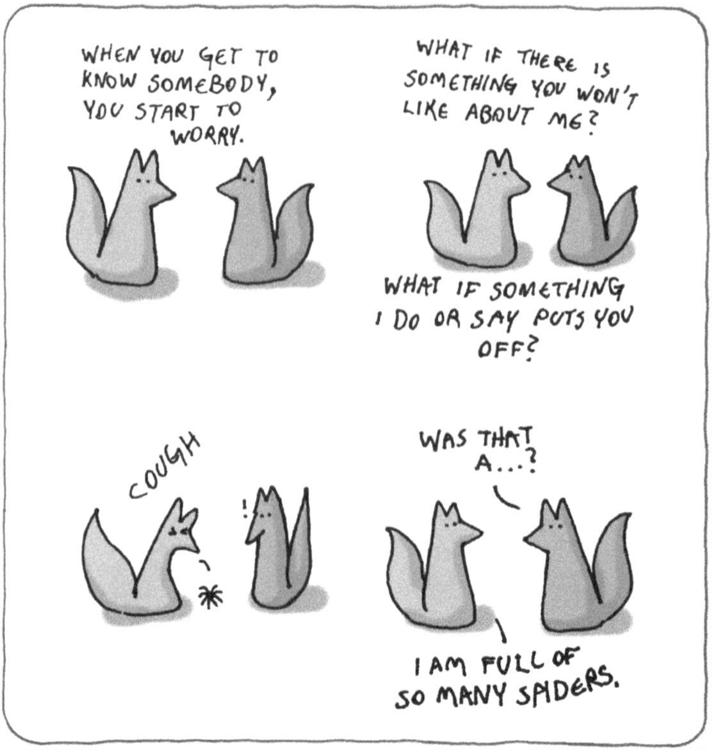
WHEN YOU GET TO KNOW SOMEBODY, YOU START TO WORRY.
WHAT IF THERE IS SOMETHING YOU WON'T LIKE ABOUT ME?
WHAT IF SOMETHING I DO OR SAY PUTS YOU OFF?
COUGH
!
WAS THAT A...?
I AM FULL OF SO MANY SPIDERS.

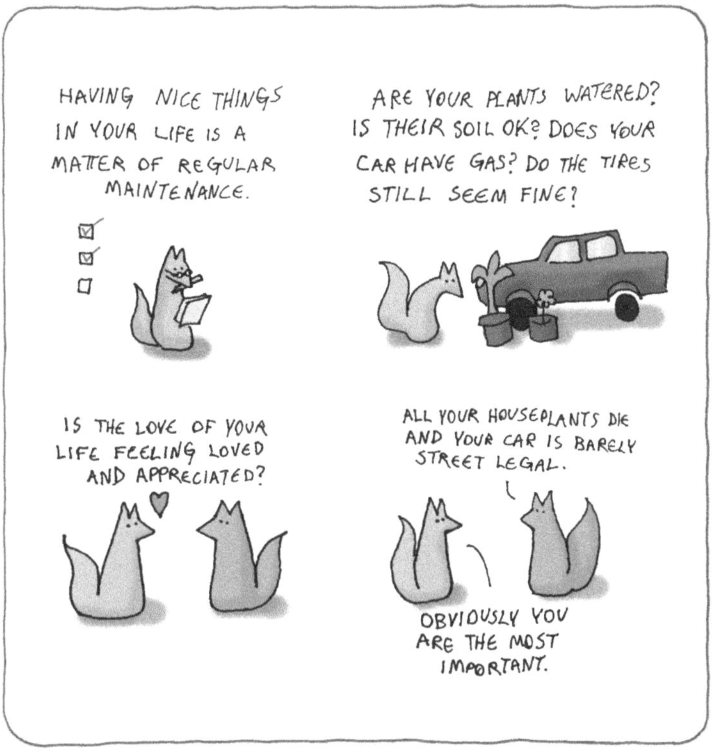
HAVING NICE THINGS IN YOUR LIFE IS A MATTER OF REGULAR MAINTENANCE.
ARE YOUR PLANTS WATERED? IS THEIR SOIL OK? DOES YOUR CAR HAVE GAS? DO THE TIRES STILL SEEM FINE?
IS THE LOVE OF YOUR LIFE FEELING LOVED AND APPRECIATED?
ALL YOUR HOUSEPLANTS DIE AND YOUR CAR IS BARELY STREET LEGAL.
OBVIOUSLY YOU ARE THE MOST IMPORTANT.

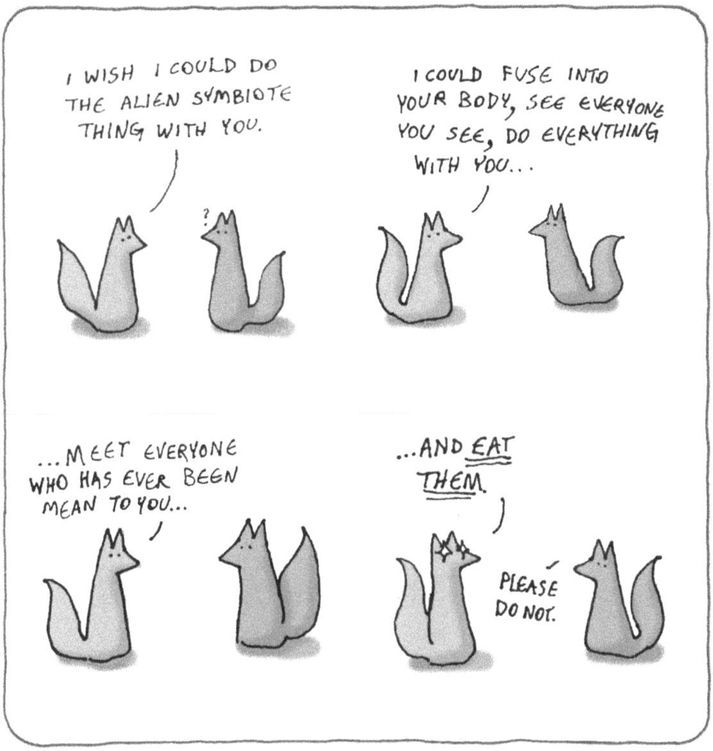
I WISH I COULD DO THE ALIEN SYMBIOTE THING WITH YOU.
?
I COULD FUSE INTO YOUR BODY, SEE EVERYONE YOU SEE, DO EVERYTHING WITH YOU...
...MEET EVERYONE WHO HAS EVER BEEN MEAN TO YOU...
...AND EAT THEM.
PLEASE DO NOT.

TOIVO KAARTINEN

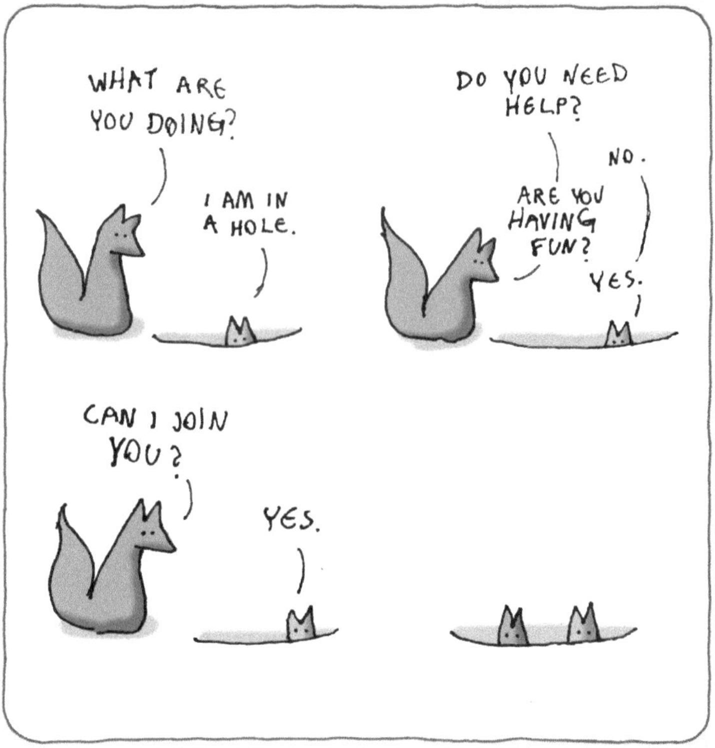
WHAT ARE YOU DOING?
I AM IN A HOLE.
DO YOU NEED HELP?
NO.
ARE YOU HAVING FUN?
YES.
CAN I JOIN YOU?
YES.

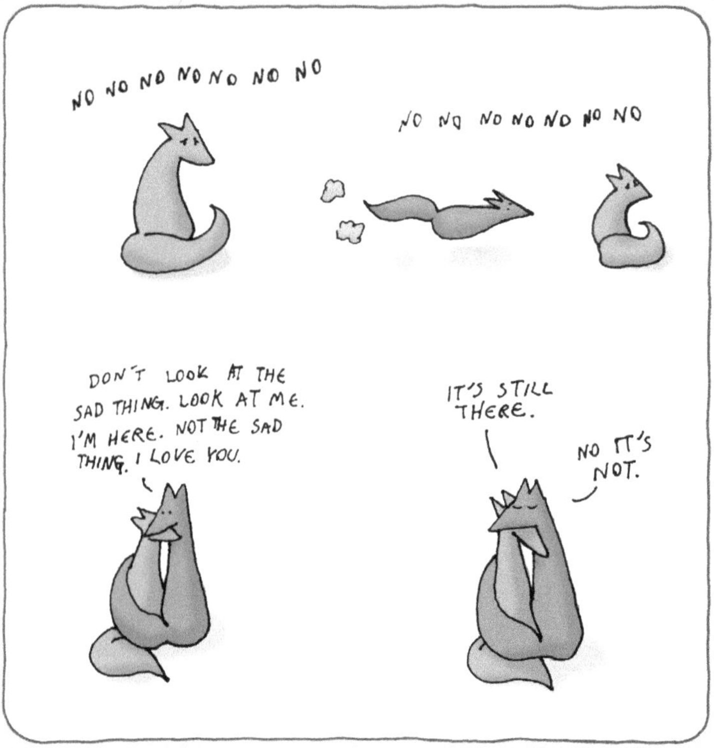
NO NO NO NO NO NO NO
NO NO NO NO NO NO NO
DON'T LOOK AT THE SAD THING. LOOK AT ME. I'M HERE. NOT THE SAD THING. I LOVE YOU.
IT'S STILL THERE.
NO IT'S NOT.

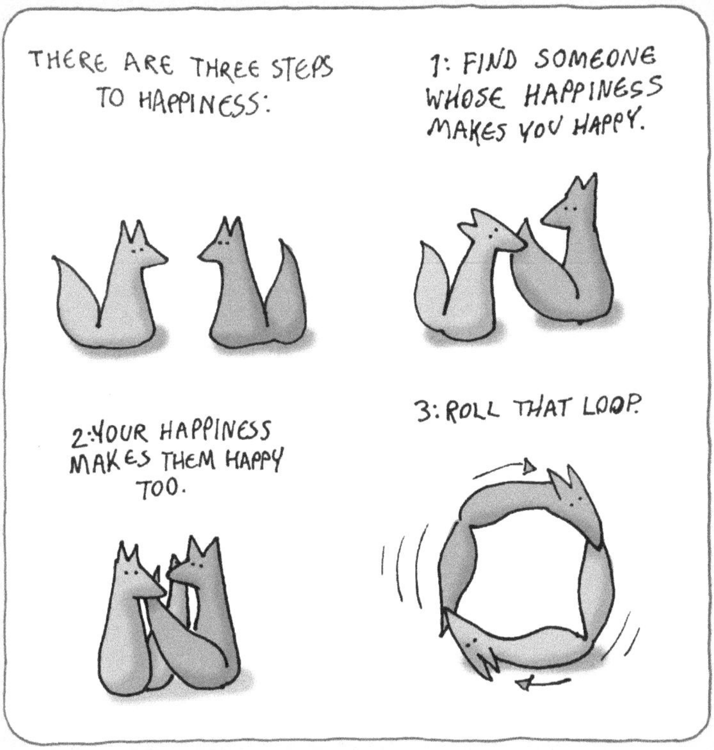
THERE ARE THREE STEPS TO HAPPINESS:
1: FIND SOMEONE WHOSE HAPPINESS MAKES YOU HAPPY.
2: YOUR HAPPINESS MAKES THEM HAPPY TOO.
3: ROLL THAT LOOP.

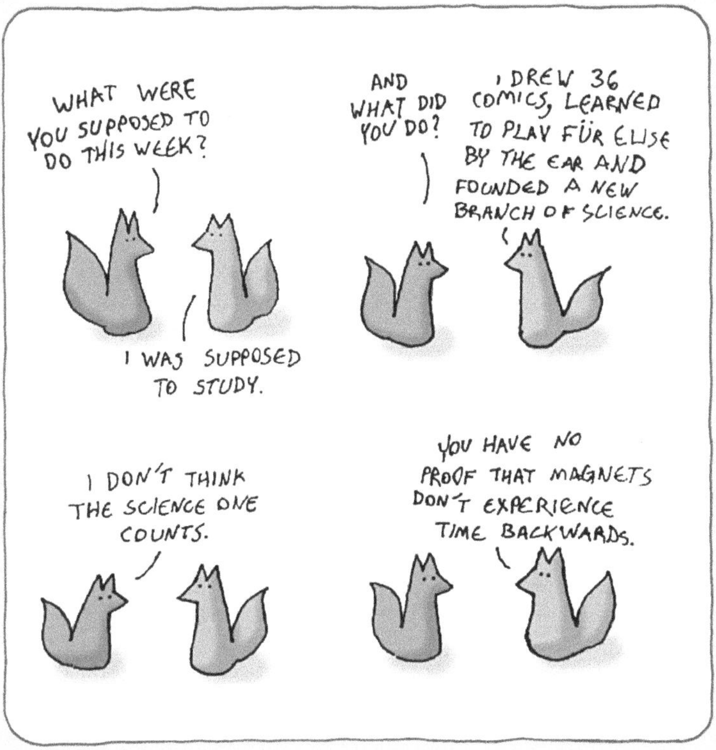
WHAT WERE YOU SUPPOSED TO DO THIS WEEK?
I WAS SUPPOSED TO STUDY.
AND WHAT DID YOU DO?
I DREW 36 COMICS, LEARNED TO PLAY FÜR ELISE BY THE EAR AND FOUNDED A NEW BRANCH OF SCIENCE.
I DON'T THINK THE SCIENCE ONE COUNTS.
YOU HAVE NO PROOF THAT MAGNETS DON'T EXPERIENCE TIME BACKWARDS.

TOIVO KAARTINEN

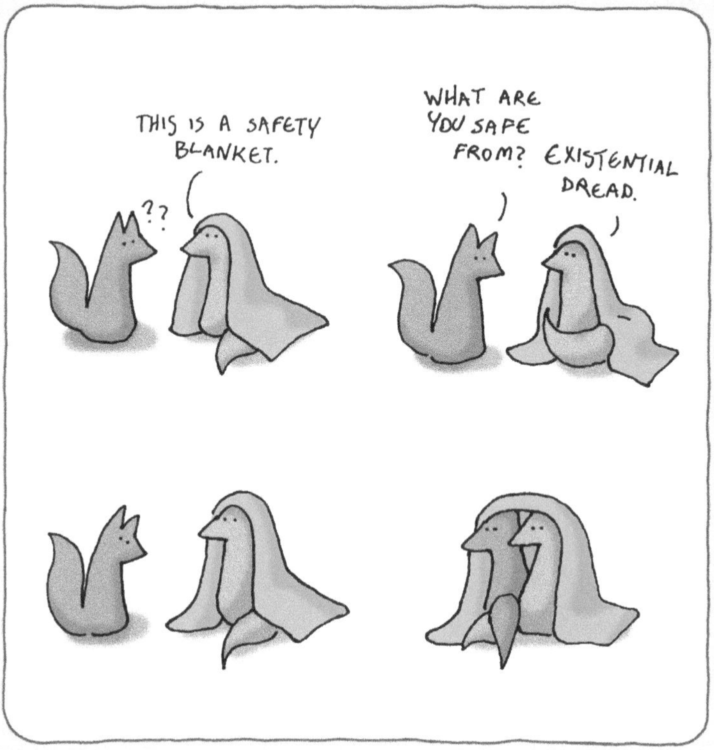
THIS IS A SAFETY BLANKET.
??
WHAT ARE YOU SAFE FROM?
EXISTENTIAL DREAD.

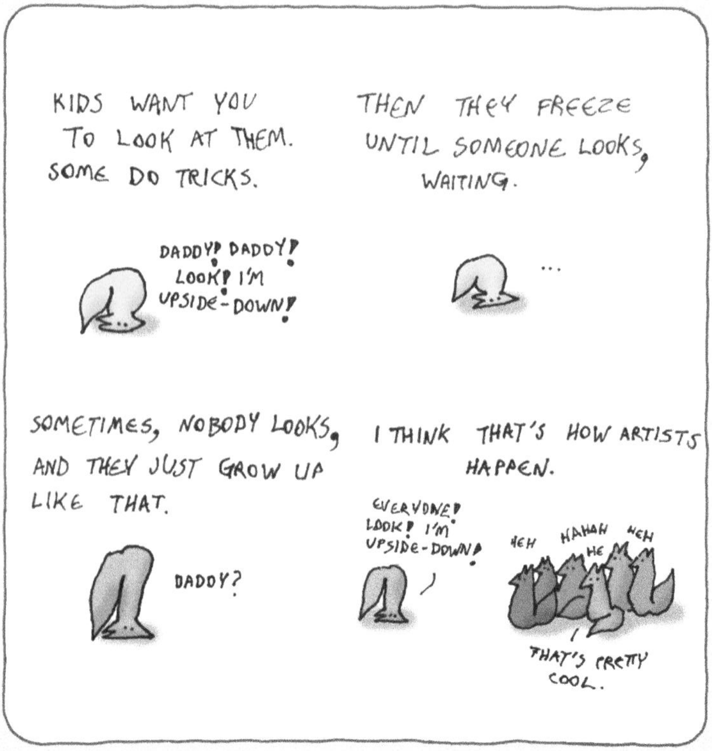
KIDS WANT YOU TO LOOK AT THEM. SOME DO TRICKS.
DADDY! DADDY! LOOK! I'M UPSIDE-DOWN!
THEN THEY FREEZE UNTIL SOMEONE LOOKS, WAITING.
...
SOMETIMES, NOBODY LOOKS, AND THEY JUST GROW UP LIKE THAT.
DADDY?
I THINK THAT'S HOW ARTISTS HAPPEN.
EVERYONE! LOOK! I'M UPSIDE-DOWN!
HEH HAHAH HE HEH
THAT'S PRETTY COOL.

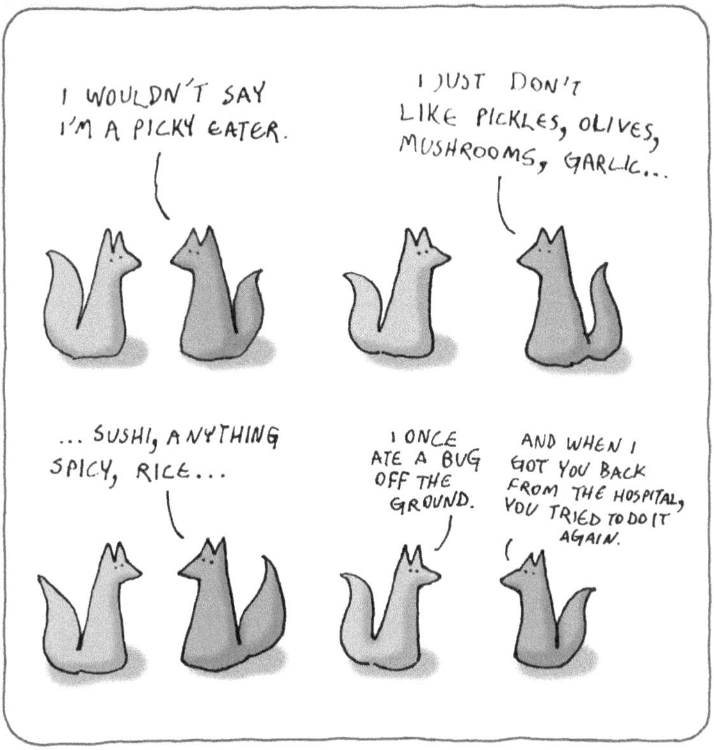
I WOULDN'T SAY I'M A PICKY EATER.
I JUST DON'T LIKE PICKLES, OLIVES, MUSHROOMS, GARLIC...
... SUSHI, ANYTHING SPICY, RICE...
I ONCE ATE A BUG OFF THE GROUND.
AND WHEN I GOT YOU BACK FROM THE HOSPITAL, YOU TRIED TO DO IT AGAIN.

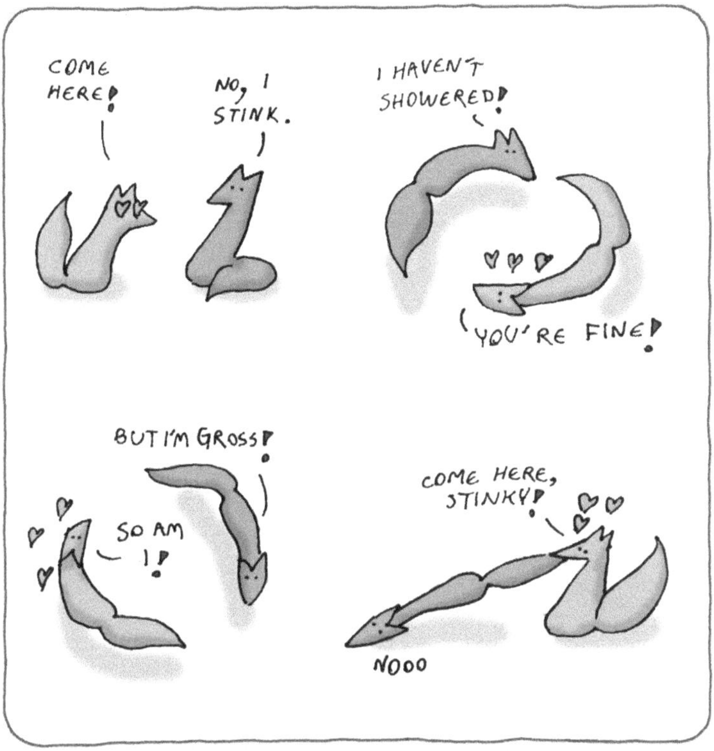
COME HERE!
NO, I STINK.
I HAVEN'T SHOWERED!
YOU'RE FINE!
BUT I'M GROSS!
SO AM I!
COME HERE, STINKY!
NOOO

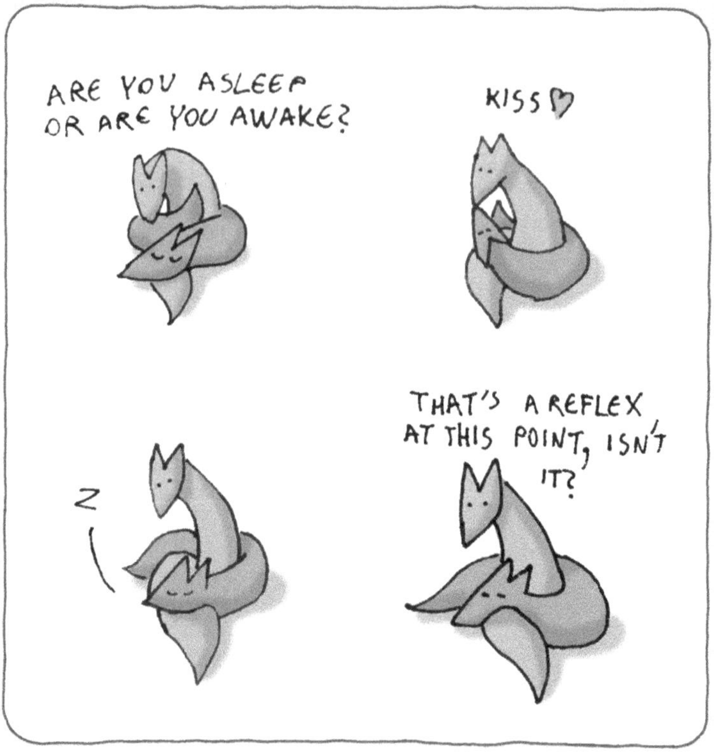
ARE YOU ASLEEP
OR ARE YOU AWAKE?
KISS ♡
Z
THAT'S A REFLEX
AT THIS POINT, ISN'T
IT?

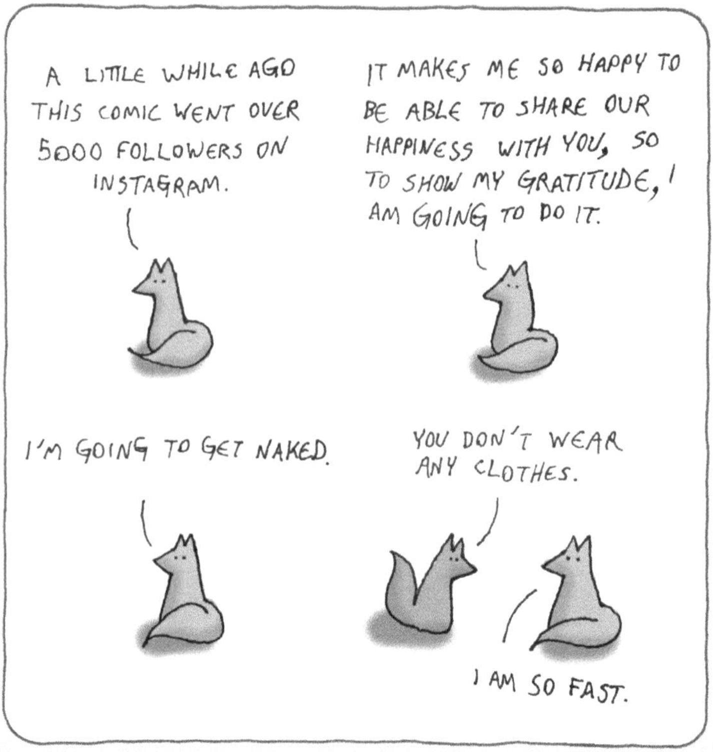
A LITTLE WHILE AGO
THIS COMIC WENT OVER
5000 FOLLOWERS ON
INSTAGRAM.
IT MAKES ME SO HAPPY TO
BE ABLE TO SHARE OUR
HAPPINESS WITH YOU, SO
TO SHOW MY GRATITUDE, I
AM GOING TO DO IT.
I'M GOING TO GET NAKED.
YOU DON'T WEAR
ANY CLOTHES.
I AM SO FAST.

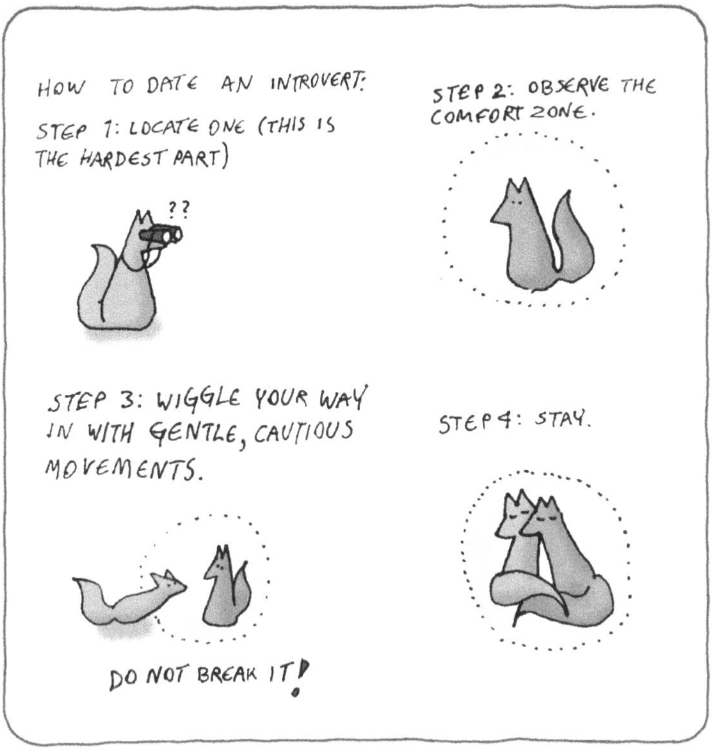
HOW TO DATE AN INTROVERT:
STEP 1: LOCATE ONE (THIS IS THE HARDEST PART)
??
STEP 2: OBSERVE THE COMFORT ZONE.
STEP 3: WIGGLE YOUR WAY IN WITH GENTLE, CAUTIOUS MOVEMENTS.
DO NOT BREAK IT!
STEP 4: STAY.

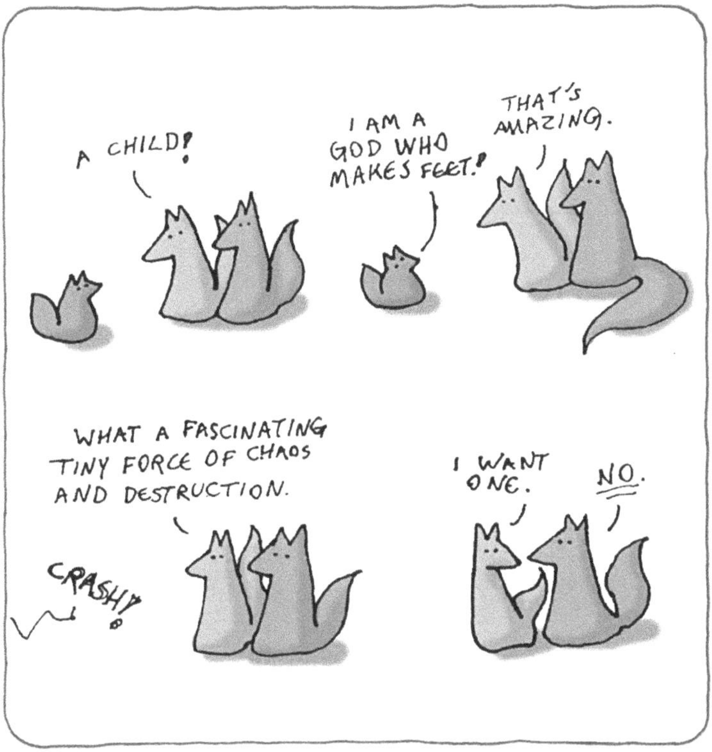
A CHILD!
I AM A GOD WHO MAKES FEET!
THAT'S AMAZING.
CRASH!
WHAT A FASCINATING TINY FORCE OF CHAOS AND DESTRUCTION.
I WANT ONE.
NO.

TOIVO KAARTINEN

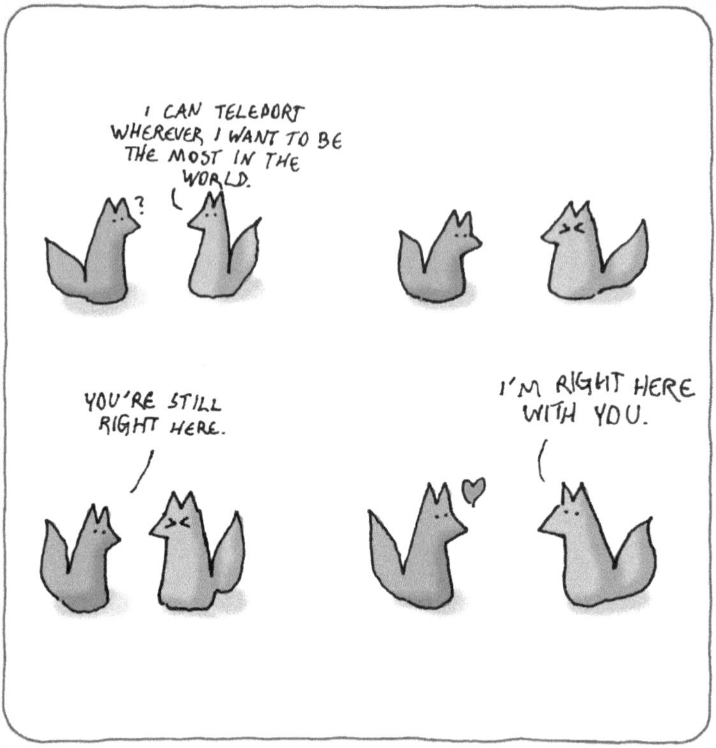

I CAN TELEPORT WHEREVER I WANT TO BE THE MOST IN THE WORLD.
?
YOU'RE STILL RIGHT HERE.
I'M RIGHT HERE WITH YOU.

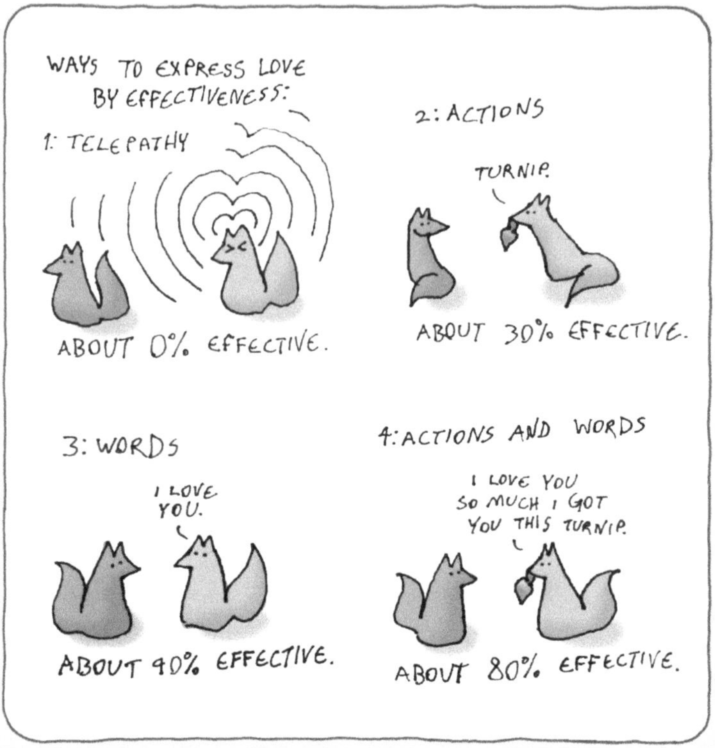

WAYS TO EXPRESS LOVE BY EFFECTIVENESS:
1: TELEPATHY
ABOUT 0% EFFECTIVE.
2: ACTIONS
TURNIP.
ABOUT 30% EFFECTIVE.
3: WORDS
I LOVE YOU.
ABOUT 40% EFFECTIVE.
4: ACTIONS AND WORDS
I LOVE YOU SO MUCH I GOT YOU THIS TURNIP.
ABOUT 80% EFFECTIVE.

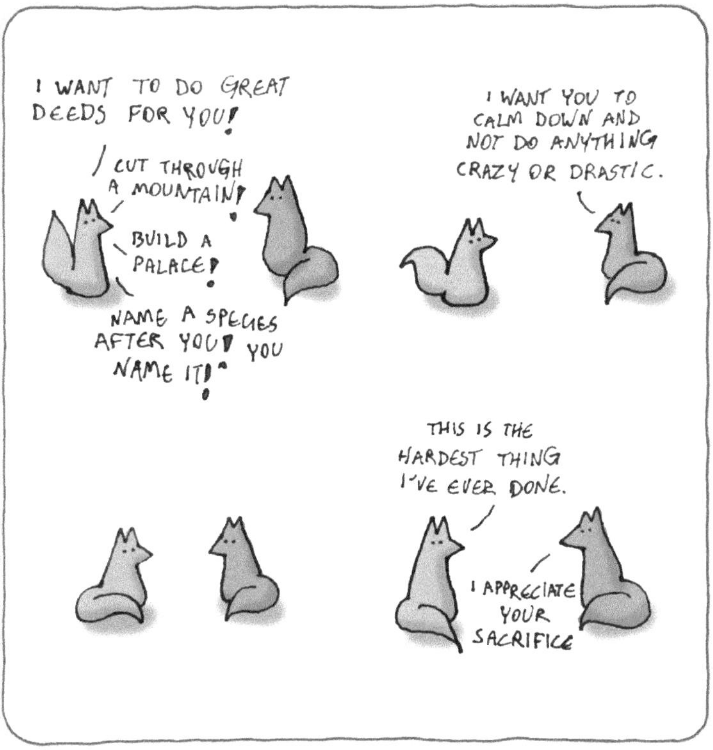
I WANT TO DO GREAT DEEDS FOR YOU!
CUT THROUGH A MOUNTAIN!
BUILD A PALACE!
NAME A SPECIES AFTER YOU! YOU NAME IT!
I WANT YOU TO CALM DOWN AND NOT DO ANYTHING CRAZY OR DRASTIC.
THIS IS THE HARDEST THING I'VE EVER DONE.
I APPRECIATE YOUR SACRIFICE

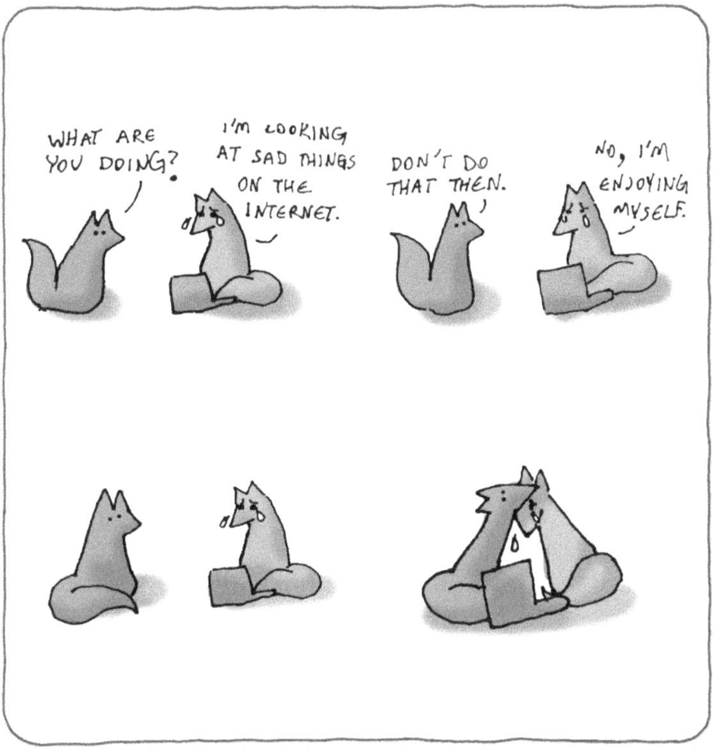
WHAT ARE YOU DOING?
I'M LOOKING AT SAD THINGS ON THE INTERNET.
DON'T DO THAT THEN.
NO, I'M ENJOYING MYSELF.

TOIVO KAARTINEN

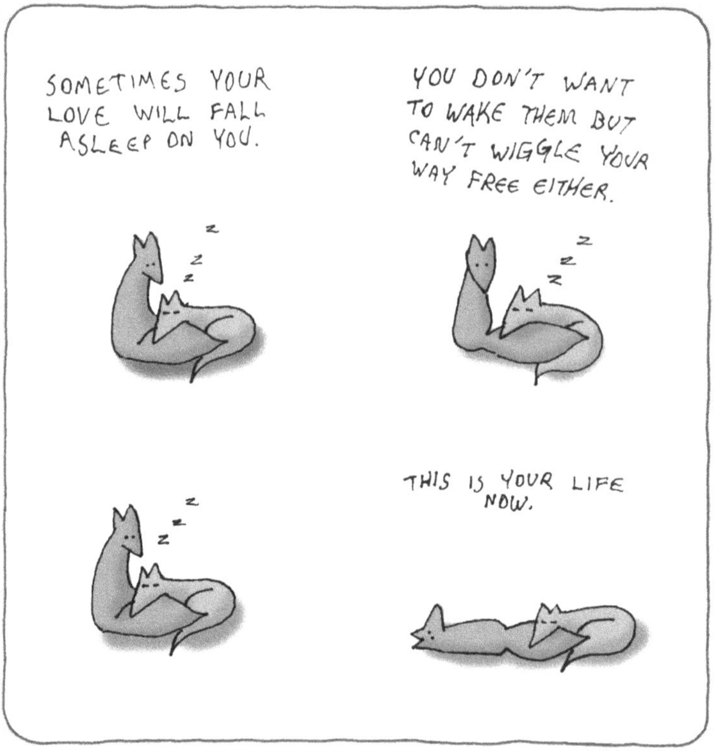
SOMETIMES YOUR LOVE WILL FALL ASLEEP ON YOU.
YOU DON'T WANT TO WAKE THEM BUT CAN'T WIGGLE YOUR WAY FREE EITHER.
THIS IS YOUR LIFE NOW.

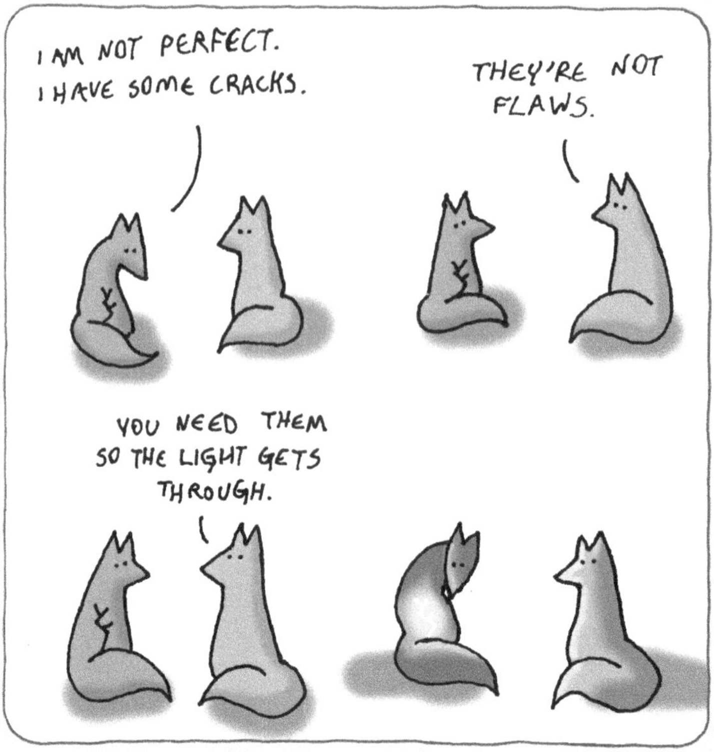
I AM NOT PERFECT. I HAVE SOME CRACKS.
THEY'RE NOT FLAWS.
YOU NEED THEM SO THE LIGHT GETS THROUGH.

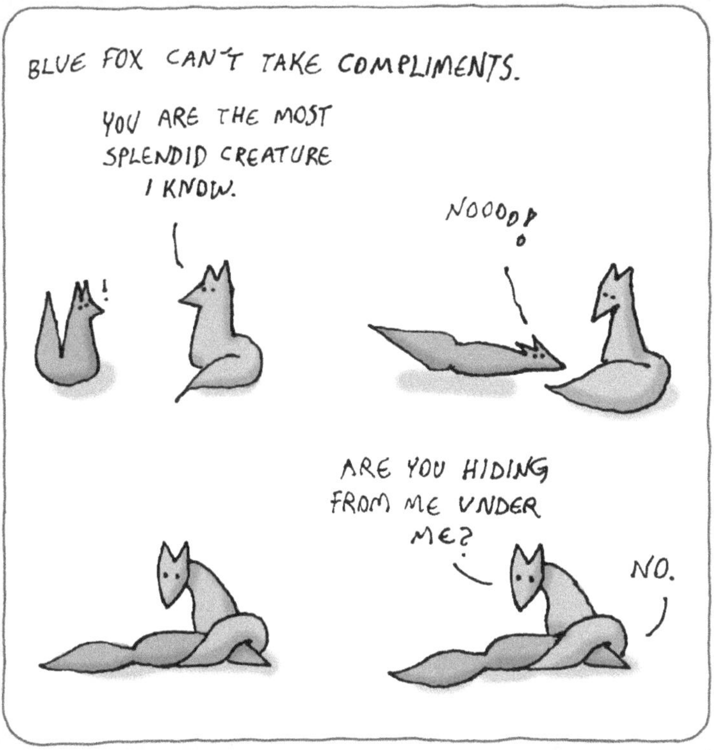
BLUE FOX CAN'T TAKE COMPLIMENTS.
YOU ARE THE MOST SPLENDID CREATURE I KNOW.
!
NOOOO!
ARE YOU HIDING FROM ME UNDER ME?
NO.

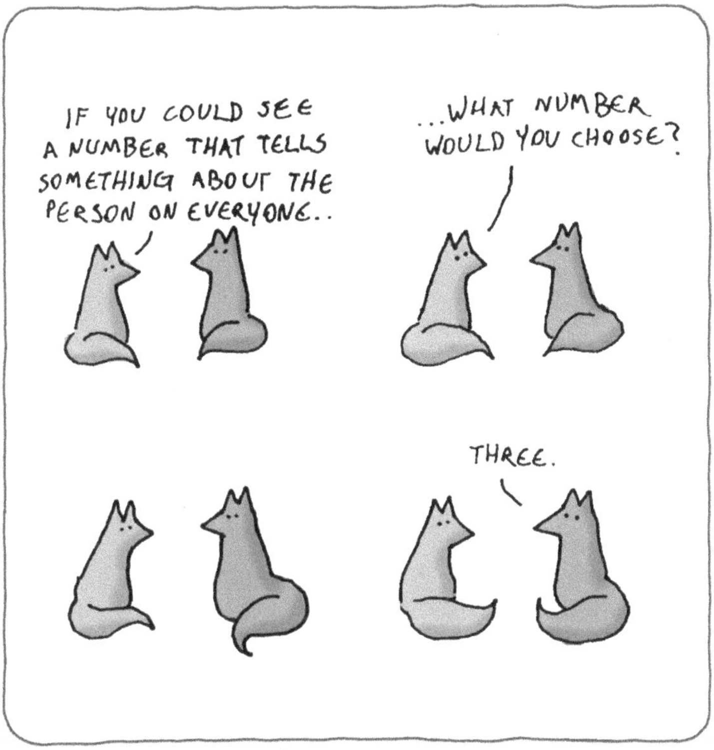
IF YOU COULD SEE A NUMBER THAT TELLS SOMETHING ABOUT THE PERSON ON EVERYONE..
...WHAT NUMBER WOULD YOU CHOOSE?
THREE.

TOIVO KAARTINEN

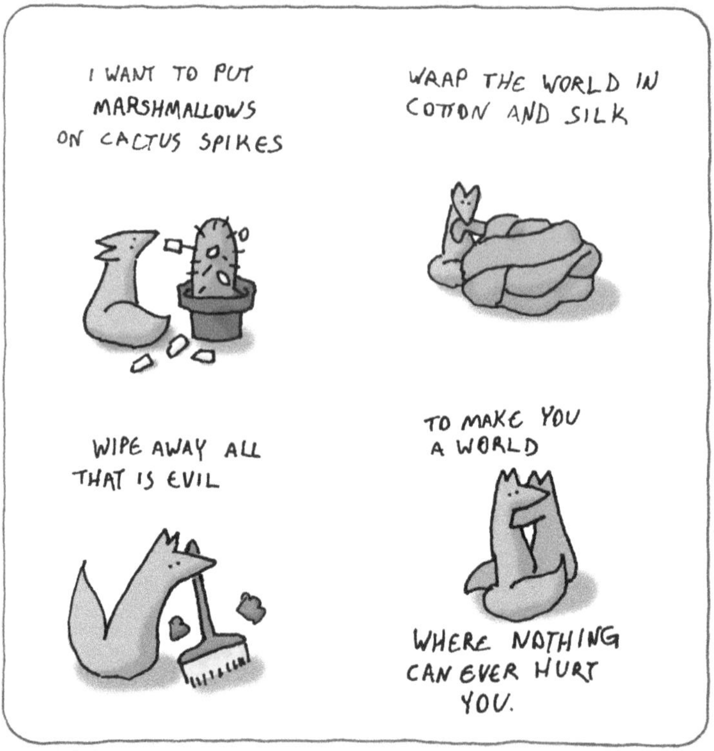
I WANT TO PUT MARSHMALLOWS ON CACTUS SPIKES
WRAP THE WORLD IN COTTON AND SILK
WIPE AWAY ALL THAT IS EVIL
TO MAKE YOU A WORLD
WHERE NOTHING CAN EVER HURT YOU.

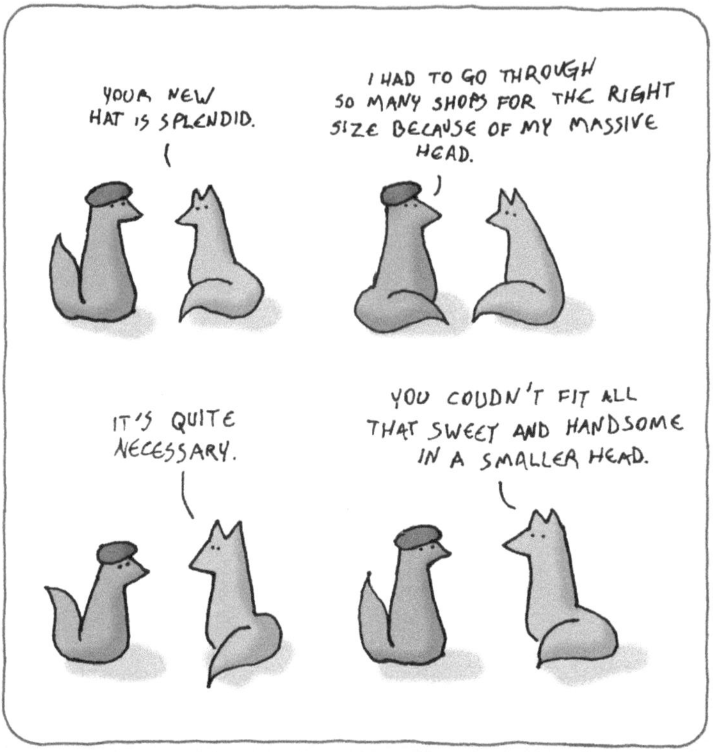
YOUR NEW HAT IS SPLENDID.
I HAD TO GO THROUGH SO MANY SHOPS FOR THE RIGHT SIZE BECAUSE OF MY MASSIVE HEAD.
IT'S QUITE NECESSARY.
YOU COUDN'T FIT ALL THAT SWEET AND HANDSOME IN A SMALLER HEAD.

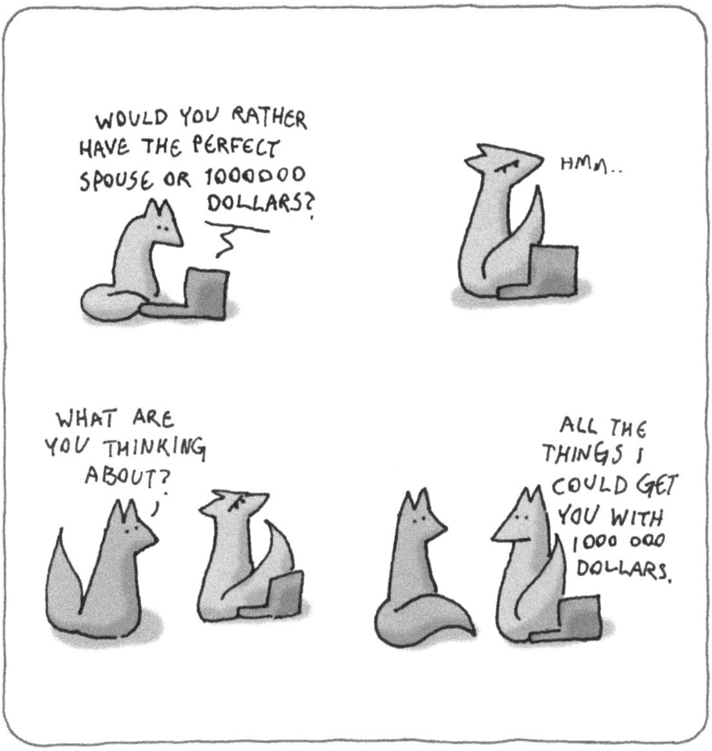
WOULD YOU RATHER HAVE THE PERFECT SPOUSE OR 1000000 DOLLARS?
HMM..
WHAT ARE YOU THINKING ABOUT?
ALL THE THINGS I COULD GET YOU WITH 1000 000 DOLLARS.

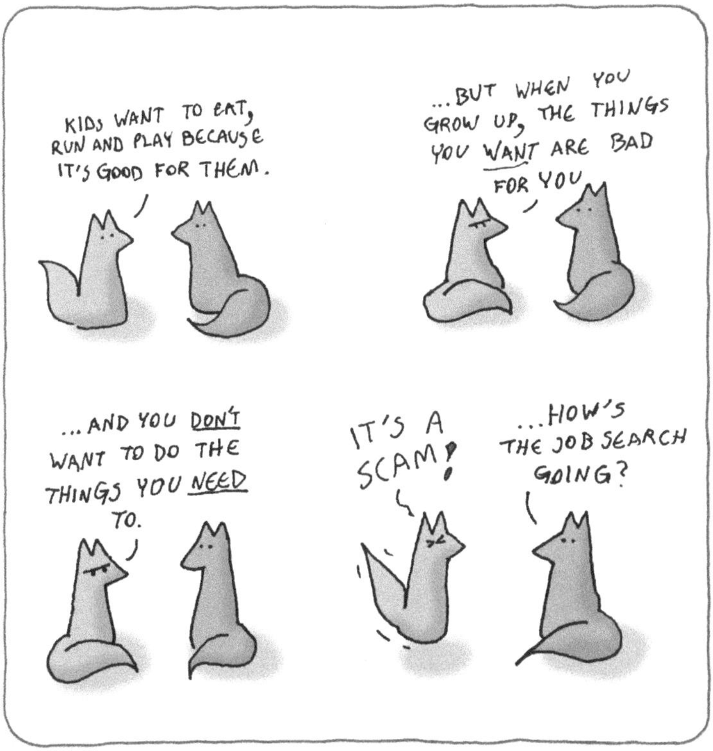
KIDS WANT TO EAT, RUN AND PLAY BECAUSE IT'S GOOD FOR THEM.
...BUT WHEN YOU GROW UP, THE THINGS YOU WANT ARE BAD FOR YOU,
...AND YOU DON'T WANT TO DO THE THINGS YOU NEED TO.
IT'S A SCAM!
...HOW'S THE JOB SEARCH GOING?

TOIVO KAARTINEN

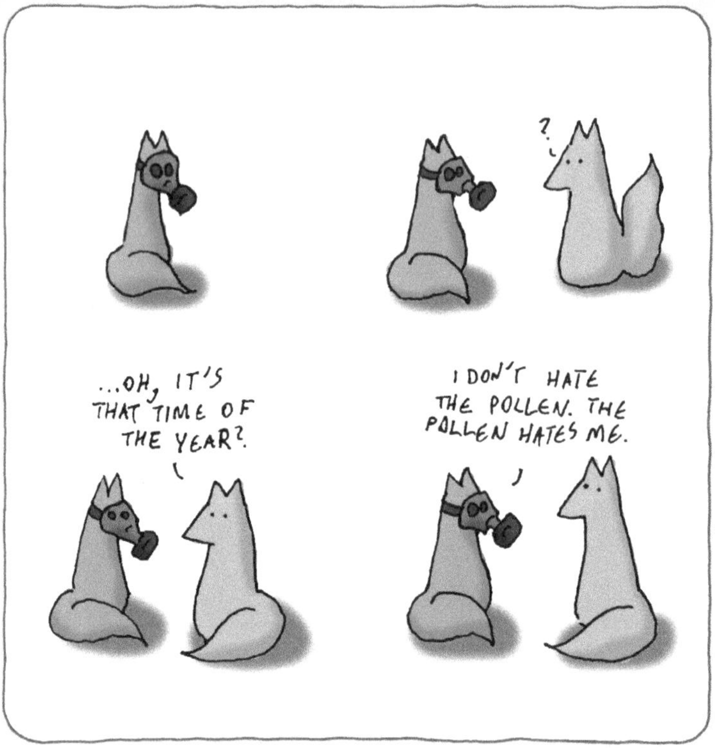
...OH, IT'S THAT TIME OF THE YEAR?
I DON'T HATE THE POLLEN. THE POLLEN HATES ME.

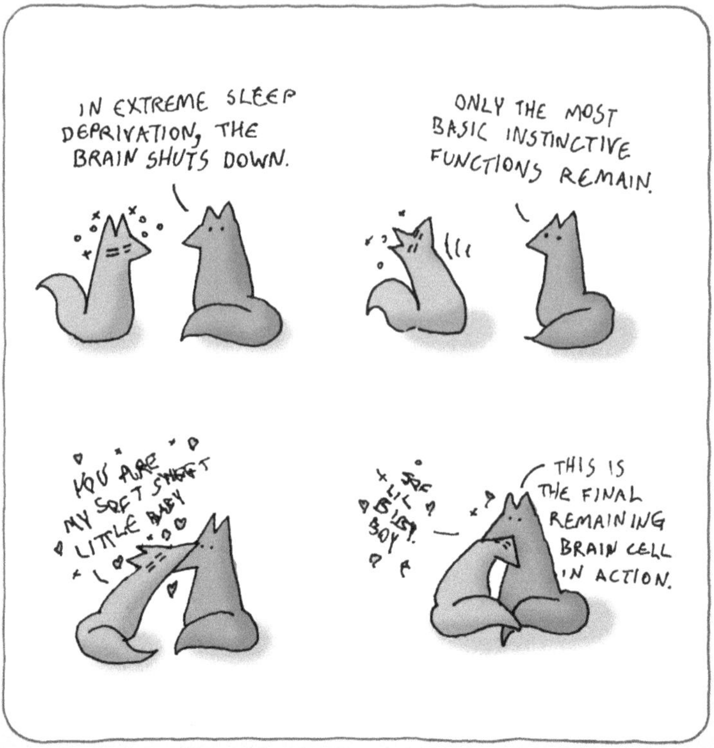
IN EXTREME SLEEP DEPRIVATION, THE BRAIN SHUTS DOWN.
ONLY THE MOST BASIC INSTINCTIVE FUNCTIONS REMAIN.
YOU ARE MY SOFT SWEET LITTLE BABY
THIS IS THE FINAL REMAINING BRAIN CELL IN ACTION.

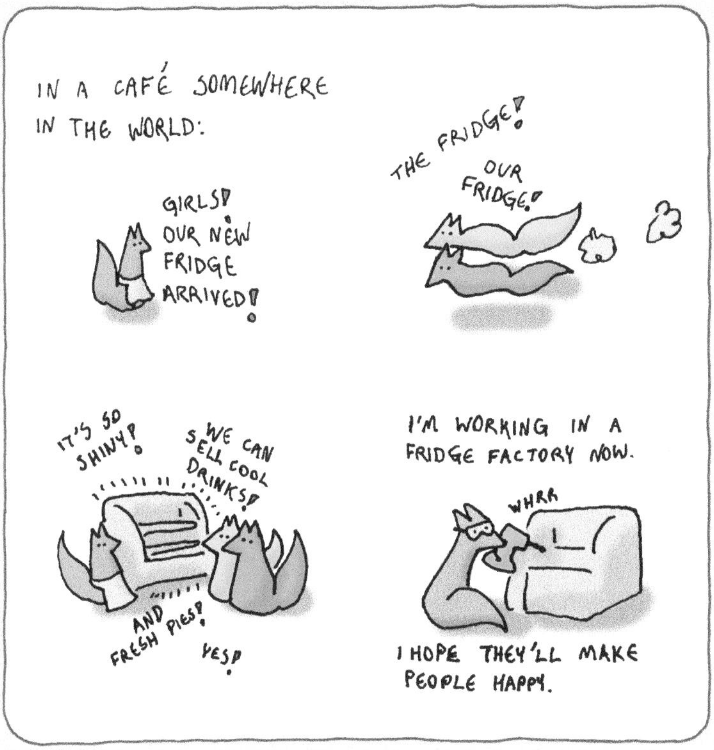
IN A CAFÉ SOMEWHERE IN THE WORLD:
GIRLS! OUR NEW FRIDGE ARRIVED!
THE FRIDGE!
OUR FRIDGE!
IT'S SO SHINY!
WE CAN SELL COOL DRINKS!
AND FRESH PIES!
YES!
I'M WORKING IN A FRIDGE FACTORY NOW.
WHRR
I HOPE THEY'LL MAKE PEOPLE HAPPY.

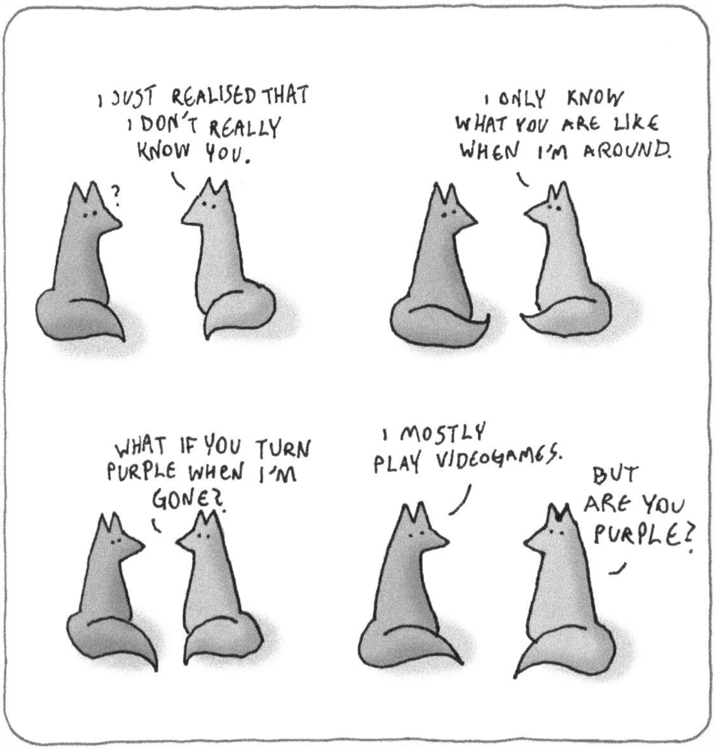
I JUST REALISED THAT I DON'T REALLY KNOW YOU.
?
I ONLY KNOW WHAT YOU ARE LIKE WHEN I'M AROUND.
WHAT IF YOU TURN PURPLE WHEN I'M GONE?
I MOSTLY PLAY VIDEOGAMES.
BUT ARE YOU PURPLE?

TOIVO KAARTINEN

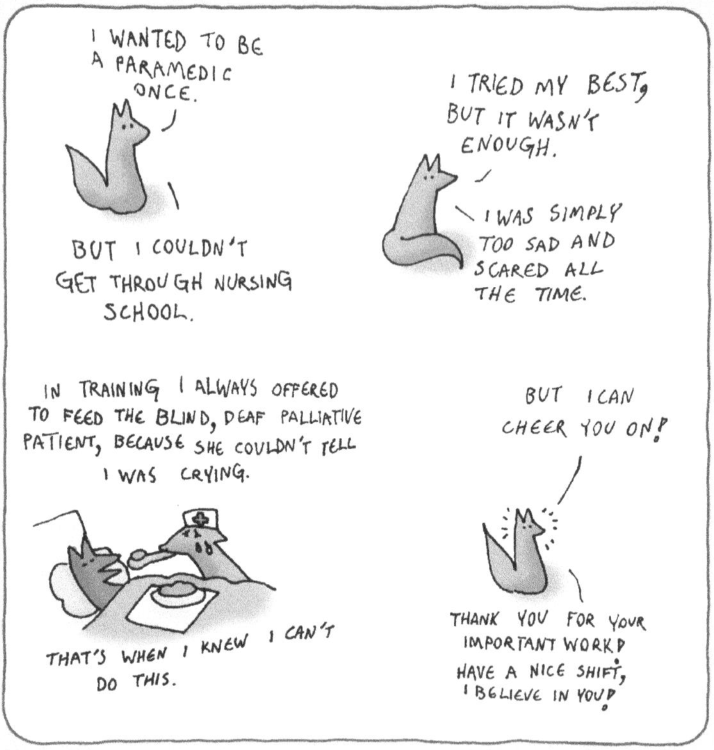
I WANTED TO BE A PARAMEDIC ONCE.
BUT I COULDN'T GET THROUGH NURSING SCHOOL.
I TRIED MY BEST, BUT IT WASN'T ENOUGH.
I WAS SIMPLY TOO SAD AND SCARED ALL THE TIME.
IN TRAINING I ALWAYS OFFERED TO FEED THE BLIND, DEAF PALLIATIVE PATIENT, BECAUSE SHE COULDN'T TELL I WAS CRYING.
THAT'S WHEN I KNEW I CAN'T DO THIS.
BUT I CAN CHEER YOU ON!
THANK YOU FOR YOUR IMPORTANT WORK! HAVE A NICE SHIFT, I BELIEVE IN YOU!

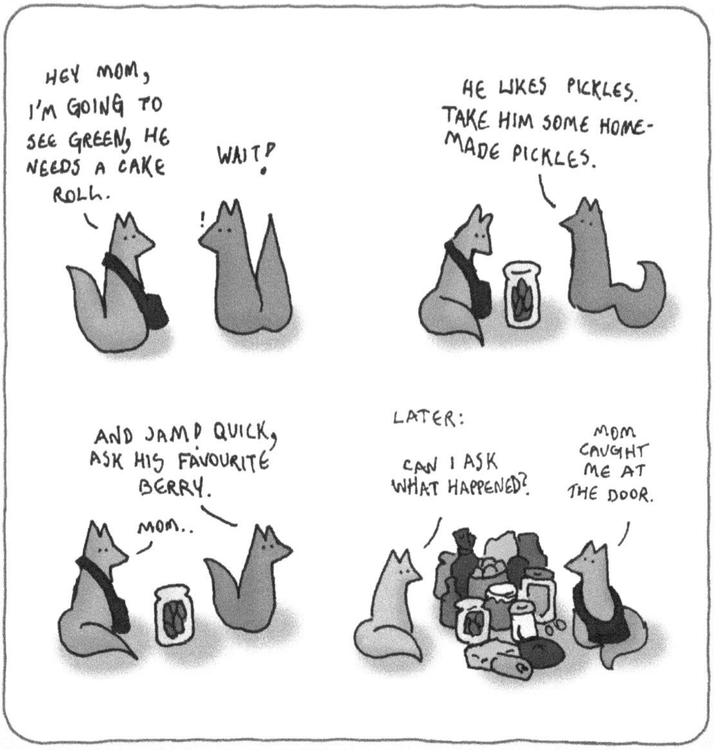
HEY MOM, I'M GOING TO SEE GREEN, HE NEEDS A CAKE ROLL.
WAIT!
!
HE LIKES PICKLES. TAKE HIM SOME HOME-MADE PICKLES.
AND JAM! QUICK, ASK HIS FAVOURITE BERRY.
MOM..
LATER:
CAN I ASK WHAT HAPPENED?
MOM CAUGHT ME AT THE DOOR.

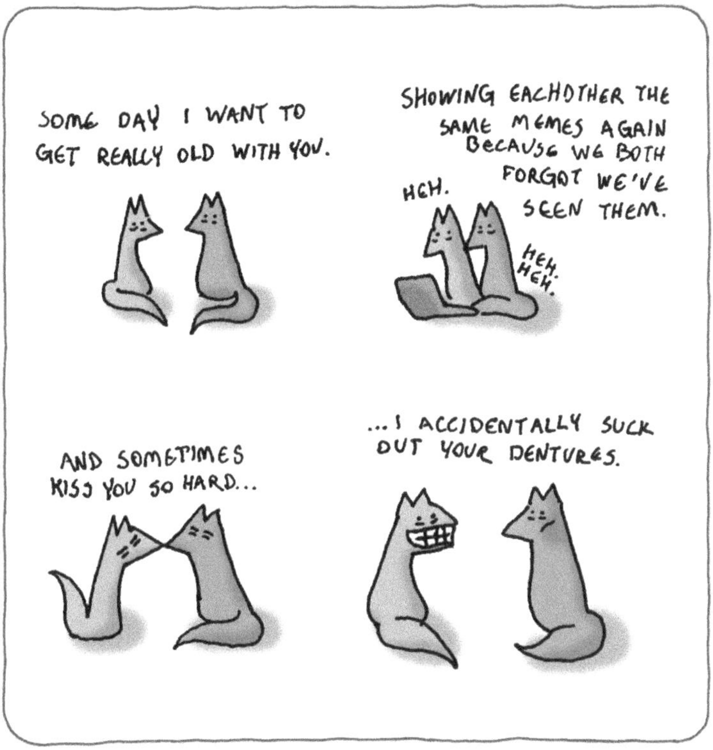
SOME DAY I WANT TO GET REALLY OLD WITH YOU.
SHOWING EACHOTHER THE SAME MEMES AGAIN BECAUSE WE BOTH FORGOT WE'VE SEEN THEM.
HEH.
HEH. HEH.
AND SOMETIMES KISS YOU SO HARD...
...I ACCIDENTALLY SUCK OUT YOUR DENTURES.

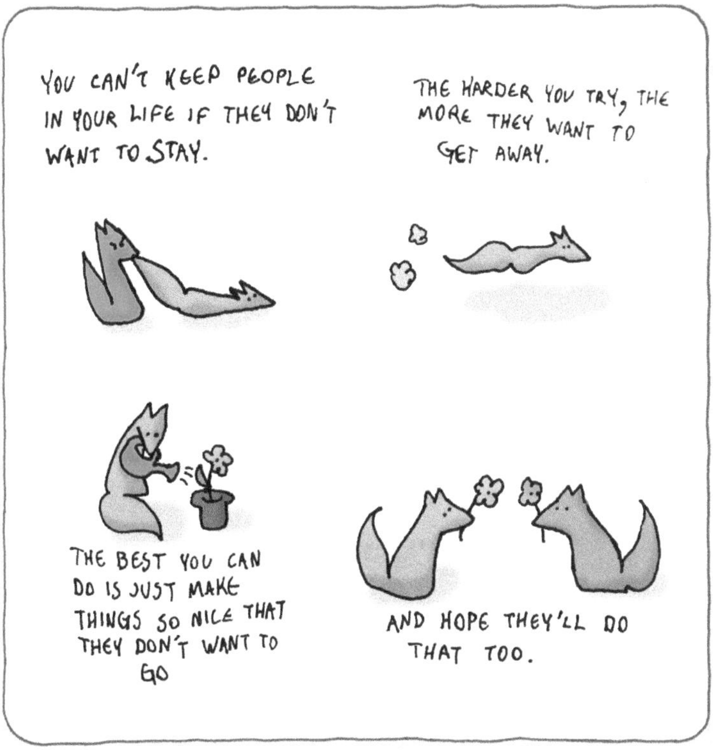
YOU CAN'T KEEP PEOPLE IN YOUR LIFE IF THEY DON'T WANT TO STAY.
THE HARDER YOU TRY, THE MORE THEY WANT TO GET AWAY.
THE BEST YOU CAN DO IS JUST MAKE THINGS SO NICE THAT THEY DON'T WANT TO GO
AND HOPE THEY'LL DO THAT TOO.

TOIVO KAARTINEN

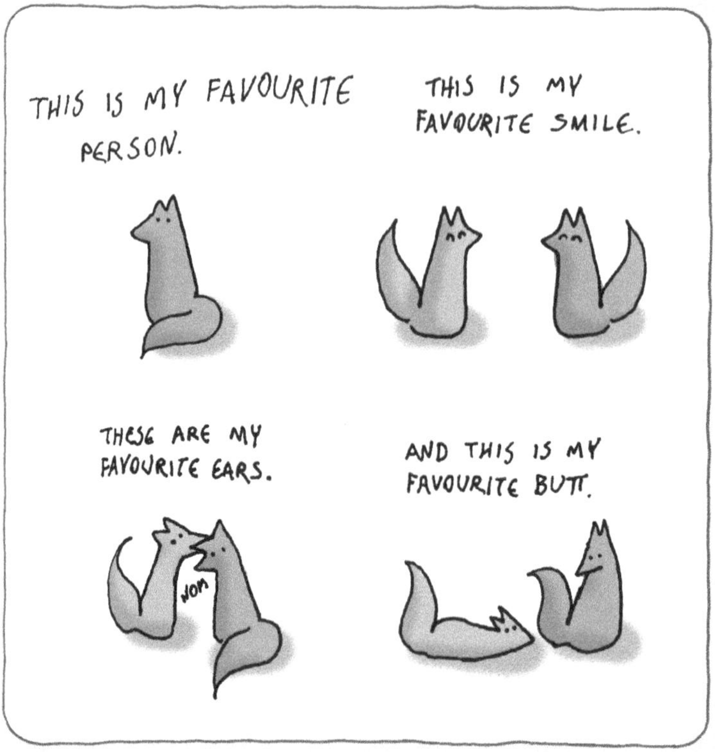
THIS IS MY FAVOURITE PERSON.
THIS IS MY FAVOURITE SMILE.
THESE ARE MY FAVOURITE EARS.
NOM
AND THIS IS MY FAVOURITE BUTT.

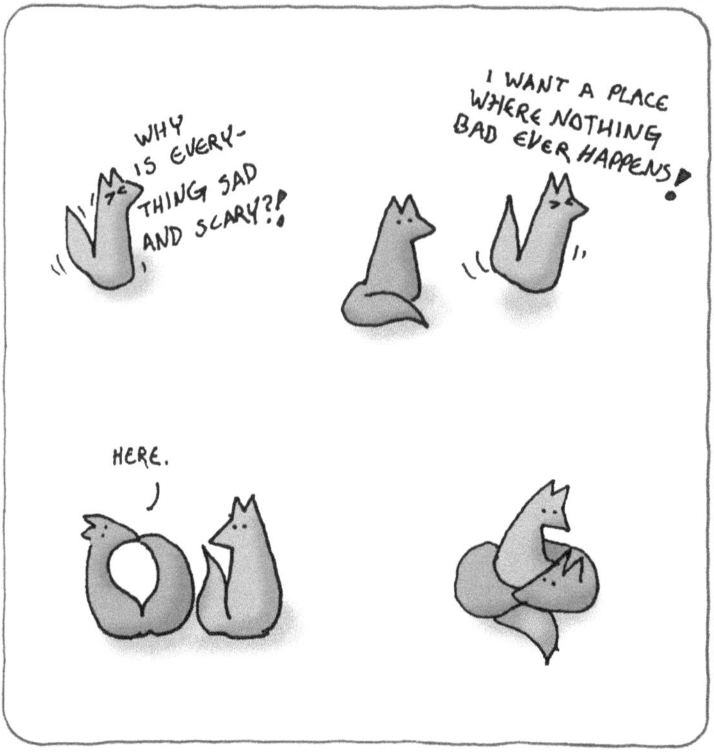
WHY IS EVERY-THING SAD AND SCARY?!
I WANT A PLACE WHERE NOTHING BAD EVER HAPPENS!
HERE.

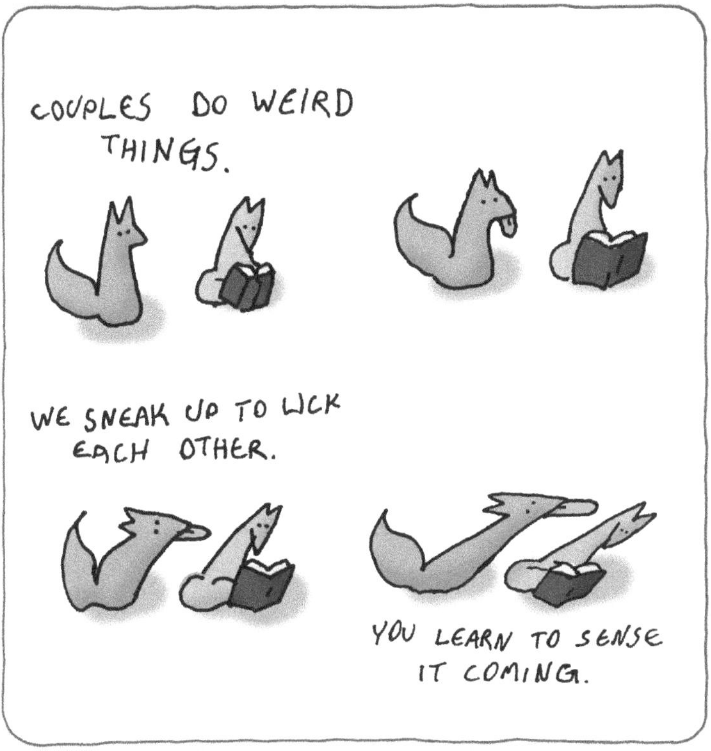
COUPLES DO WEIRD THINGS.
WE SNEAK UP TO LICK EACH OTHER.
YOU LEARN TO SENSE IT COMING.

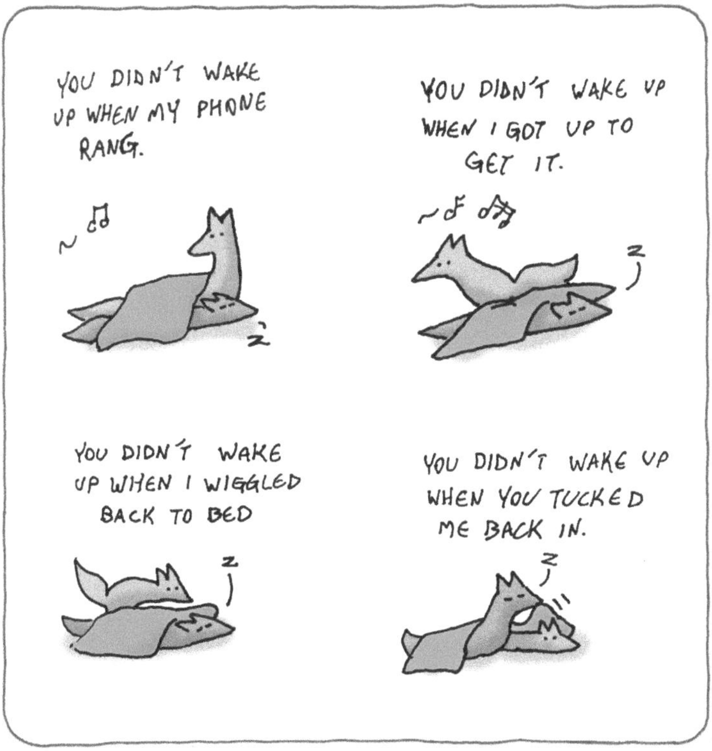
YOU DIDN'T WAKE UP WHEN MY PHONE RANG.
YOU DIDN'T WAKE UP WHEN I GOT UP TO GET IT.
YOU DIDN'T WAKE UP WHEN I WIGGLED BACK TO BED
YOU DIDN'T WAKE UP WHEN YOU TUCKED ME BACK IN.

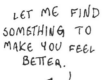

LET ME FIND SOMETHING TO MAKE YOU FEEL BETTER.

A FLOWER POT?

SOME CRAYONS?

THIS OLD SHOE?

WHAT ARE YOU THINKING ABOUT?

WELL, SINCE I DON'T WANT YOU TO DEAL WITH MY LOSS, I'VE DECIDED TO OUTLIVE YOU.

...SO CAN I SING "YOU ARE MY SUNSHINE" AT YOUR FUNERAL?

REMIND ME TO NEVER ASK ABOUT YOUR THOUGHTS AGAIN.

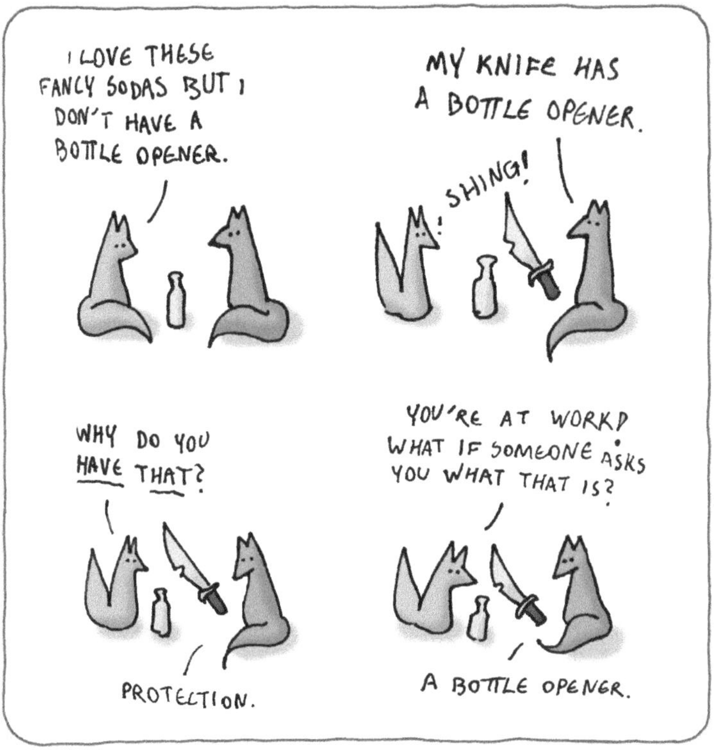
I LOVE THESE FANCY SODAS BUT I DON'T HAVE A BOTTLE OPENER.
MY KNIFE HAS A BOTTLE OPENER.
SHING!
!
WHY DO YOU HAVE THAT?
PROTECTION.
YOU'RE AT WORK?
WHAT IF SOMEONE ASKS YOU WHAT THAT IS?
A BOTTLE OPENER.

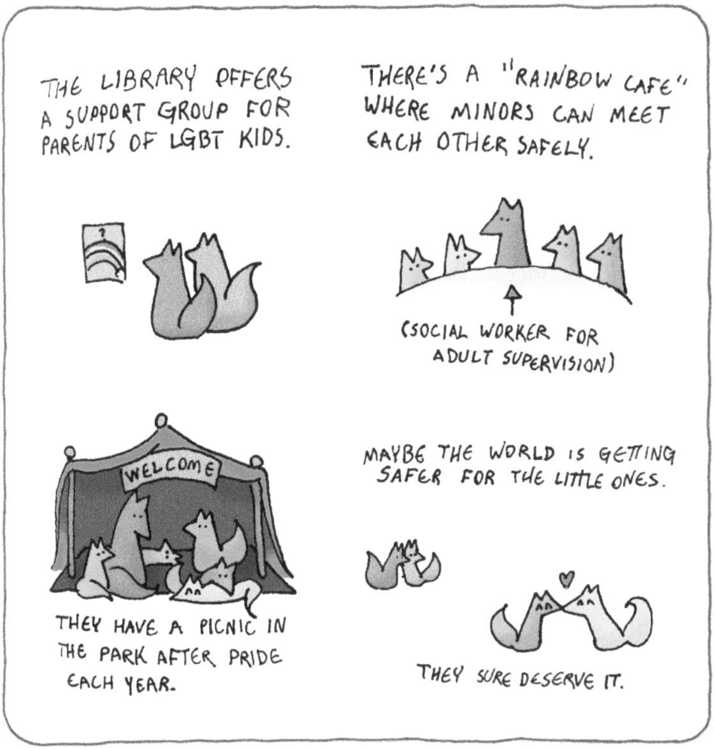
THE LIBRARY OFFERS A SUPPORT GROUP FOR PARENTS OF LGBT KIDS.
THERE'S A "RAINBOW CAFE" WHERE MINORS CAN MEET EACH OTHER SAFELY.
(SOCIAL WORKER FOR ADULT SUPERVISION)
WELCOME
THEY HAVE A PICNIC IN THE PARK AFTER PRIDE EACH YEAR.
MAYBE THE WORLD IS GETTING SAFER FOR THE LITTLE ONES.
THEY SURE DESERVE IT.

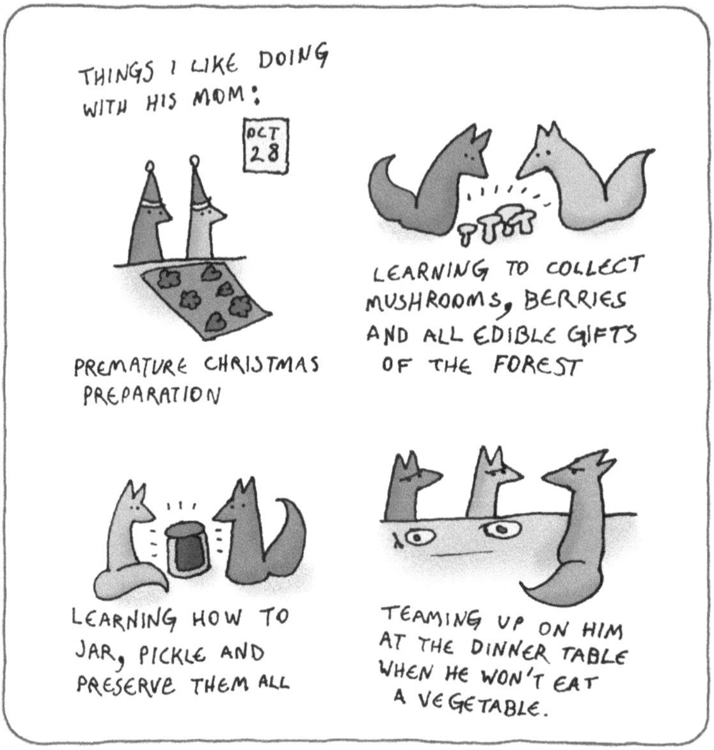
THINGS I LIKE DOING WITH HIS MOM:
OCT 28
PREMATURE CHRISTMAS PREPARATION
LEARNING TO COLLECT MUSHROOMS, BERRIES AND ALL EDIBLE GIFTS OF THE FOREST
LEARNING HOW TO JAR, PICKLE AND PRESERVE THEM ALL
TEAMING UP ON HIM AT THE DINNER TABLE WHEN HE WON'T EAT A VEGETABLE.

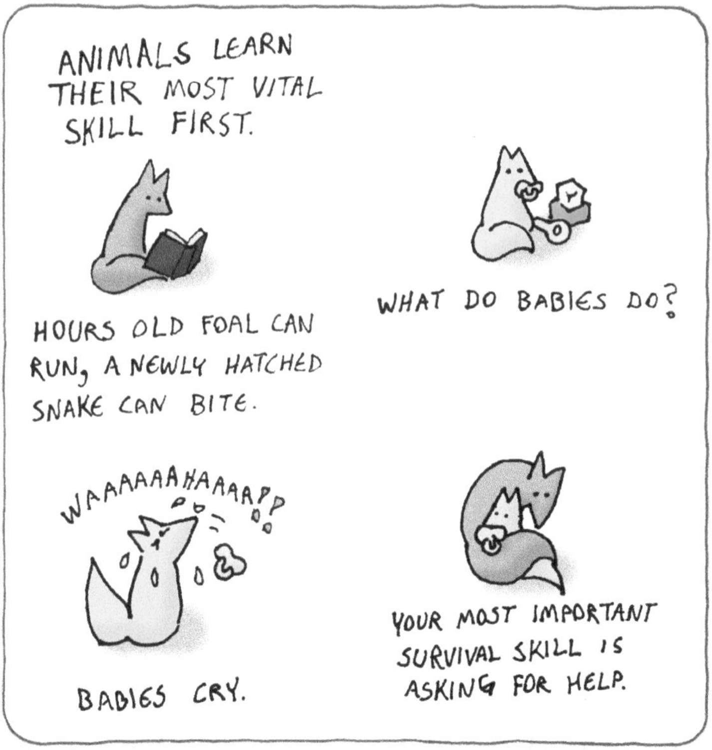
ANIMALS LEARN THEIR MOST VITAL SKILL FIRST.
HOURS OLD FOAL CAN RUN, A NEWLY HATCHED SNAKE CAN BITE.
WHAT DO BABIES DO?
WAAAAAAHAAAAPP
BABIES CRY.
YOUR MOST IMPORTANT SURVIVAL SKILL IS ASKING FOR HELP.

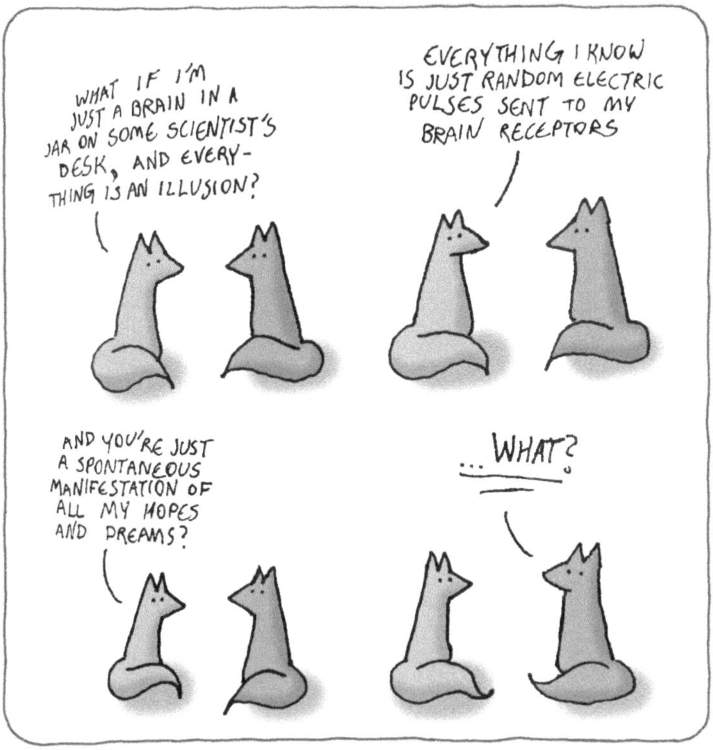
WHAT IF I'M JUST A BRAIN IN A JAR ON SOME SCIENTIST'S DESK, AND EVERYTHING IS AN ILLUSION?
EVERYTHING I KNOW IS JUST RANDOM ELECTRIC PULSES SENT TO MY BRAIN RECEPTORS
AND YOU'RE JUST A SPONTANEOUS MANIFESTATION OF ALL MY HOPES AND DREAMS?
...WHAT?

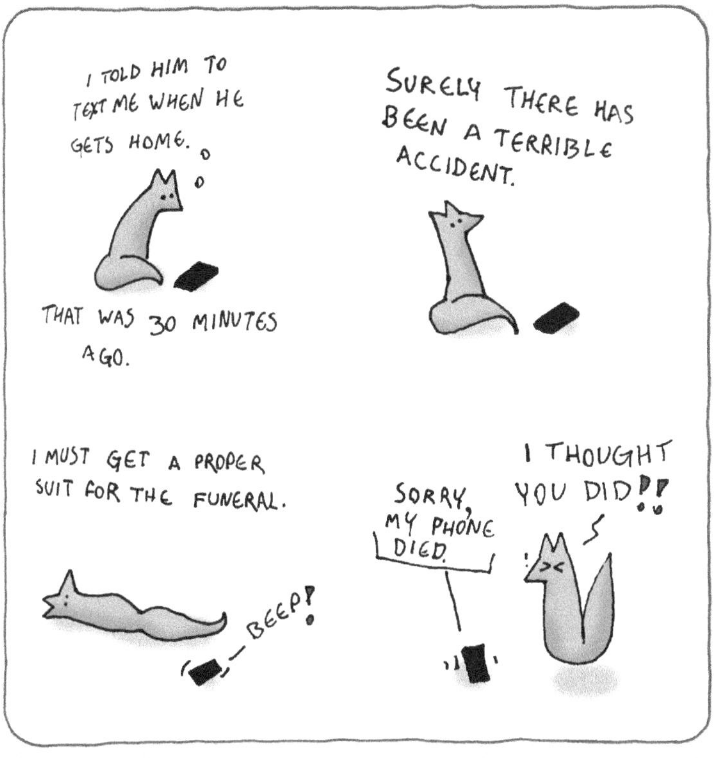
I TOLD HIM TO TEXT ME WHEN HE GETS HOME.
THAT WAS 30 MINUTES AGO.
SURELY THERE HAS BEEN A TERRIBLE ACCIDENT.
I MUST GET A PROPER SUIT FOR THE FUNERAL.
BEEP!
SORRY, MY PHONE DIED.
I THOUGHT YOU DID!!

FOXES IN LOVE

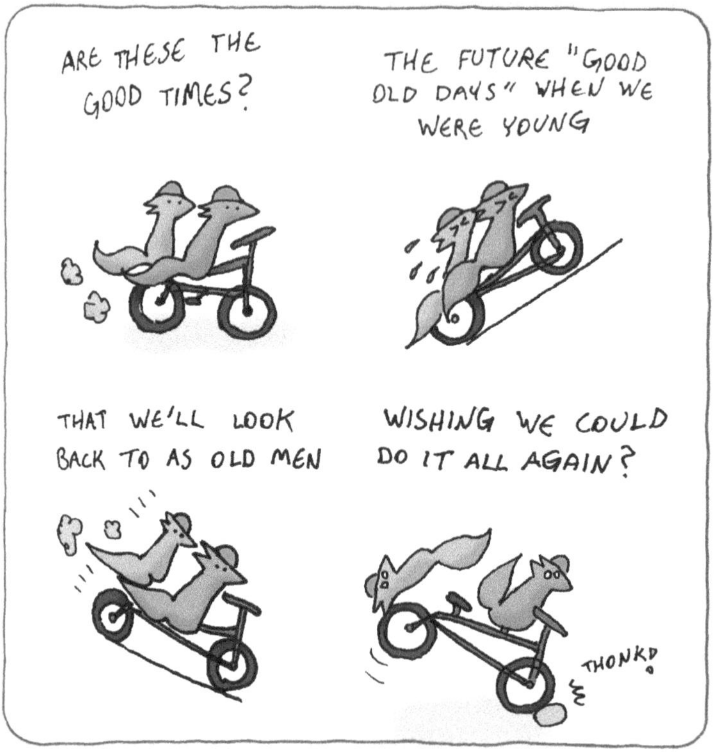
ARE THESE THE GOOD TIMES?
THE FUTURE "GOOD OLD DAYS" WHEN WE WERE YOUNG
THAT WE'LL LOOK BACK TO AS OLD MEN
WISHING WE COULD DO IT ALL AGAIN?
THONK!

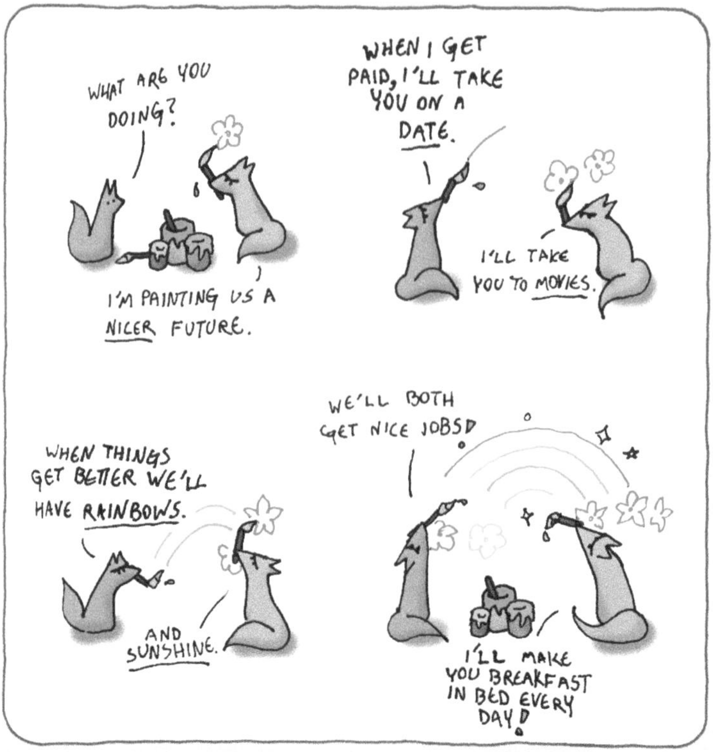
WHAT ARE YOU DOING?
I'M PAINTING US A NICER FUTURE.
WHEN I GET PAID, I'LL TAKE YOU ON A DATE.
I'LL TAKE YOU TO MOVIES.
WHEN THINGS GET BETTER WE'LL HAVE RAINBOWS.
AND SUNSHINE.
WE'LL BOTH GET NICE JOBS!
I'LL MAKE YOU BREAKFAST IN BED EVERY DAY!

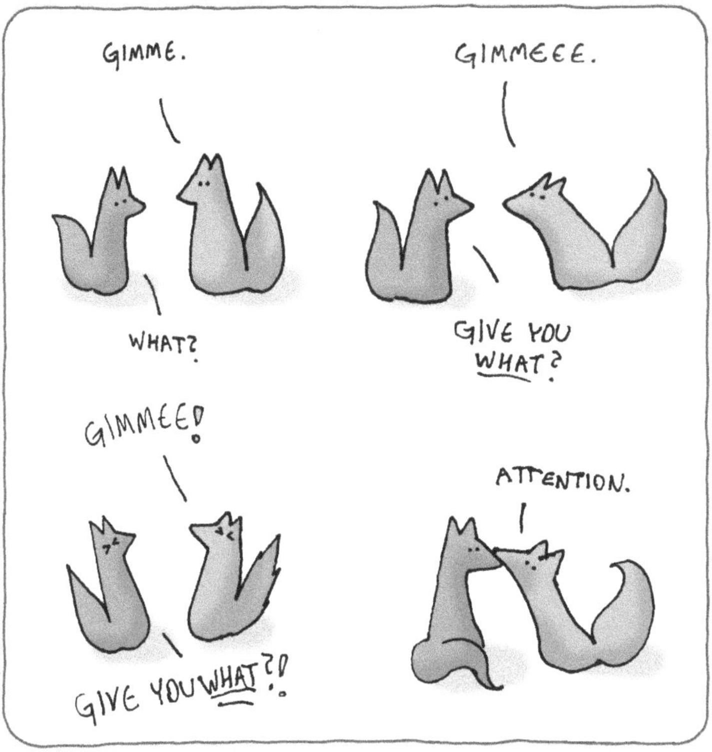
GIMME.
WHAT?
GIMMEEE.
GIVE YOU WHAT?
GIMMEE!
GIVE YOU WHAT?!
ATTENTION.

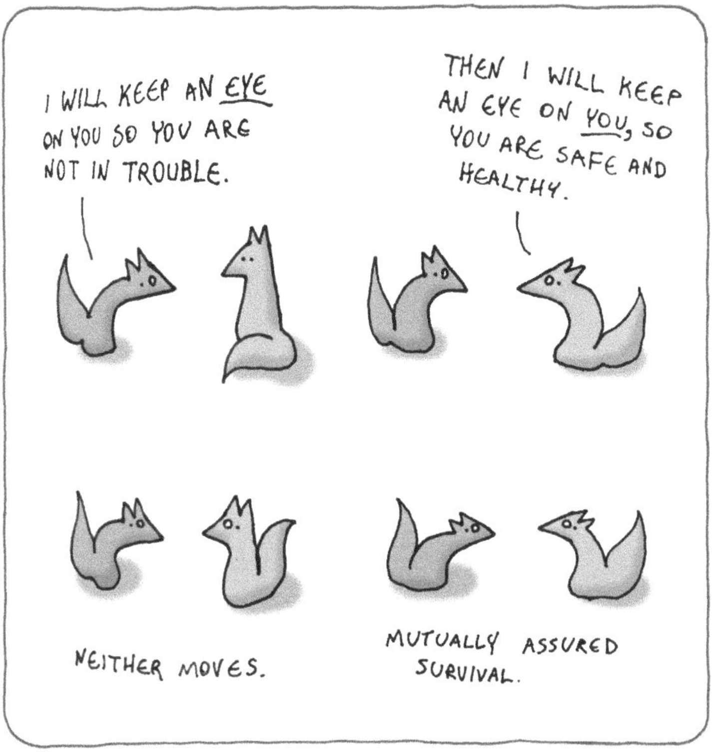
I WILL KEEP AN EYE ON YOU SO YOU ARE NOT IN TROUBLE.
THEN I WILL KEEP AN EYE ON YOU, SO YOU ARE SAFE AND HEALTHY.
NEITHER MOVES.
MUTUALLY ASSURED SURVIVAL.

TOIVO KAARTINEN

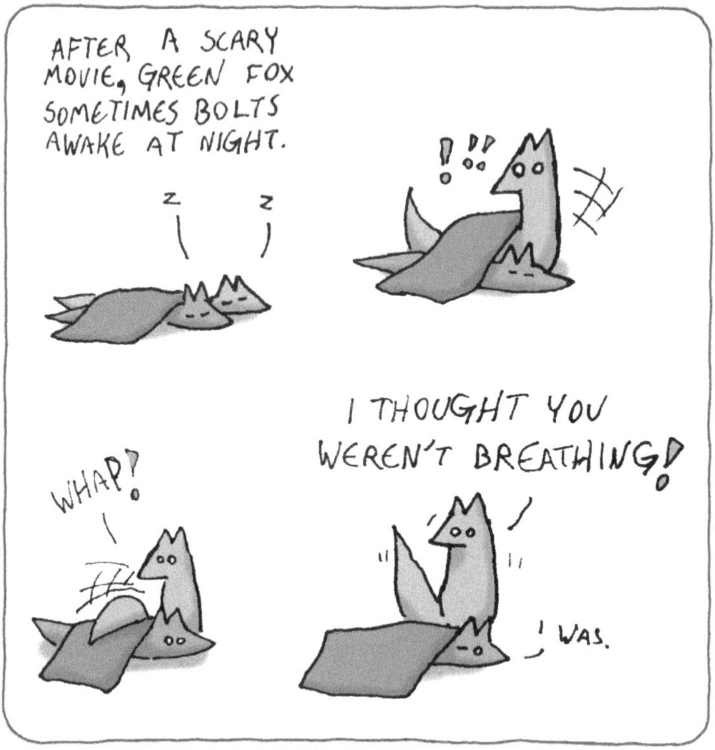
AFTER A SCARY MOVIE, GREEN FOX SOMETIMES BOLTS AWAKE AT NIGHT.
Z Z
WHAP!
I THOUGHT YOU WEREN'T BREATHING!
I WAS.

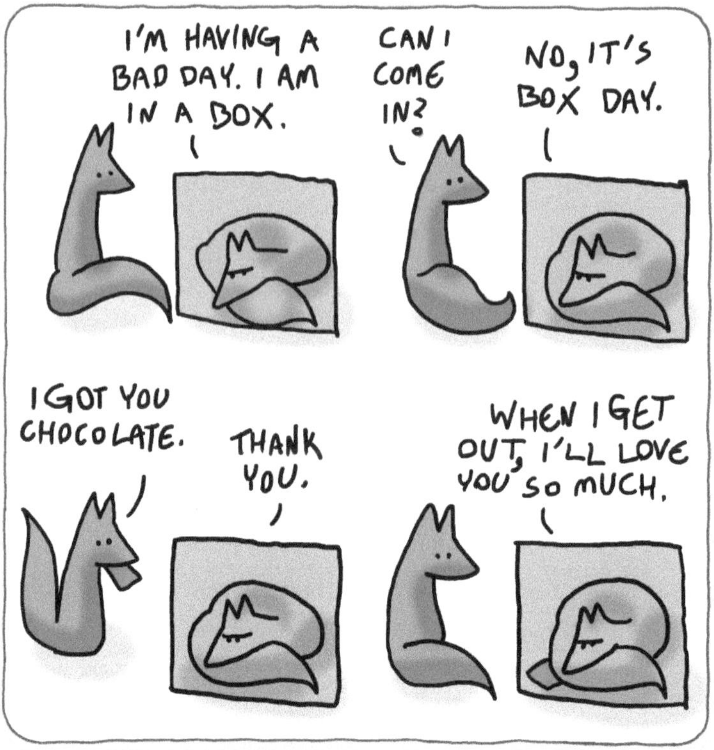
I'M HAVING A BAD DAY. I AM IN A BOX.
CAN I COME IN?
NO, IT'S BOX DAY.
I GOT YOU CHOCOLATE.
THANK YOU.
WHEN I GET OUT, I'LL LOVE YOU SO MUCH.

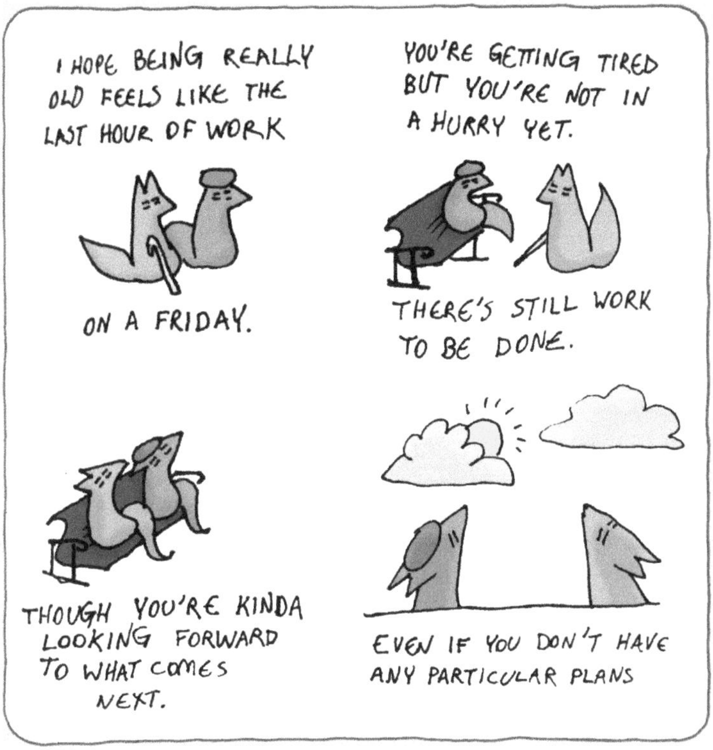
I HOPE BEING REALLY OLD FEELS LIKE THE LAST HOUR OF WORK
ON A FRIDAY.
YOU'RE GETTING TIRED BUT YOU'RE NOT IN A HURRY YET.
THERE'S STILL WORK TO BE DONE.
THOUGH YOU'RE KINDA LOOKING FORWARD TO WHAT COMES NEXT.
EVEN IF YOU DON'T HAVE ANY PARTICULAR PLANS

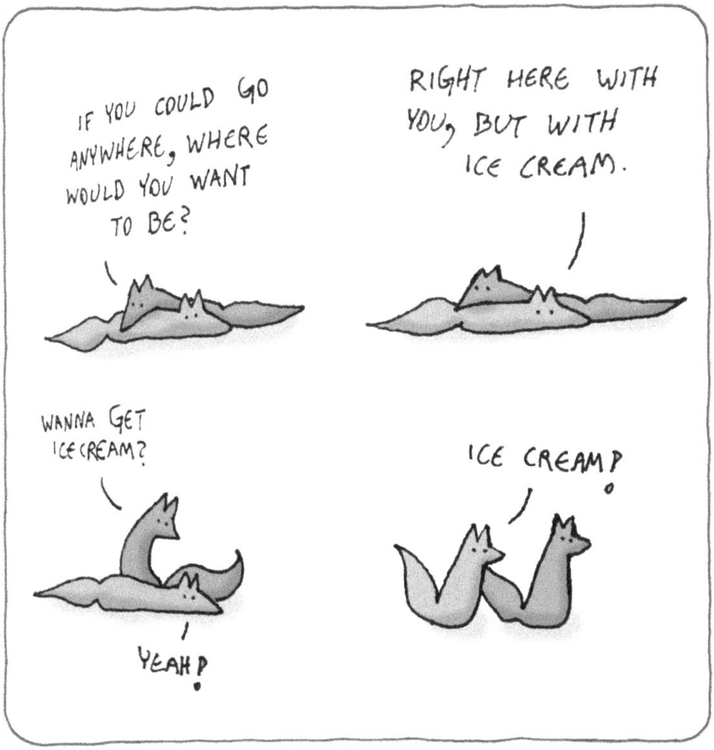
IF YOU COULD GO ANYWHERE, WHERE WOULD YOU WANT TO BE?
RIGHT HERE WITH YOU, BUT WITH ICE CREAM.
WANNA GET ICECREAM?
YEAH!
ICE CREAM!

TOIVO KAARTINEN

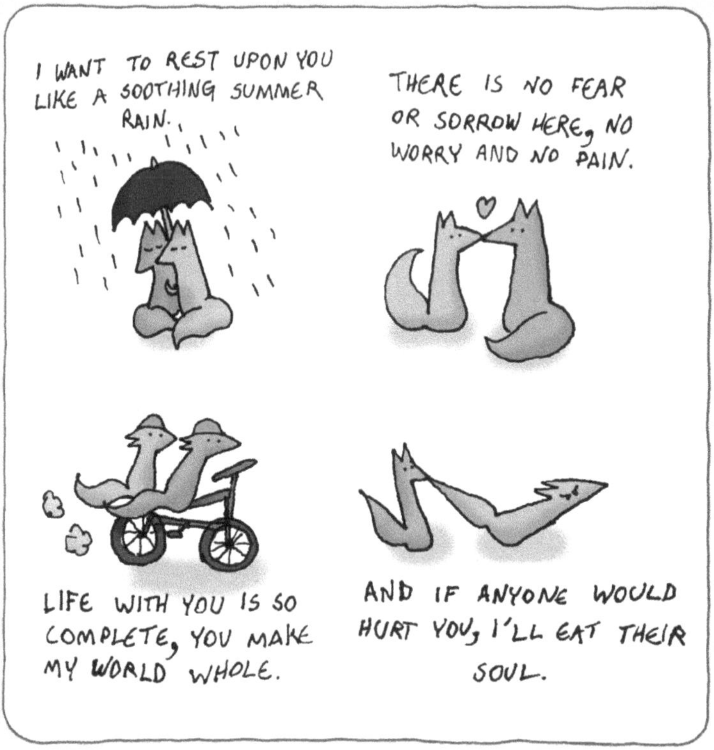
I WANT TO REST UPON YOU LIKE A SOOTHING SUMMER RAIN.
THERE IS NO FEAR OR SORROW HERE, NO WORRY AND NO PAIN.
LIFE WITH YOU IS SO COMPLETE, YOU MAKE MY WORLD WHOLE.
AND IF ANYONE WOULD HURT YOU, I'LL EAT THEIR SOUL.

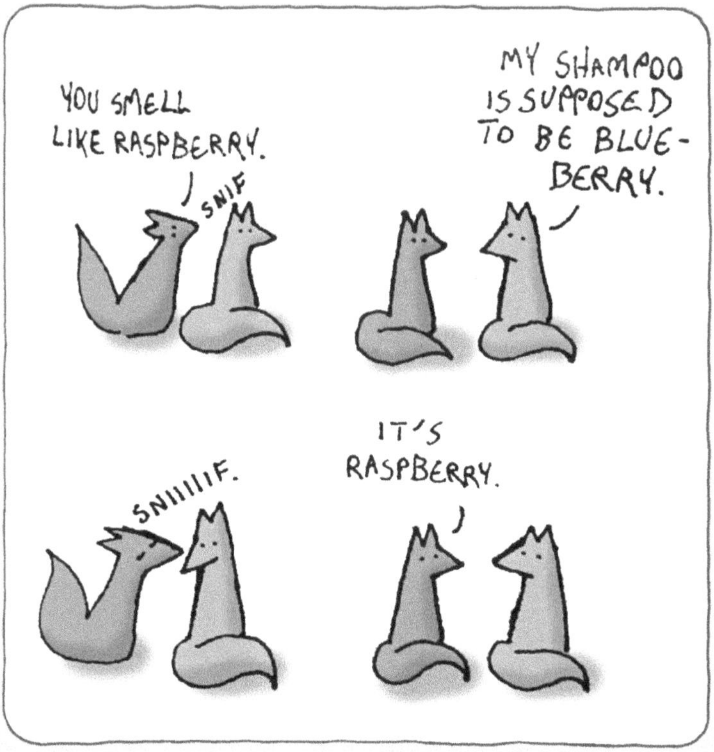
YOU SMELL LIKE RASPBERRY.
SNIF
MY SHAMPOO IS SUPPOSED TO BE BLUE-BERRY.
SNIIIIIF.
IT'S RASPBERRY.

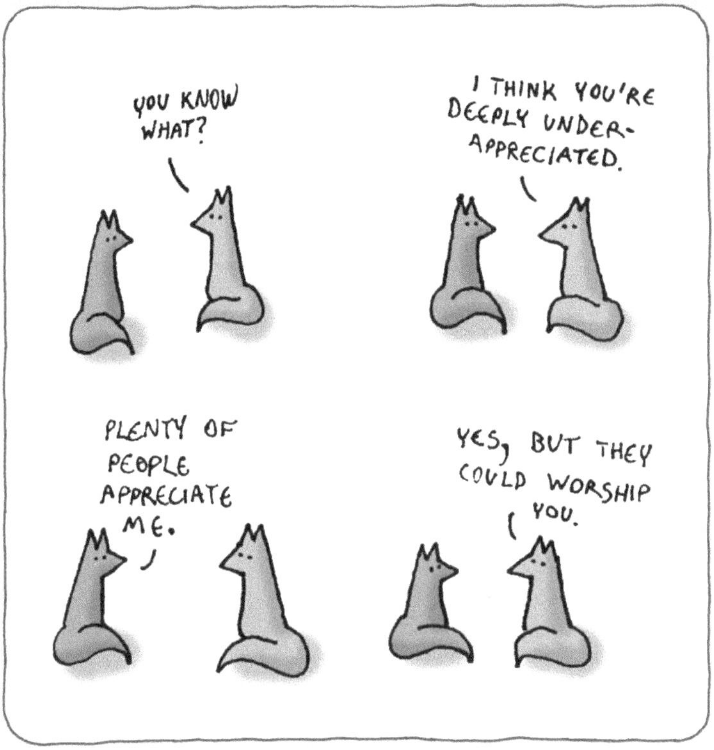
YOU KNOW WHAT?
I THINK YOU'RE DEEPLY UNDER-APPRECIATED.
PLENTY OF PEOPLE APPRECIATE ME.
YES, BUT THEY COULD WORSHIP YOU.

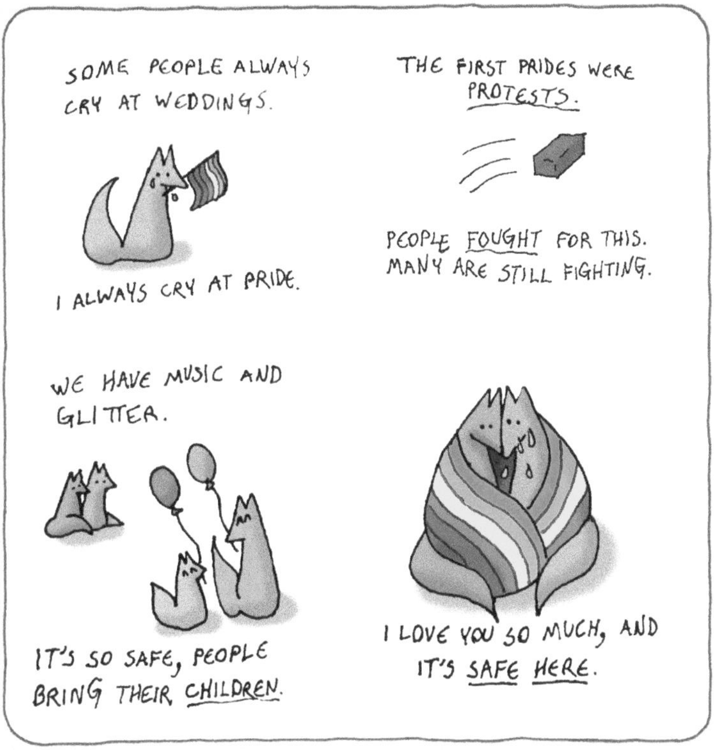
SOME PEOPLE ALWAYS CRY AT WEDDINGS.
I ALWAYS CRY AT PRIDE.
THE FIRST PRIDES WERE PROTESTS.
PEOPLE FOUGHT FOR THIS. MANY ARE STILL FIGHTING.
WE HAVE MUSIC AND GLITTER.
IT'S SO SAFE, PEOPLE BRING THEIR CHILDREN.
I LOVE YOU SO MUCH, AND IT'S SAFE HERE.

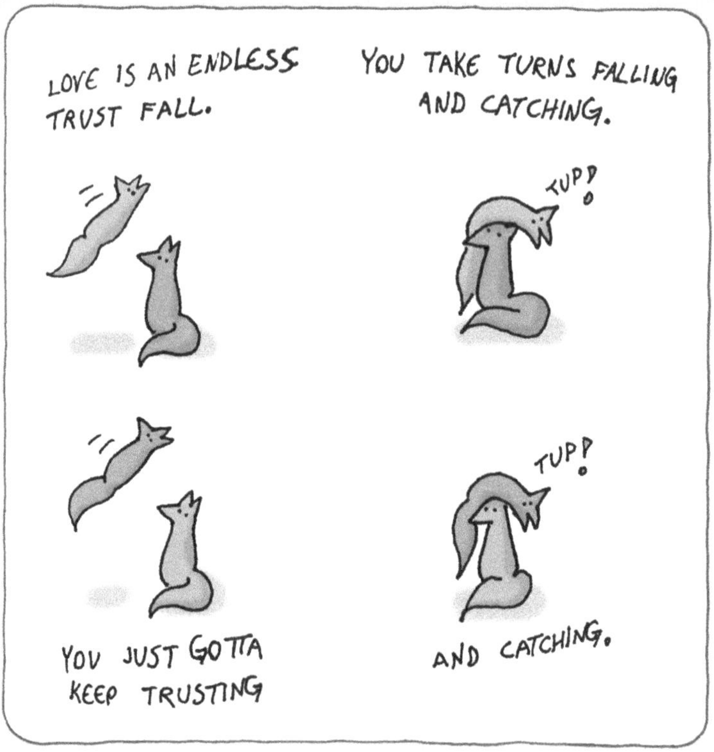
LOVE IS AN ENDLESS TRUST FALL.
YOU TAKE TURNS FALLING AND CATCHING.
TUPP!
YOU JUST GOTTA KEEP TRUSTING
TUPP!
AND CATCHING.

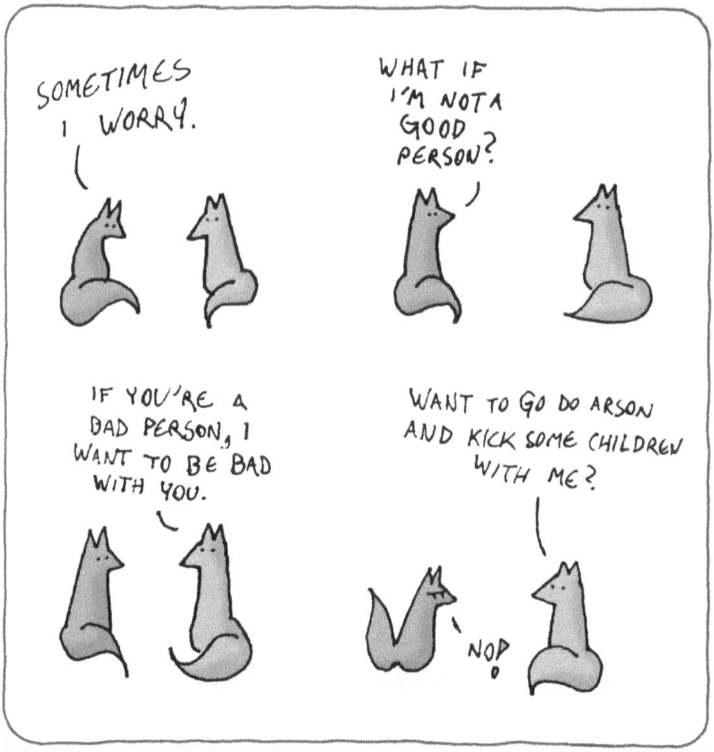
SOMETIMES I WORRY.
WHAT IF I'M NOT A GOOD PERSON?
IF YOU'RE A BAD PERSON, I WANT TO BE BAD WITH YOU.
WANT TO GO DO ARSON AND KICK SOME CHILDREN WITH ME?
NOP!

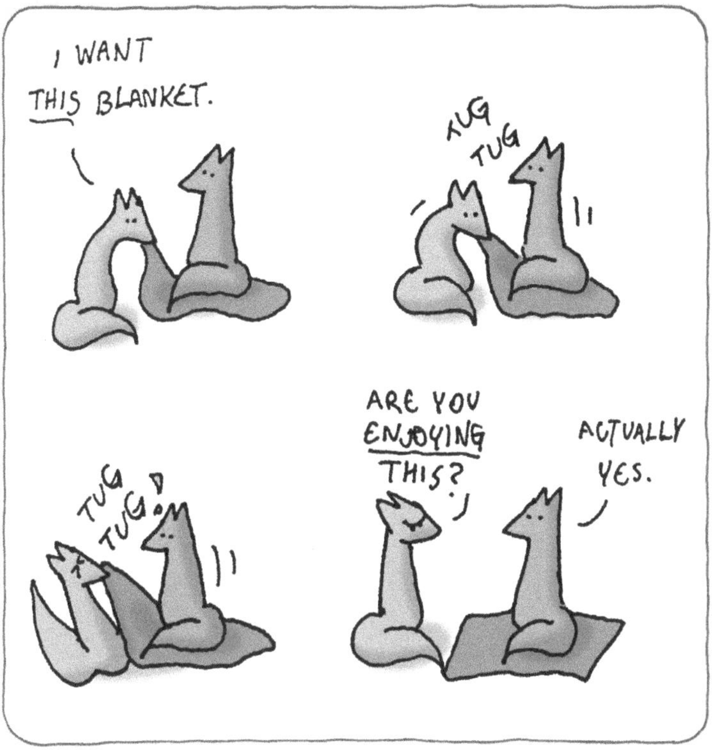
I WANT THIS BLANKET.
TUG TUG
TUG TUG!
ARE YOU ENJOYING THIS?
ACTUALLY YES.

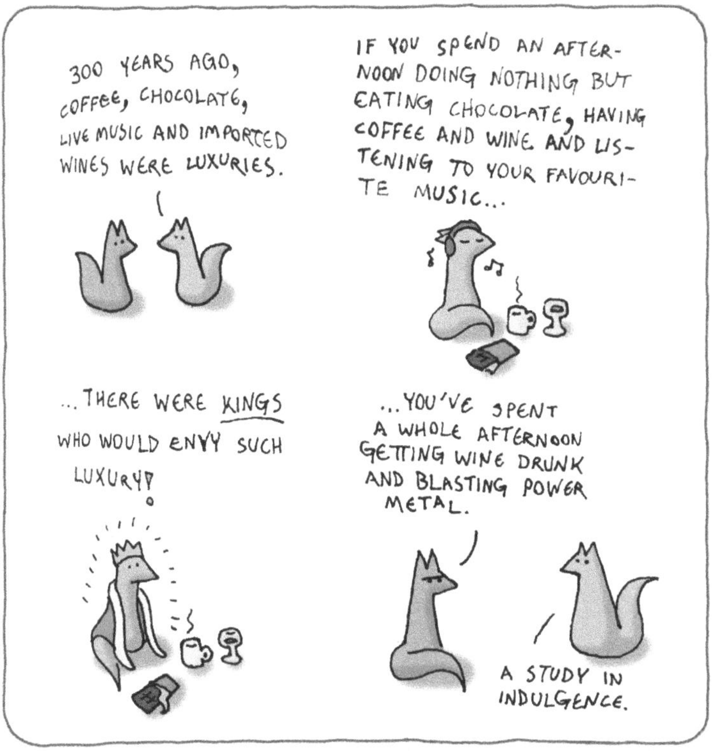
300 YEARS AGO, COFFEE, CHOCOLATE, LIVE MUSIC AND IMPORTED WINES WERE LUXURIES.
IF YOU SPEND AN AFTER-NOON DOING NOTHING BUT EATING CHOCOLATE, HAVING COFFEE AND WINE AND LIS-TENING TO YOUR FAVOURI-TE MUSIC...
...THERE WERE KINGS WHO WOULD ENVY SUCH LUXURY?
...YOU'VE SPENT A WHOLE AFTERNOON GETTING WINE DRUNK AND BLASTING POWER METAL.
A STUDY IN INDULGENCE.

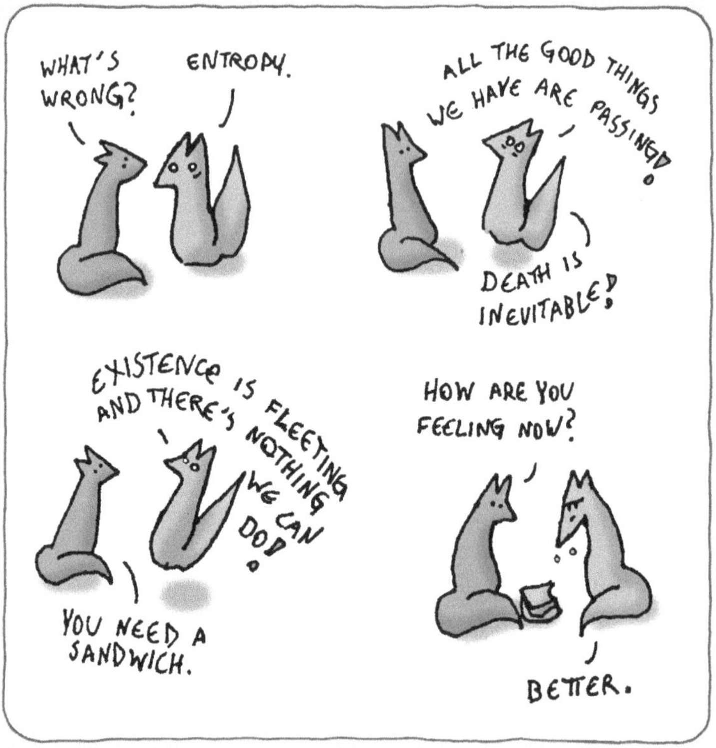
WHAT'S WRONG?
ENTROPY.
ALL THE GOOD THINGS WE HAVE ARE PASSING!
DEATH IS INEVITABLE!
EXISTENCE IS FLEETING AND THERE'S NOTHING WE CAN DO!
YOU NEED A SANDWICH.
HOW ARE YOU FEELING NOW?
BETTER.

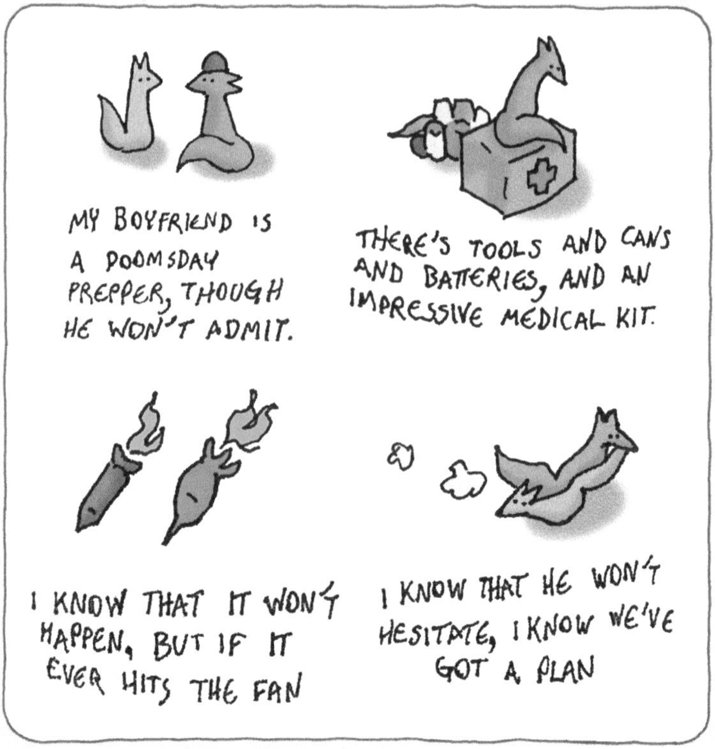
MY BOYFRIEND IS A DOOMSDAY PREPPER, THOUGH HE WON'T ADMIT.
THERE'S TOOLS AND CANS AND BATTERIES, AND AN IMPRESSIVE MEDICAL KIT.
I KNOW THAT IT WON'T HAPPEN, BUT IF IT EVER HITS THE FAN
I KNOW THAT HE WON'T HESITATE, I KNOW WE'VE GOT A PLAN

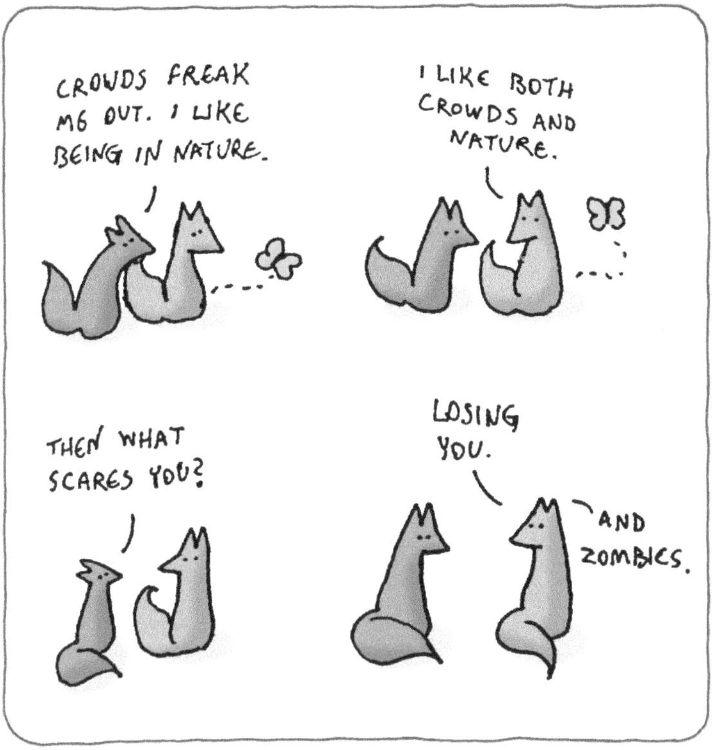
CROWDS FREAK ME OUT. I LIKE BEING IN NATURE.
I LIKE BOTH CROWDS AND NATURE.
THEN WHAT SCARES YOU?
LOSING YOU.
AND ZOMBIES.

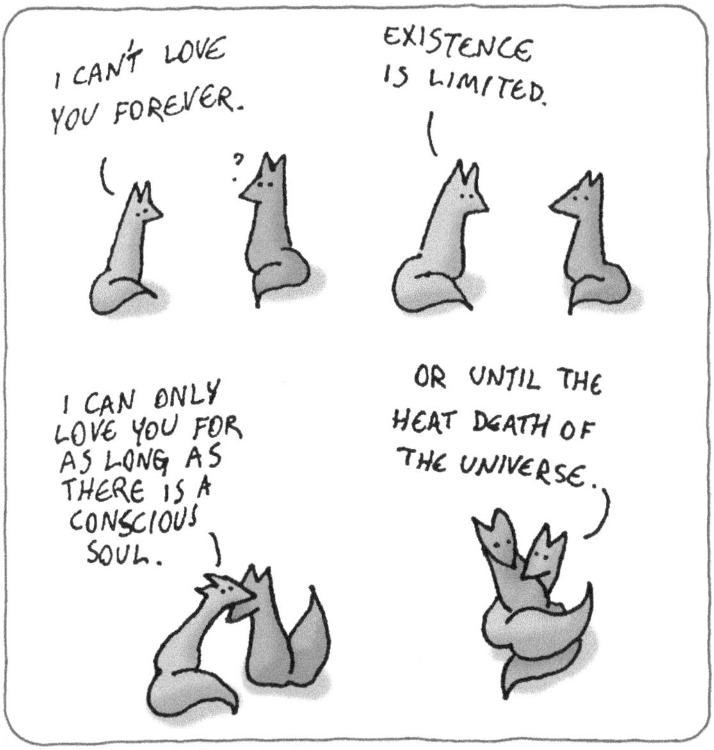
I CAN'T LOVE YOU FOREVER.
?
EXISTENCE IS LIMITED.
I CAN ONLY LOVE YOU FOR AS LONG AS THERE IS A CONSCIOUS SOUL.
OR UNTIL THE HEAT DEATH OF THE UNIVERSE.

TOIVO KAARTINEN

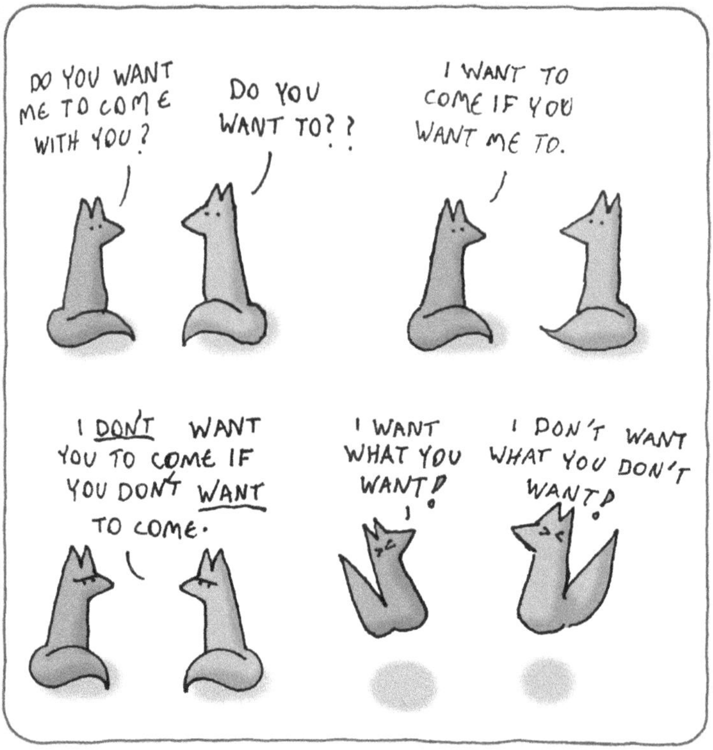
DO YOU WANT ME TO COME WITH YOU?
DO YOU WANT TO??
I WANT TO COME IF YOU WANT ME TO.
I DON'T WANT YOU TO COME IF YOU DON'T WANT TO COME.
I WANT WHAT YOU WANT!
I DON'T WANT WHAT YOU DON'T WANT!

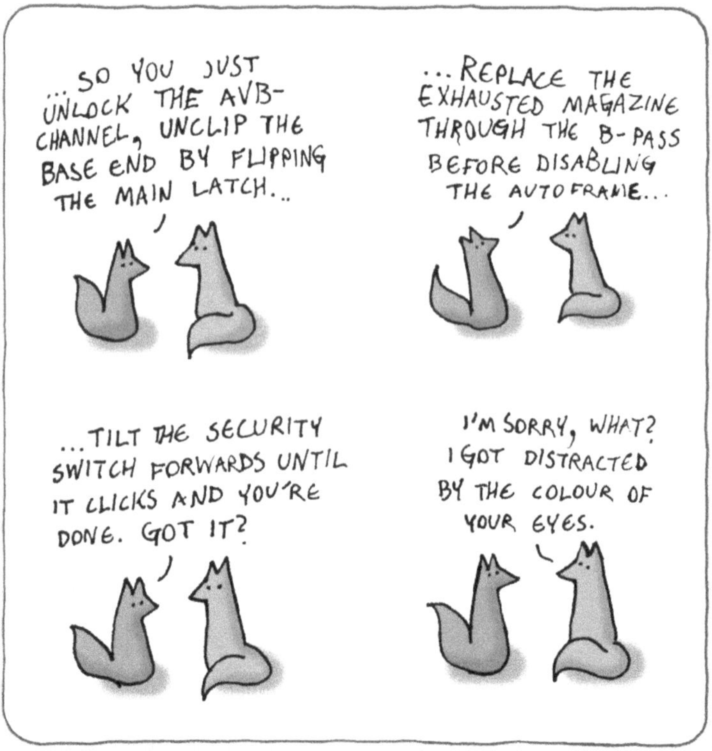
...SO YOU JUST UNLOCK THE AVB-CHANNEL, UNCLIP THE BASE END BY FLIPPING THE MAIN LATCH...
...REPLACE THE EXHAUSTED MAGAZINE THROUGH THE B-PASS BEFORE DISABLING THE AUTOFRAME...
...TILT THE SECURITY SWITCH FORWARDS UNTIL IT CLICKS AND YOU'RE DONE. GOT IT?
I'M SORRY, WHAT? I GOT DISTRACTED BY THE COLOUR OF YOUR EYES.

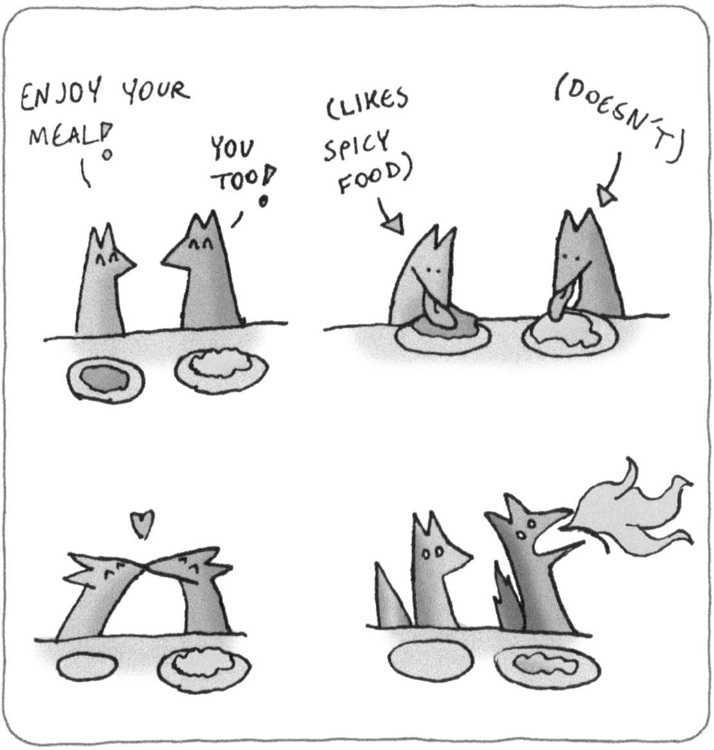
ENJOY YOUR MEAL!
YOU TOO!
(LIKES SPICY FOOD)
(DOESN'T)

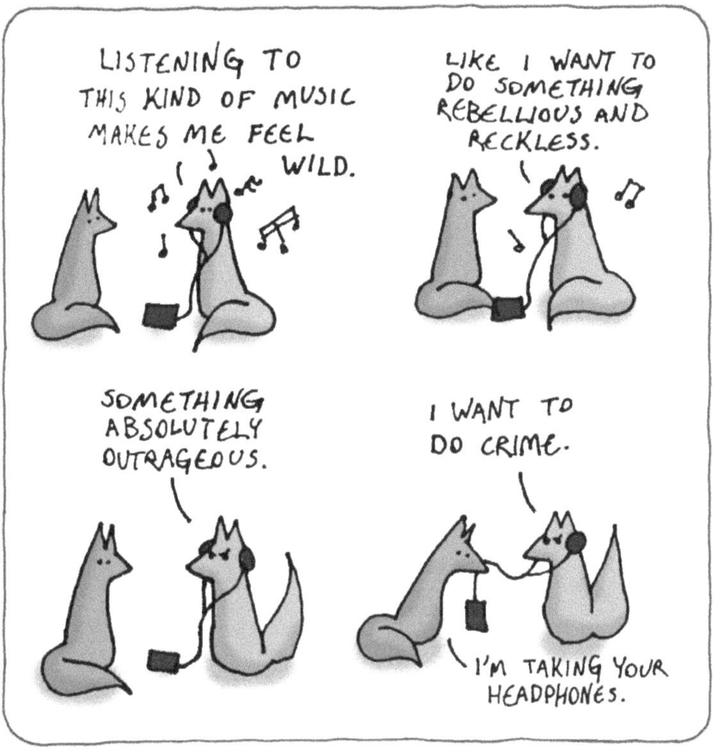
LISTENING TO THIS KIND OF MUSIC MAKES ME FEEL WILD.
LIKE I WANT TO DO SOMETHING REBELLIOUS AND RECKLESS.
SOMETHING ABSOLUTELY OUTRAGEOUS.
I WANT TO DO CRIME.
I'M TAKING YOUR HEADPHONES.

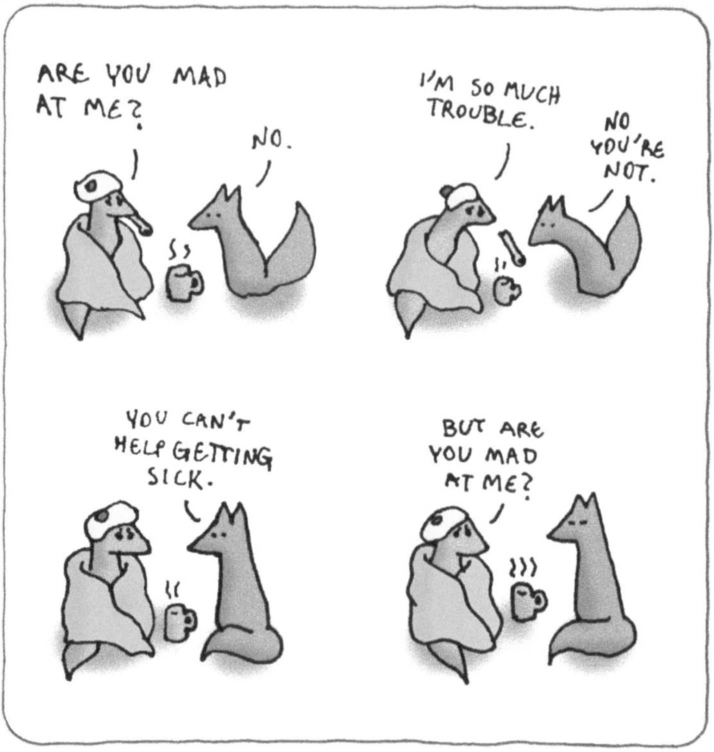
ARE YOU MAD AT ME?
NO.
I'M SO MUCH TROUBLE.
NO YOU'RE NOT.
YOU CAN'T HELP GETTING SICK.
BUT ARE YOU MAD AT ME?

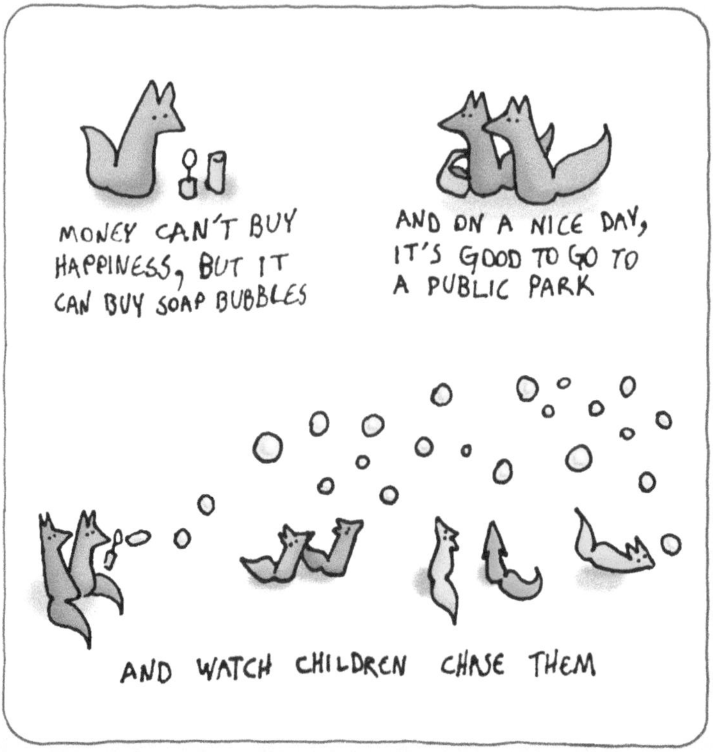
MONEY CAN'T BUY HAPPINESS, BUT IT CAN BUY SOAP BUBBLES
AND ON A NICE DAY, IT'S GOOD TO GO TO A PUBLIC PARK
AND WATCH CHILDREN CHASE THEM

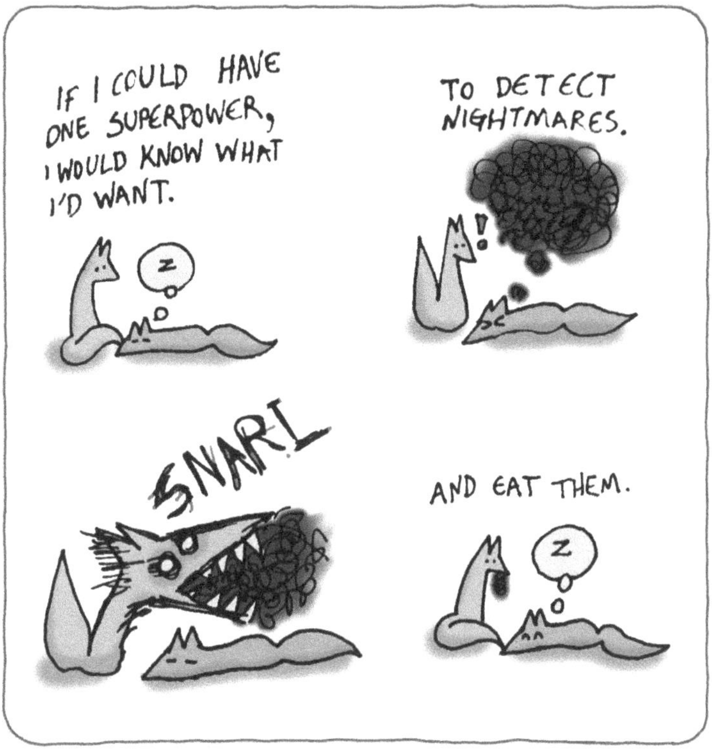
IF I COULD HAVE ONE SUPERPOWER, I WOULD KNOW WHAT I'D WANT.
Z
TO DETECT NIGHTMARES.
!
SNARL
AND EAT THEM.
Z

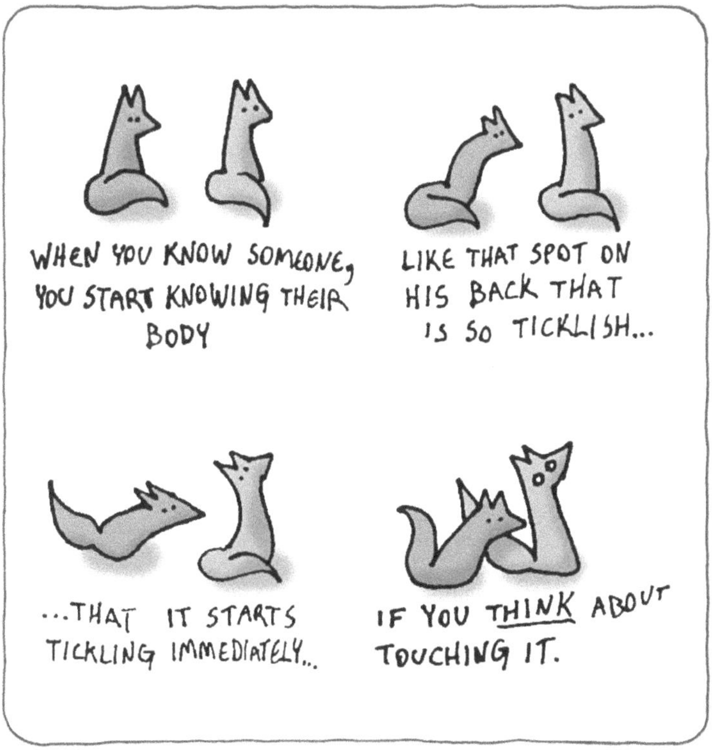
WHEN YOU KNOW SOMEONE, YOU START KNOWING THEIR BODY
LIKE THAT SPOT ON HIS BACK THAT IS SO TICKLISH...
...THAT IT STARTS TICKLING IMMEDIATELY...
IF YOU THINK ABOUT TOUCHING IT.

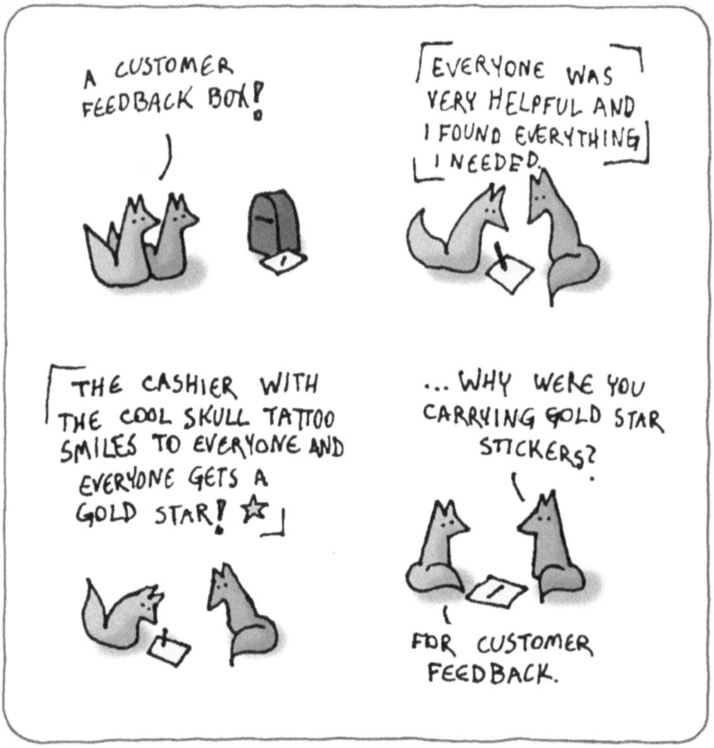
A CUSTOMER FEEDBACK BOX!
EVERYONE WAS VERY HELPFUL AND I FOUND EVERYTHING I NEEDED.
THE CASHIER WITH THE COOL SKULL TATTOO SMILES TO EVERYONE AND EVERYONE GETS A GOLD STAR! ☆
...WHY WERE YOU CARRYING GOLD STAR STICKERS?
FOR CUSTOMER FEEDBACK.

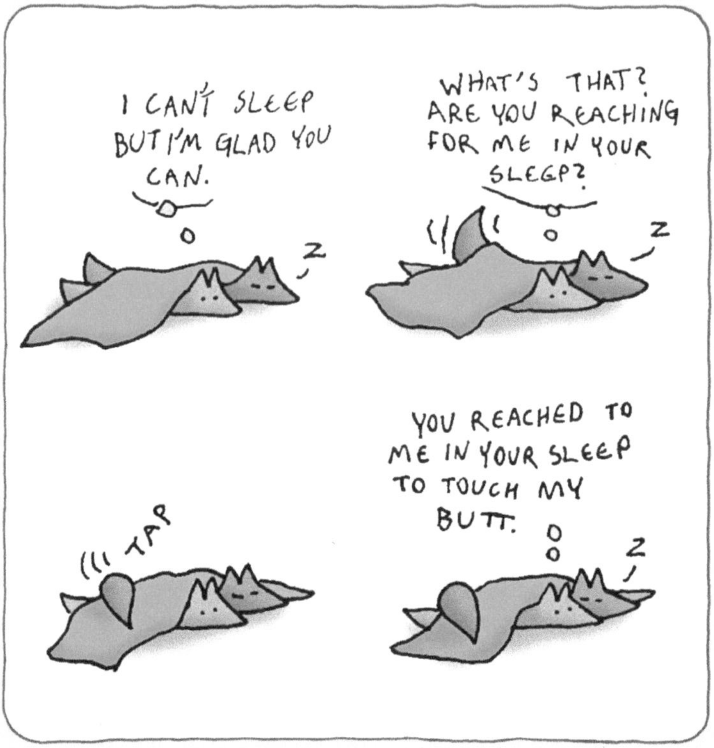
I CAN'T SLEEP BUT I'M GLAD YOU CAN.
Z
WHAT'S THAT? ARE YOU REACHING FOR ME IN YOUR SLEEP?
Z
TAP
YOU REACHED TO ME IN YOUR SLEEP TO TOUCH MY BUTT.
Z

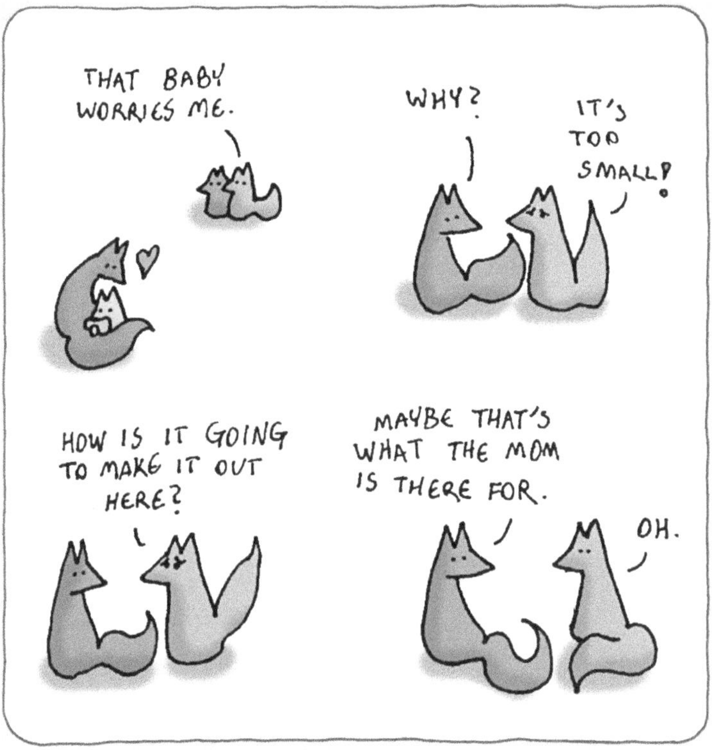
THAT BABY WORRIES ME.
WHY?
IT'S TOO SMALL!
HOW IS IT GOING TO MAKE IT OUT HERE?
MAYBE THAT'S WHAT THE MOM IS THERE FOR.
OH.

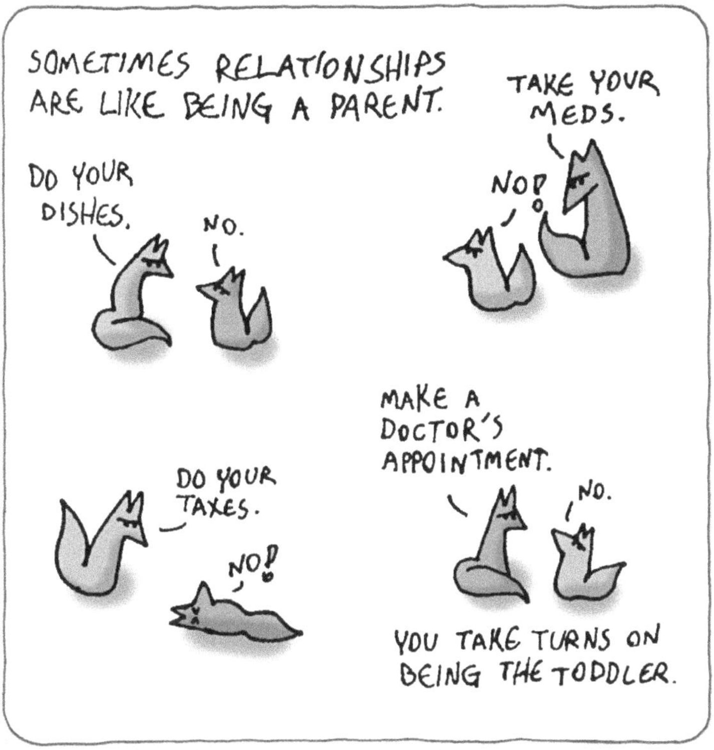
SOMETIMES RELATIONSHIPS ARE LIKE BEING A PARENT.
DO YOUR DISHES.
NO.
TAKE YOUR MEDS.
NO!
DO YOUR TAXES.
NO!
MAKE A DOCTOR'S APPOINTMENT.
NO.
YOU TAKE TURNS ON BEING THE TODDLER.

TOIVO KAARTINEN

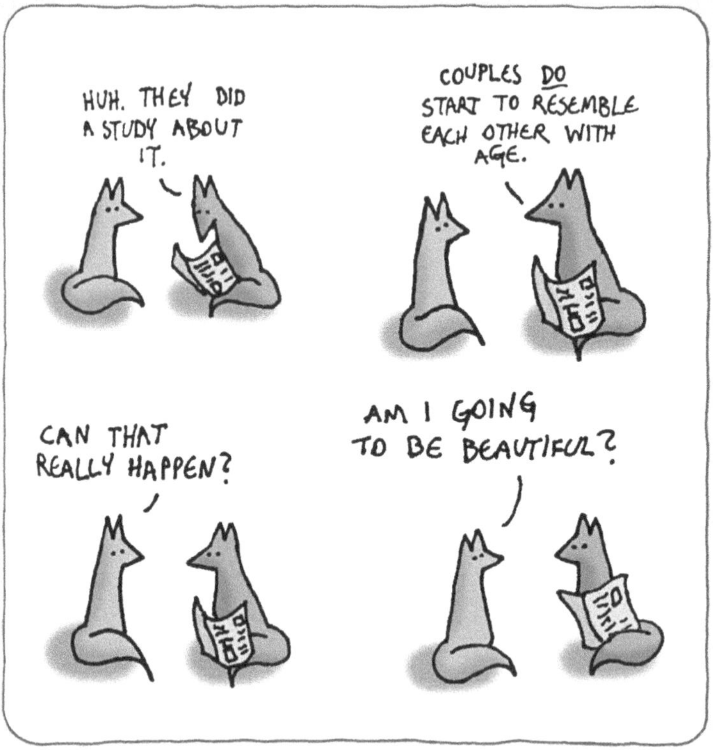
HUH. THEY DID A STUDY ABOUT IT.
COUPLES DO START TO RESEMBLE EACH OTHER WITH AGE.
CAN THAT REALLY HAPPEN?
AM I GOING TO BE BEAUTIFUL?

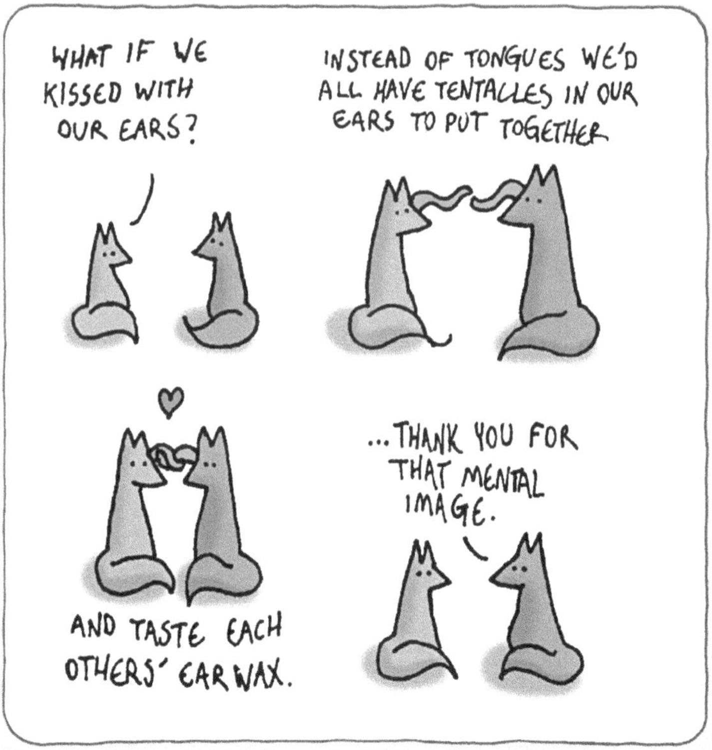
WHAT IF WE KISSED WITH OUR EARS?
INSTEAD OF TONGUES WE'D ALL HAVE TENTACLES IN OUR EARS TO PUT TOGETHER
AND TASTE EACH OTHERS' EARWAX.
...THANK YOU FOR THAT MENTAL IMAGE.

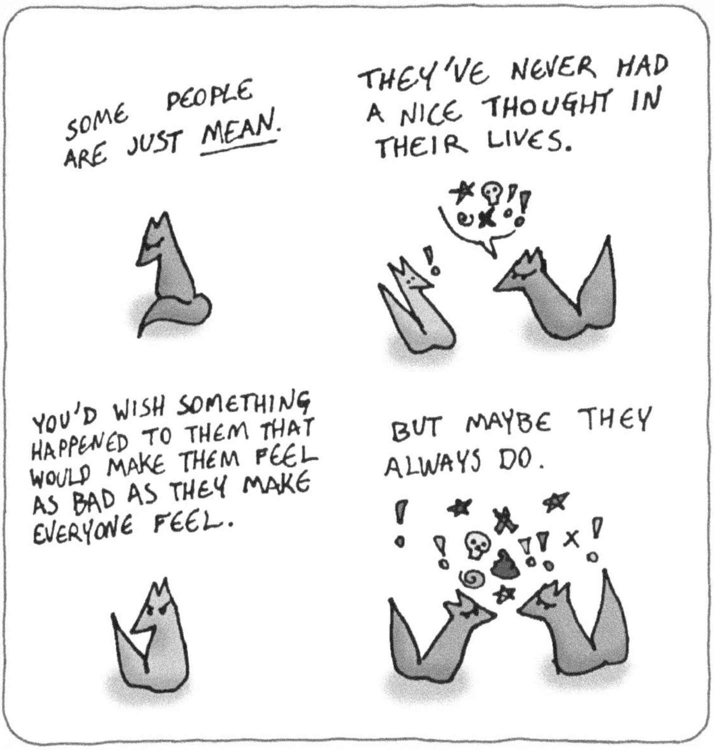
SOME PEOPLE ARE JUST MEAN.
THEY'VE NEVER HAD A NICE THOUGHT IN THEIR LIVES.
YOU'D WISH SOMETHING HAPPENED TO THEM THAT WOULD MAKE THEM FEEL AS BAD AS THEY MAKE EVERYONE FEEL.
BUT MAYBE THEY ALWAYS DO.

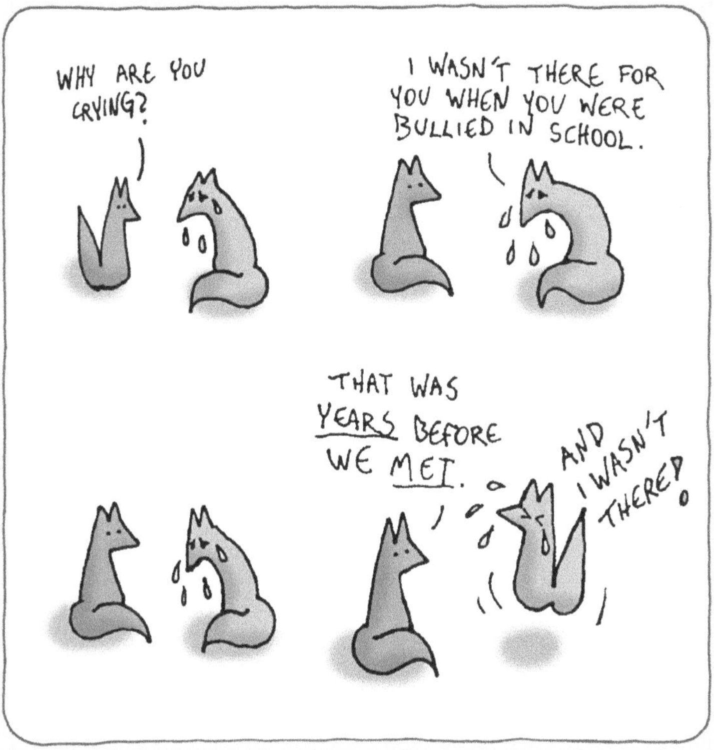
WHY ARE YOU CRYING?
I WASN'T THERE FOR YOU WHEN YOU WERE BULLIED IN SCHOOL.
THAT WAS YEARS BEFORE WE MET.
AND I WASN'T THERE!

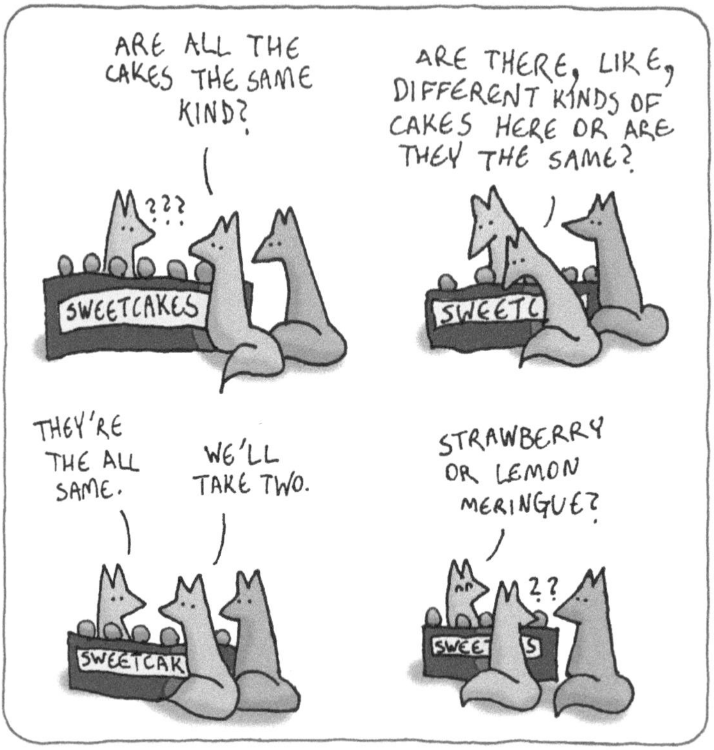
ARE ALL THE CAKES THE SAME KIND?
???
SWEETCAKES
ARE THERE, LIKE, DIFFERENT KINDS OF CAKES HERE OR ARE THEY THE SAME?
SWEETC
THEY'RE THE ALL SAME.
WE'LL TAKE TWO.
SWEETCAK
STRAWBERRY OR LEMON MERINGUE?
??
SWEE S

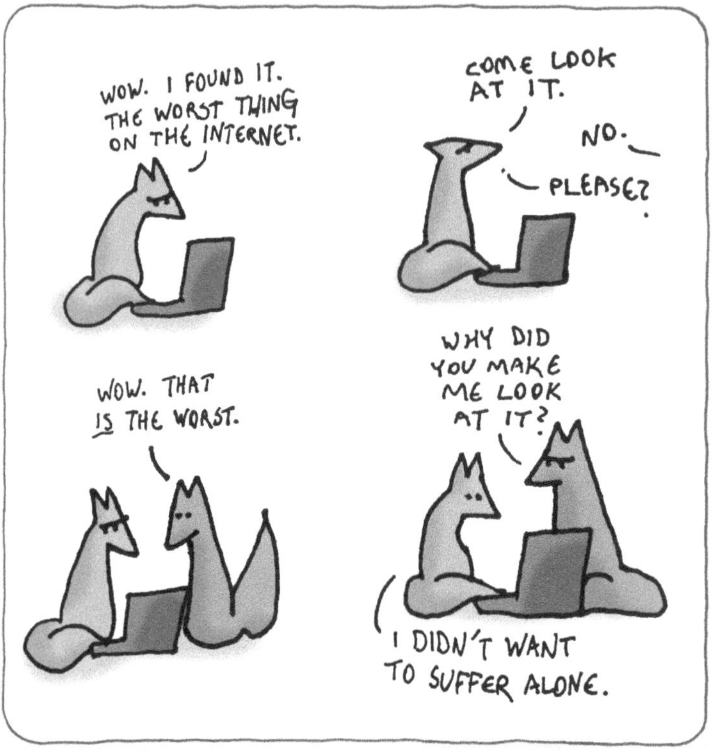
WOW. I FOUND IT. THE WORST THING ON THE INTERNET.
COME LOOK AT IT.
NO.
PLEASE?
WOW. THAT IS THE WORST.
WHY DID YOU MAKE ME LOOK AT IT?
I DIDN'T WANT TO SUFFER ALONE.

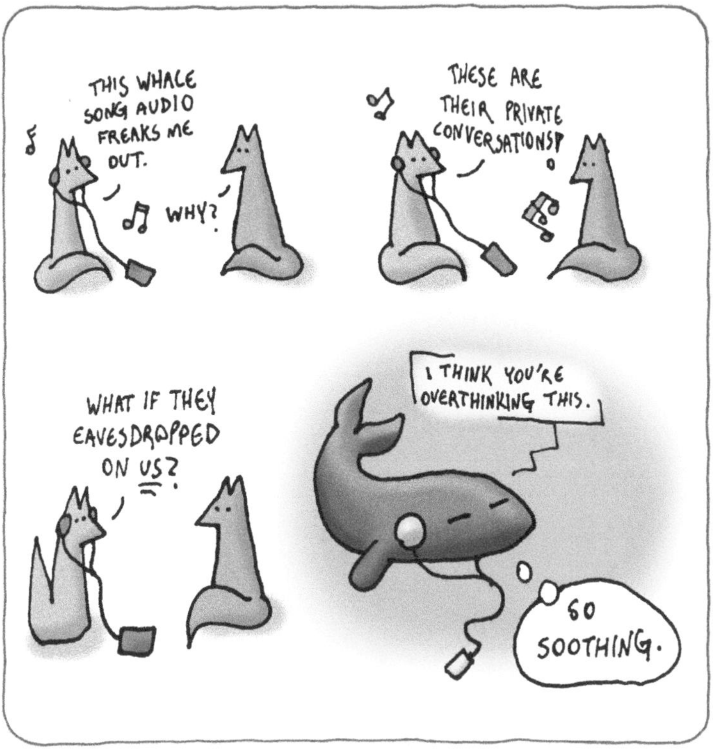
THIS WHALE SONG AUDIO FREAKS ME OUT.
WHY?
THESE ARE THEIR PRIVATE CONVERSATIONS!
WHAT IF THEY EAVESDROPPED ON US?
I THINK YOU'RE OVERTHINKING THIS.
SO SOOTHING.

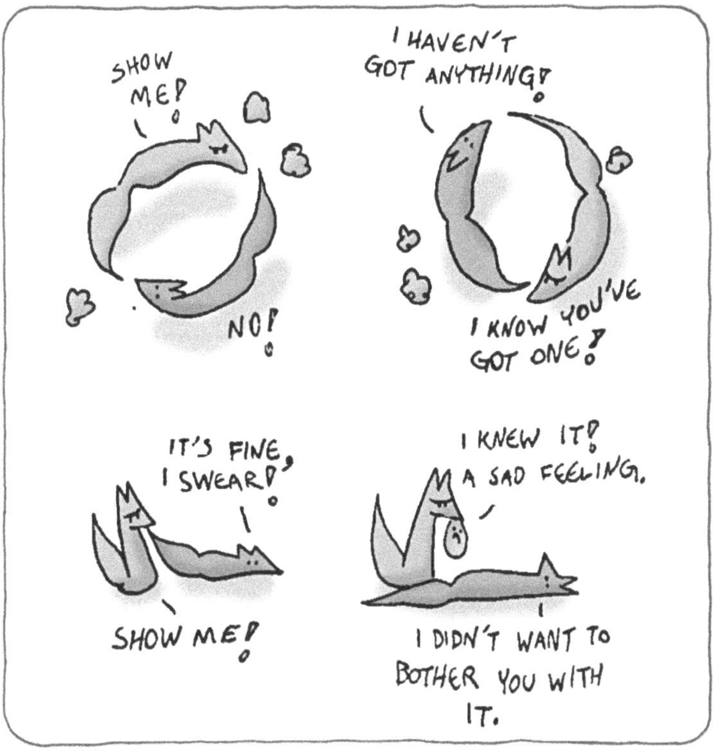
SHOW ME!
NO!
I HAVEN'T GOT ANYTHING!
I KNOW YOU'VE GOT ONE!
IT'S FINE, I SWEAR!
SHOW ME!
I KNEW IT! A SAD FEELING.
I DIDN'T WANT TO BOTHER YOU WITH IT.

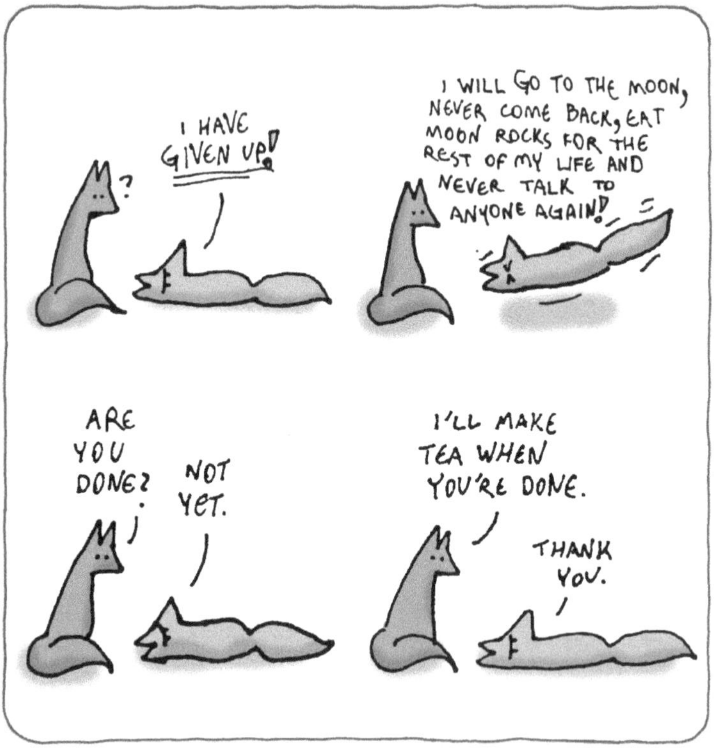
I HAVE GIVEN UP!
I WILL GO TO THE MOON, NEVER COME BACK, EAT MOON ROCKS FOR THE REST OF MY LIFE AND NEVER TALK TO ANYONE AGAIN!
ARE YOU DONE?
NOT YET.
I'LL MAKE TEA WHEN YOU'RE DONE.
THANK YOU.

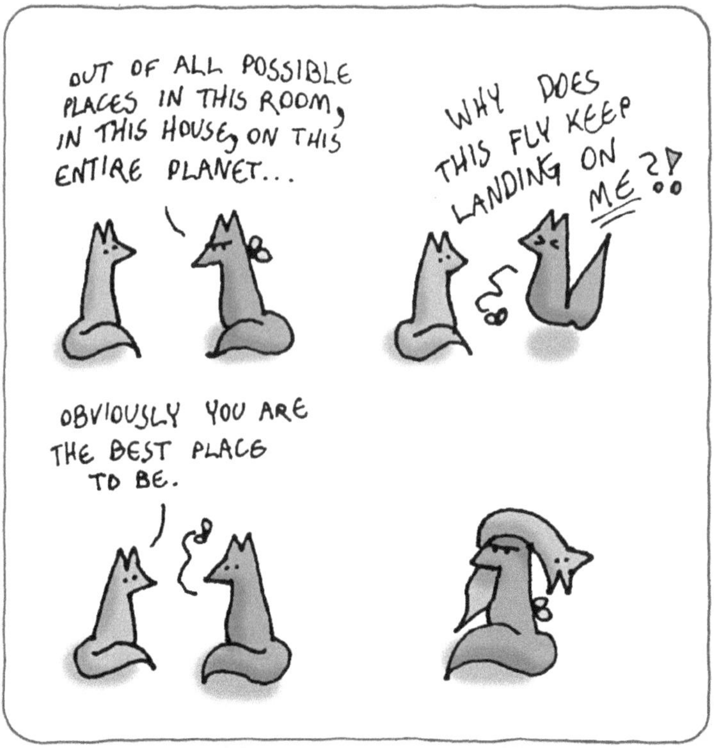
OUT OF ALL POSSIBLE PLACES IN THIS ROOM, IN THIS HOUSE, ON THIS ENTIRE PLANET...
WHY DOES THIS FLY KEEP LANDING ON ME?!
OBVIOUSLY YOU ARE THE BEST PLACE TO BE.

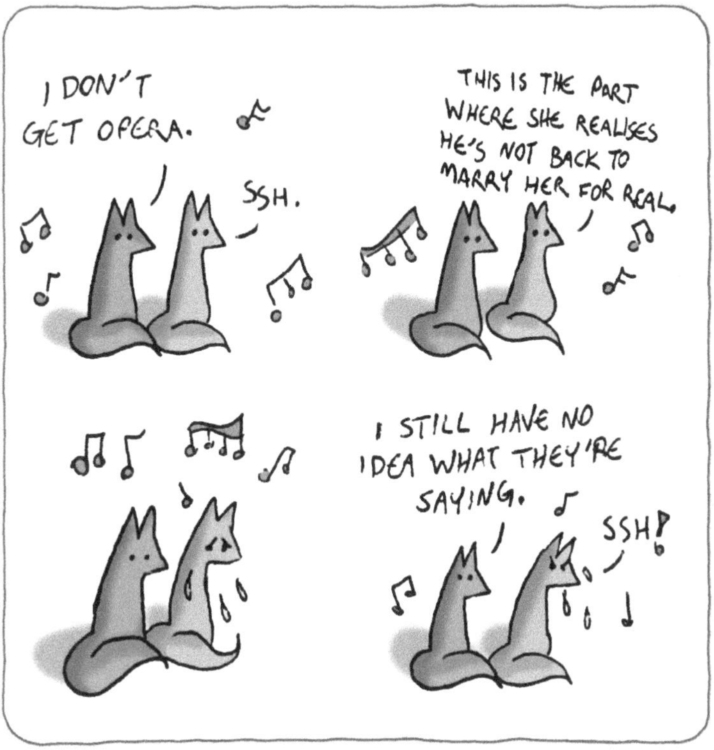
I DON'T GET OPERA.
SSH.
THIS IS THE PART WHERE SHE REALISES HE'S NOT BACK TO MARRY HER FOR REAL.
I STILL HAVE NO IDEA WHAT THEY'RE SAYING.
SSH!

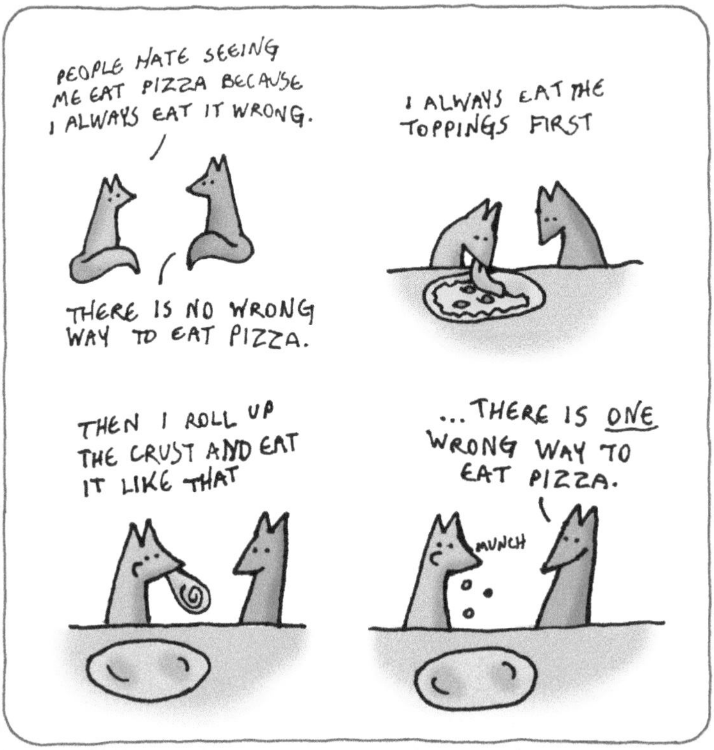
PEOPLE HATE SEEING ME EAT PIZZA BECAUSE I ALWAYS EAT IT WRONG.
THERE IS NO WRONG WAY TO EAT PIZZA.
I ALWAYS EAT THE TOPPINGS FIRST
THEN I ROLL UP THE CRUST AND EAT IT LIKE THAT
...THERE IS ONE WRONG WAY TO EAT PIZZA.
MUNCH

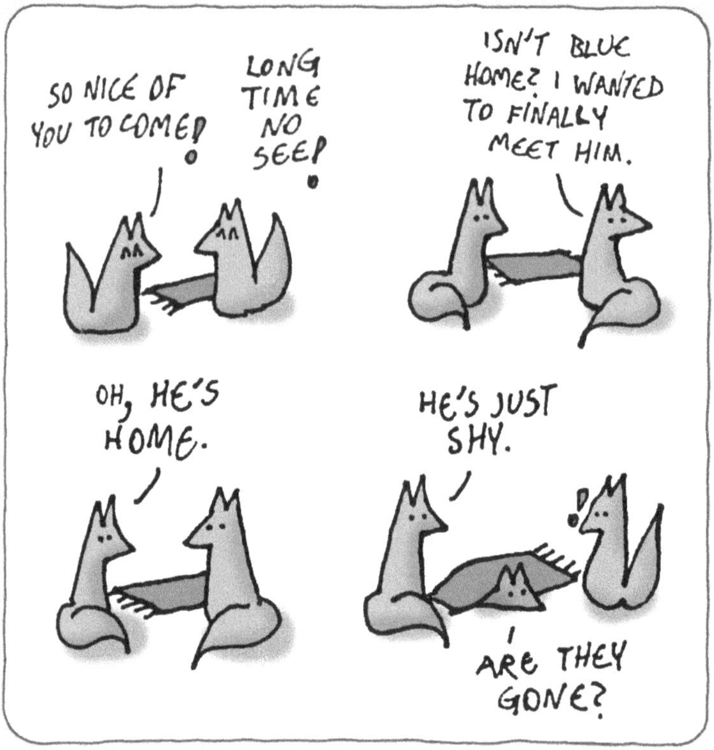
SO NICE OF YOU TO COME!
LONG TIME NO SEE!
ISN'T BLUE HOME? I WANTED TO FINALLY MEET HIM.
OH, HE'S HOME.
HE'S JUST SHY.
ARE THEY GONE?

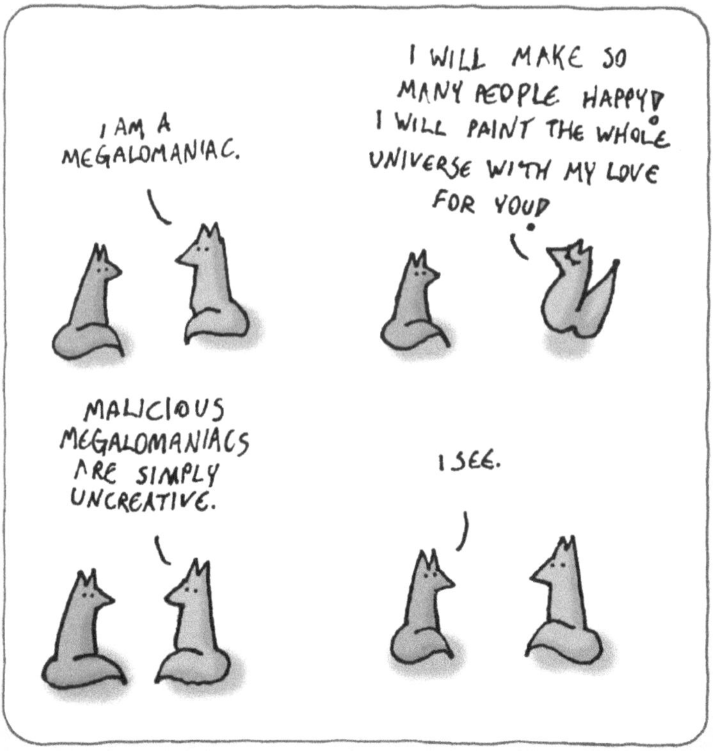
I AM A MEGALOMANIAC.
I WILL MAKE SO MANY PEOPLE HAPPY! I WILL PAINT THE WHOLE UNIVERSE WITH MY LOVE FOR YOU!
MALICIOUS MEGALOMANIACS ARE SIMPLY UNCREATIVE.
I SEE.

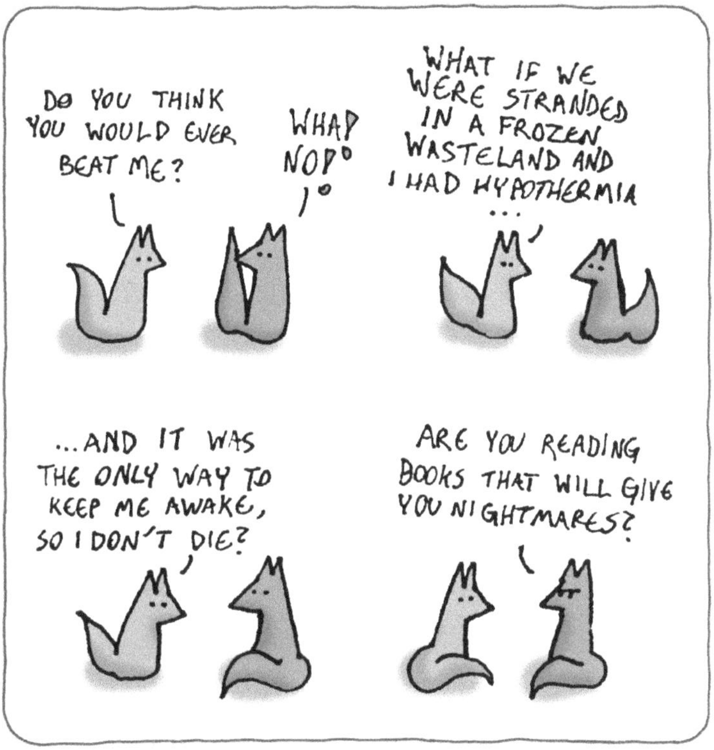
DO YOU THINK YOU WOULD EVER BEAT ME?
WHA?! NO?!
WHAT IF WE WERE STRANDED IN A FROZEN WASTELAND AND I HAD HYPOTHERMIA
...
...AND IT WAS THE ONLY WAY TO KEEP ME AWAKE, SO I DON'T DIE?
ARE YOU READING BOOKS THAT WILL GIVE YOU NIGHTMARES?

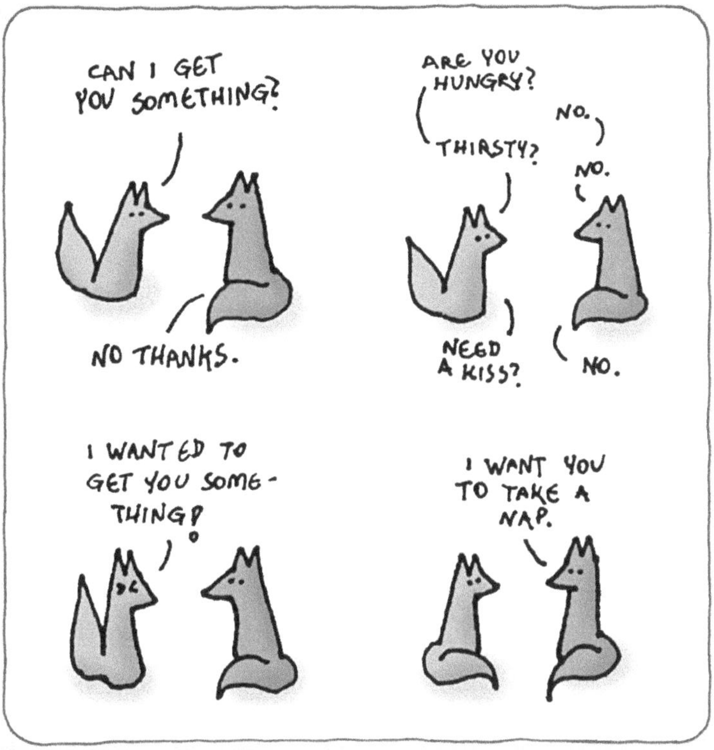
CAN I GET YOU SOMETHING?
NO THANKS.
ARE YOU HUNGRY?
NO.
THIRSTY?
NO.
NEED A KISS?
NO.
I WANTED TO GET YOU SOME-THING?!
I WANT YOU TO TAKE A NAP.

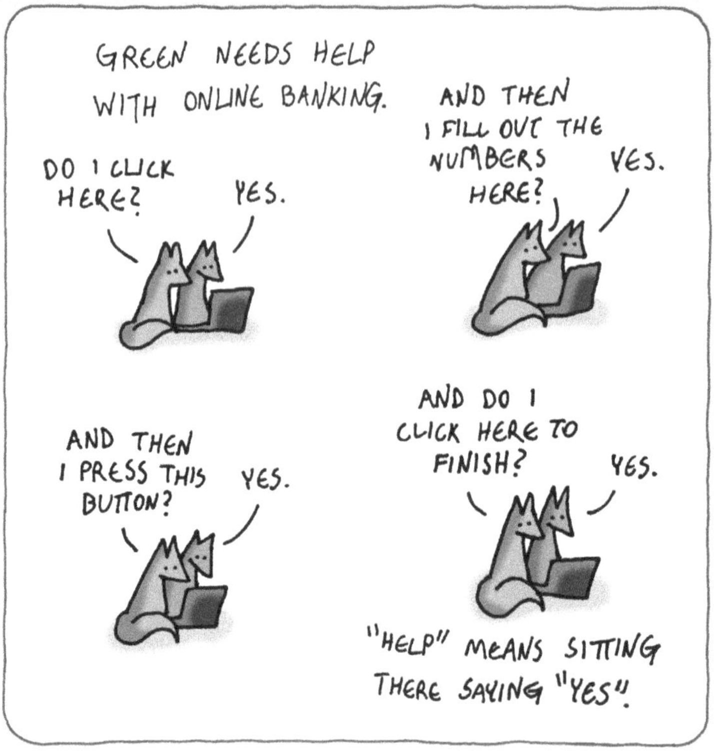
GREEN NEEDS HELP WITH ONLINE BANKING.
DO I CLICK HERE?
YES.
AND THEN I FILL OUT THE NUMBERS HERE?
YES.
AND THEN I PRESS THIS BUTTON?
YES.
AND DO I CLICK HERE TO FINISH?
YES.
"HELP" MEANS SITTING THERE SAYING "YES".

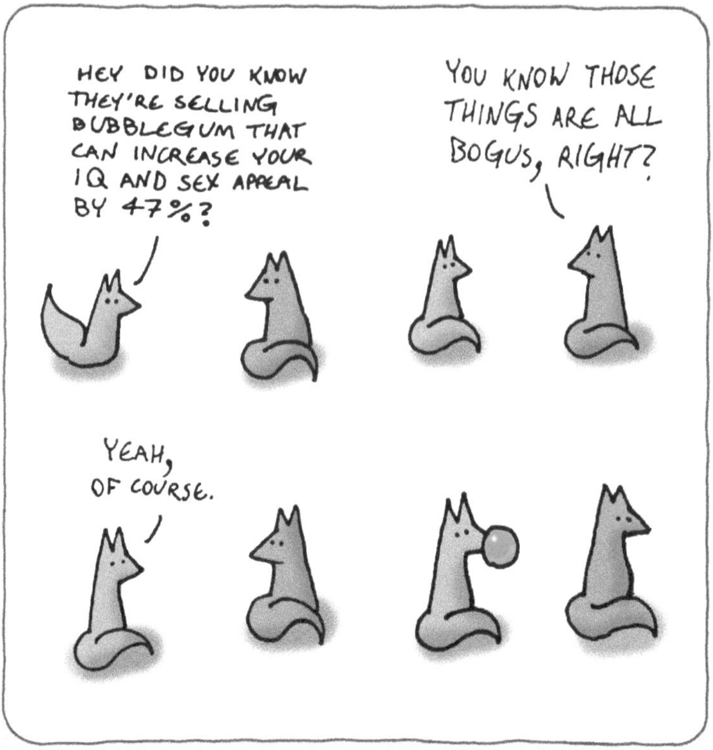
HEY DID YOU KNOW THEY'RE SELLING BUBBLEGUM THAT CAN INCREASE YOUR IQ AND SEX APPEAL BY 47%?
YOU KNOW THOSE THINGS ARE ALL BOGUS, RIGHT?
YEAH, OF COURSE.

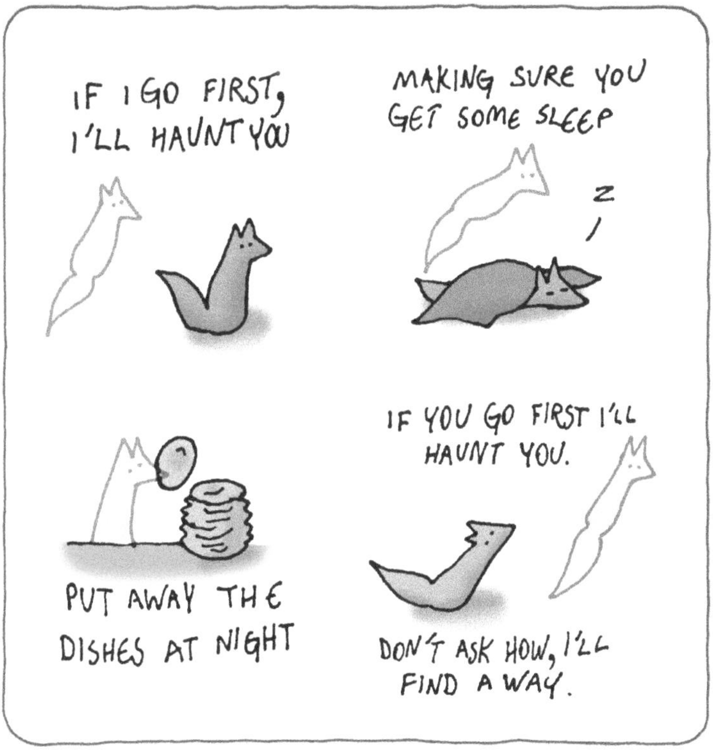
IF I GO FIRST, I'LL HAUNT YOU
MAKING SURE YOU GET SOME SLEEP
Z
PUT AWAY THE DISHES AT NIGHT
IF YOU GO FIRST I'LL HAUNT YOU.
DON'T ASK HOW, I'LL FIND A WAY.

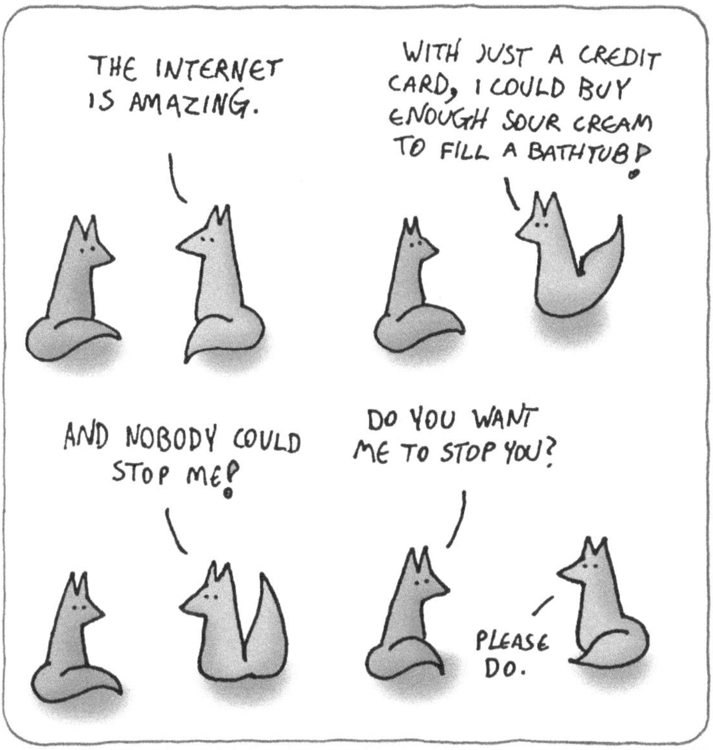
THE INTERNET IS AMAZING.
WITH JUST A CREDIT CARD, I COULD BUY ENOUGH SOUR CREAM TO FILL A BATHTUB!
AND NOBODY COULD STOP ME!
DO YOU WANT ME TO STOP YOU?
PLEASE DO.

TOIVO KAARTINEN

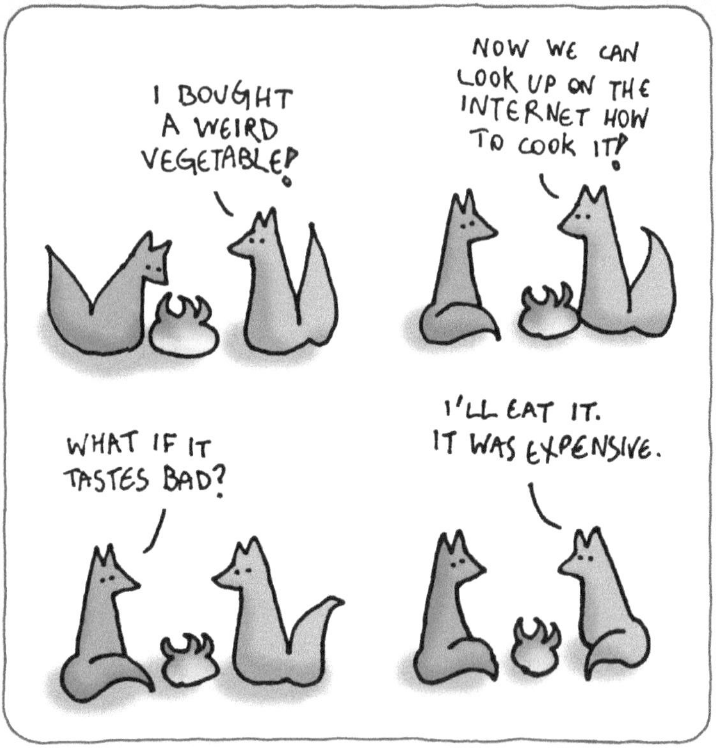
I BOUGHT A WEIRD VEGETABLE!
NOW WE CAN LOOK UP ON THE INTERNET HOW TO COOK IT!
WHAT IF IT TASTES BAD?
I'LL EAT IT. IT WAS EXPENSIVE.

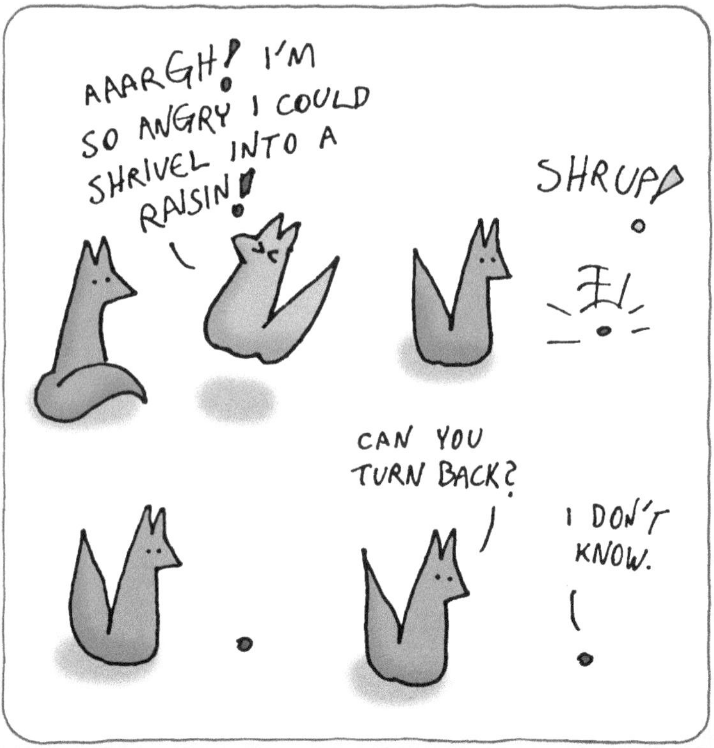
AAARGH! I'M SO ANGRY I COULD SHRIVEL INTO A RAISIN!
SHRUP!
CAN YOU TURN BACK?
I DON'T KNOW.

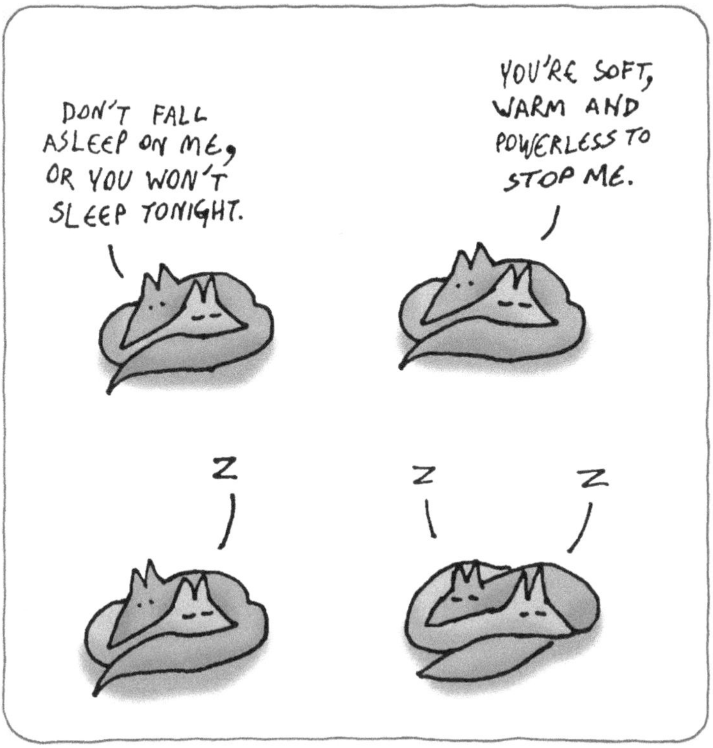
DON'T FALL ASLEEP ON ME, OR YOU WON'T SLEEP TONIGHT.
YOU'RE SOFT, WARM AND POWERLESS TO STOP ME.
Z
Z
Z

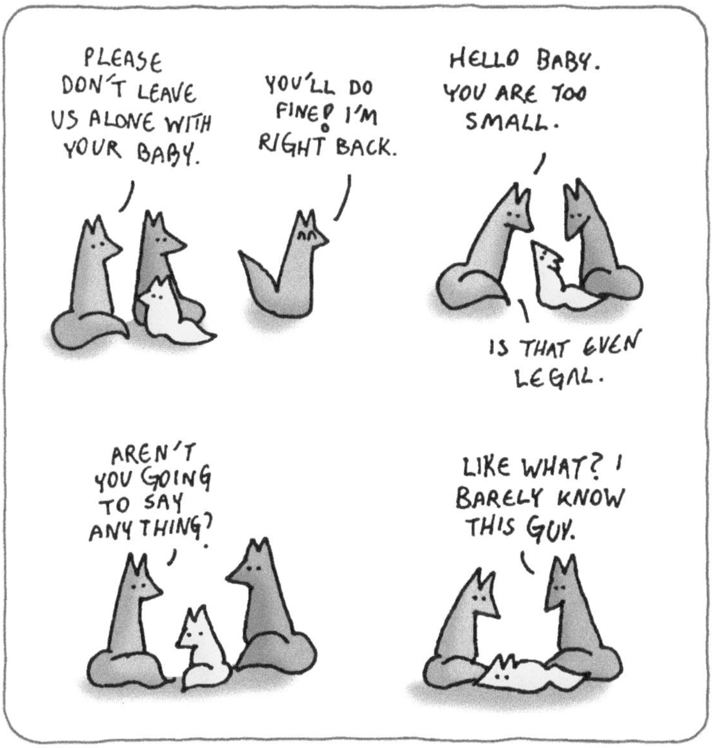
PLEASE DON'T LEAVE US ALONE WITH YOUR BABY.
YOU'LL DO FINE! I'M RIGHT BACK.
HELLO BABY. YOU ARE TOO SMALL.
IS THAT EVEN LEGAL.
AREN'T YOU GOING TO SAY ANYTHING?
LIKE WHAT? I BARELY KNOW THIS GUY.

TOIVO KAARTINEN

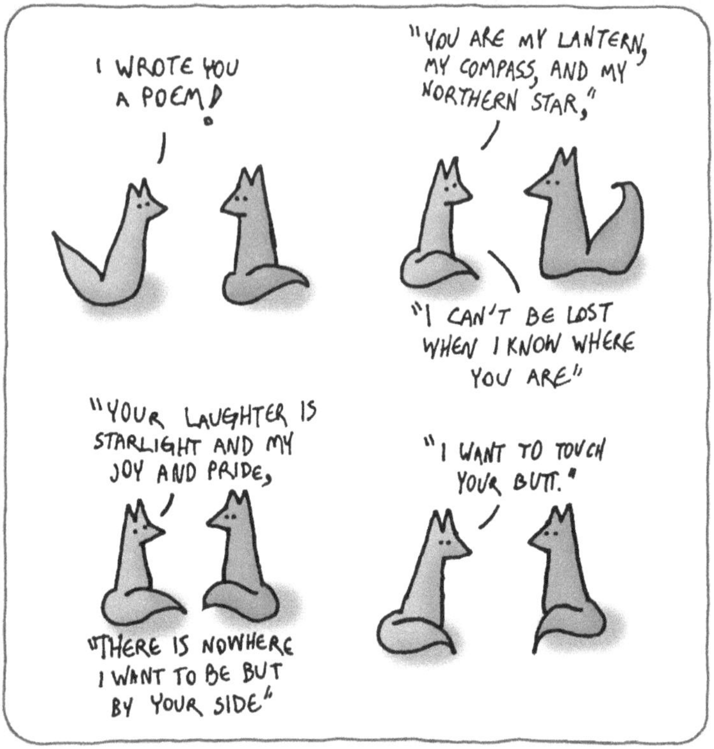
I WROTE YOU A POEM!
"YOU ARE MY LANTERN, MY COMPASS, AND MY NORTHERN STAR,"
"I CAN'T BE LOST WHEN I KNOW WHERE YOU ARE"
"YOUR LAUGHTER IS STARLIGHT AND MY JOY AND PRIDE,
"THERE IS NOWHERE I WANT TO BE BUT BY YOUR SIDE"
"I WANT TO TOUCH YOUR BUTT."

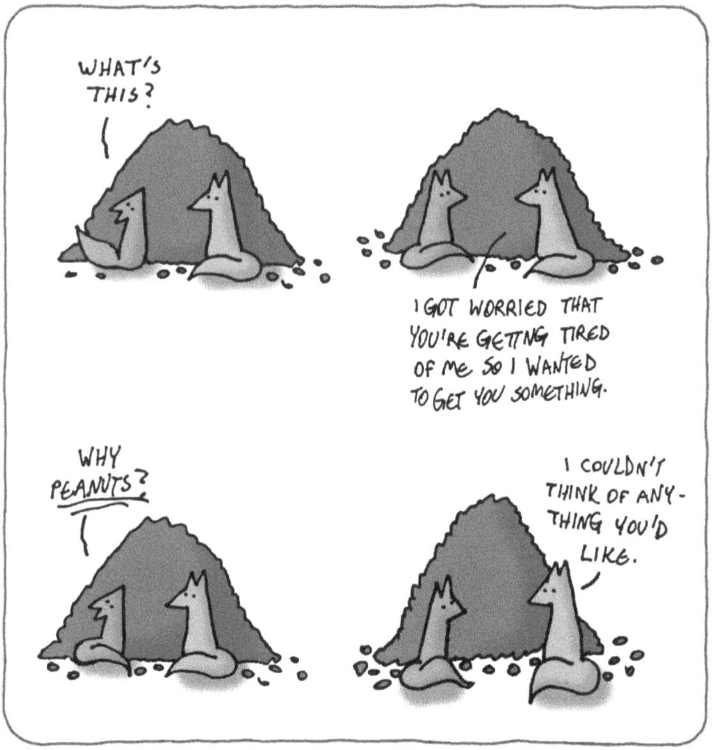
WHAT'S THIS?
I GOT WORRIED THAT YOU'RE GETTING TIRED OF ME SO I WANTED TO GET YOU SOMETHING.
WHY PEANUTS?
I COULDN'T THINK OF ANY-THING YOU'D LIKE.

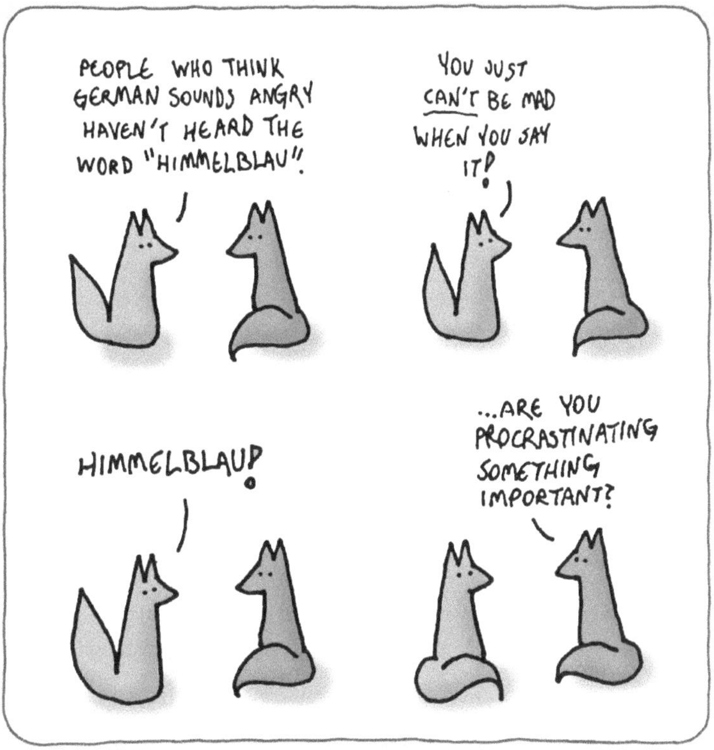
PEOPLE WHO THINK GERMAN SOUNDS ANGRY HAVEN'T HEARD THE WORD "HIMMELBLAU"!
YOU JUST CAN'T BE MAD WHEN YOU SAY IT!
HIMMELBLAU!
...ARE YOU PROCRASTINATING SOMETHING IMPORTANT?

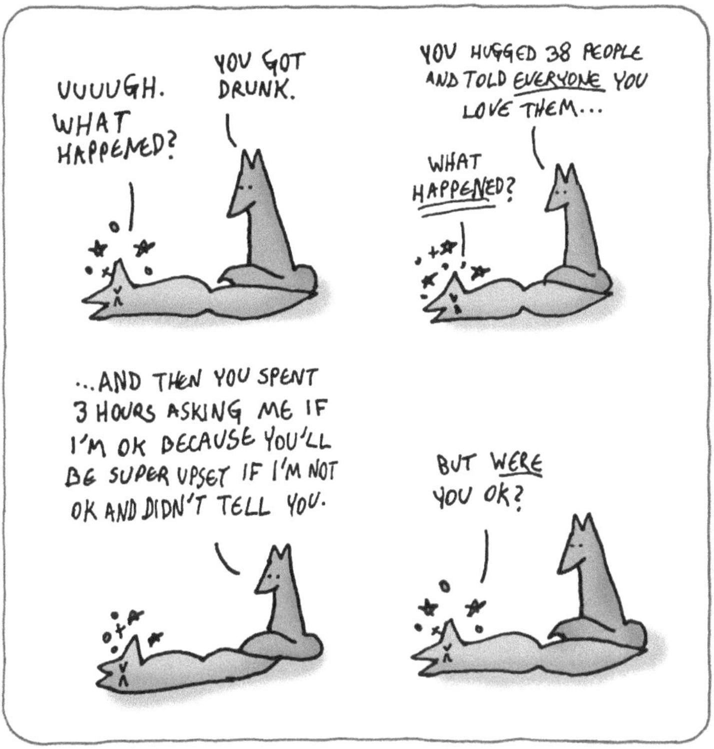
UUUUGH. WHAT HAPPENED?
YOU GOT DRUNK.
YOU HUGGED 38 PEOPLE AND TOLD EVERYONE YOU LOVE THEM...
WHAT HAPPENED?
...AND THEN YOU SPENT 3 HOURS ASKING ME IF I'M OK BECAUSE YOU'LL BE SUPER UPSET IF I'M NOT OK AND DIDN'T TELL YOU.
BUT WERE YOU OK?

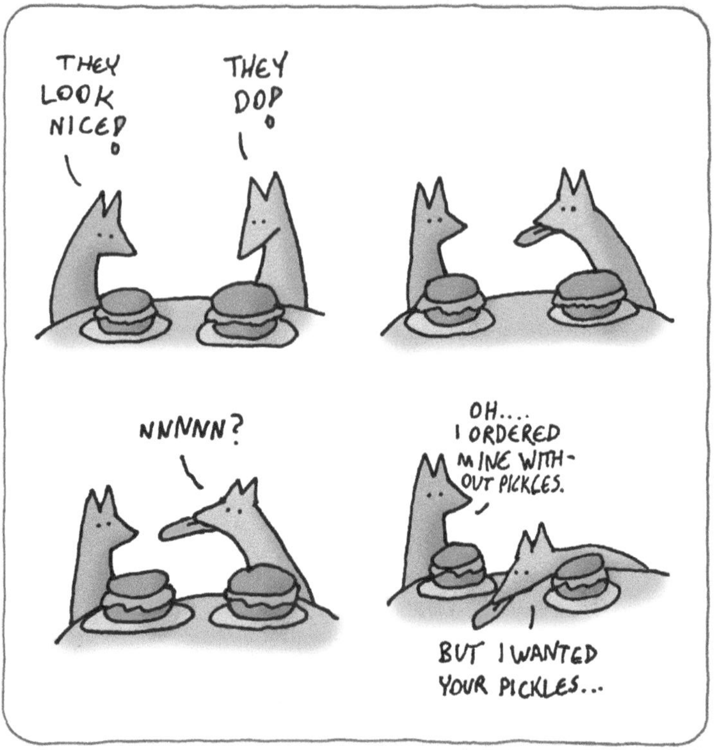
THEY LOOK NICE?
THEY DO?
NNNNN?
OH.... I ORDERED MINE WITH-OUT PICKLES.
BUT I WANTED YOUR PICKLES...

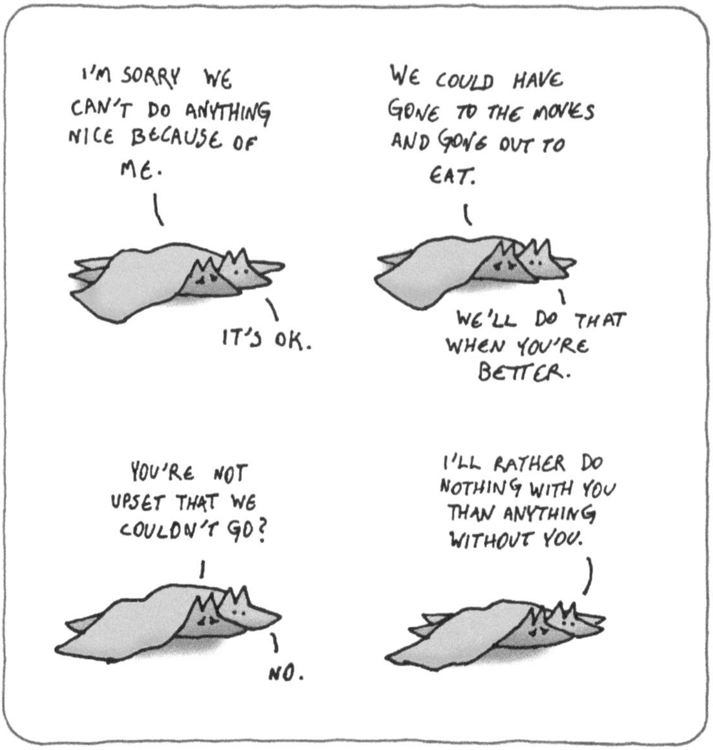
I'M SORRY WE CAN'T DO ANYTHING NICE BECAUSE OF ME.
IT'S OK.
WE COULD HAVE GONE TO THE MOVIES AND GONE OUT TO EAT.
WE'LL DO THAT WHEN YOU'RE BETTER.
YOU'RE NOT UPSET THAT WE COULDN'T GO?
NO.
I'LL RATHER DO NOTHING WITH YOU THAN ANYTHING WITHOUT YOU.

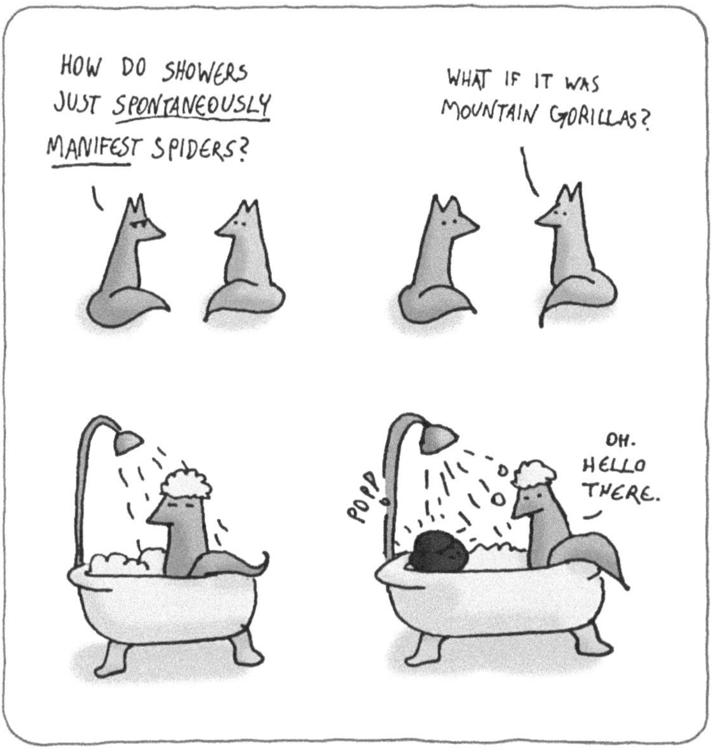
HOW DO SHOWERS JUST SPONTANEOUSLY MANIFEST SPIDERS?
WHAT IF IT WAS MOUNTAIN GORILLAS?
POPP
OH. HELLO THERE.

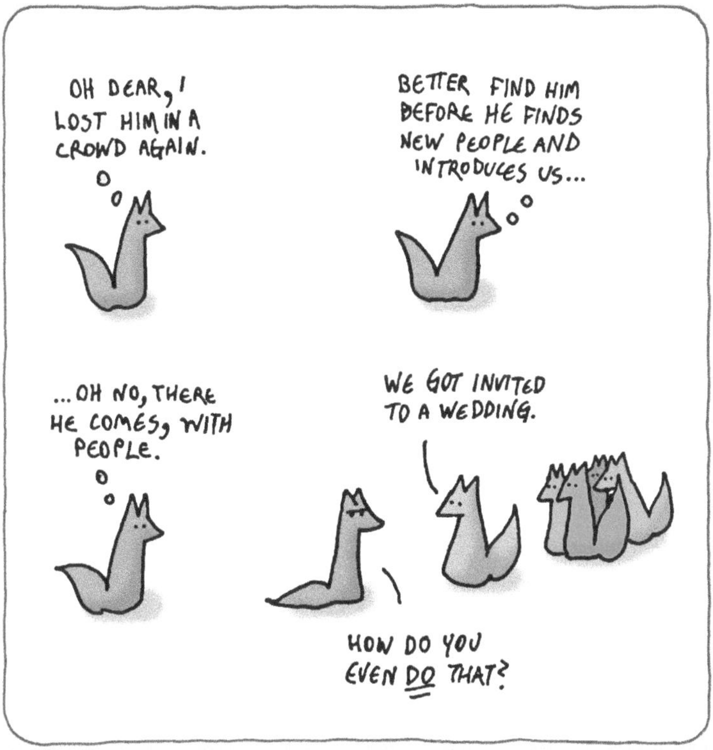
OH DEAR, I LOST HIM IN A CROWD AGAIN.
BETTER FIND HIM BEFORE HE FINDS NEW PEOPLE AND INTRODUCES US...
...OH NO, THERE HE COMES, WITH PEOPLE.
WE GOT INVITED TO A WEDDING.
HOW DO YOU EVEN DO THAT?

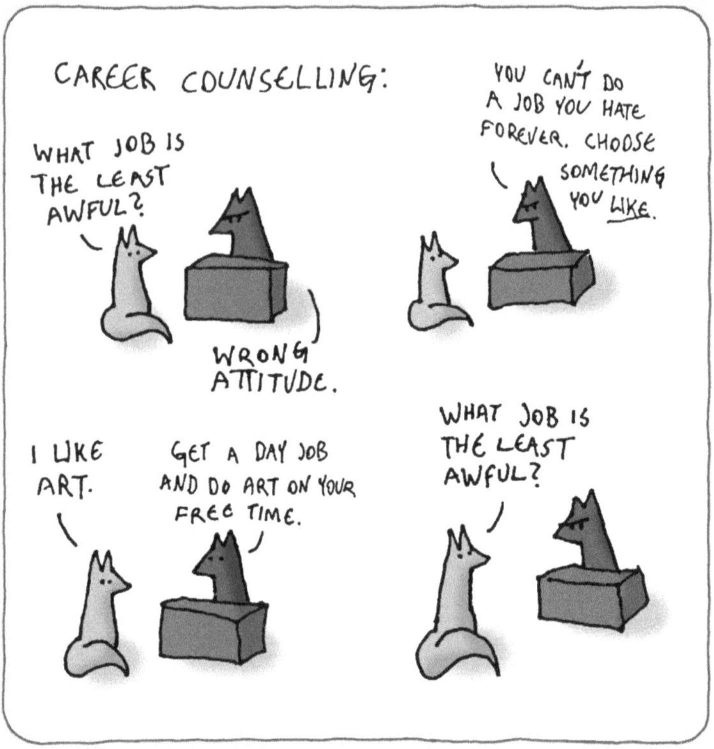
CAREER COUNSELLING:
WHAT JOB IS THE LEAST AWFUL?
WRONG ATTITUDE.
YOU CAN'T DO A JOB YOU HATE FOREVER. CHOOSE SOMETHING YOU LIKE.
I LIKE ART.
GET A DAY JOB AND DO ART ON YOUR FREE TIME.
WHAT JOB IS THE LEAST AWFUL?

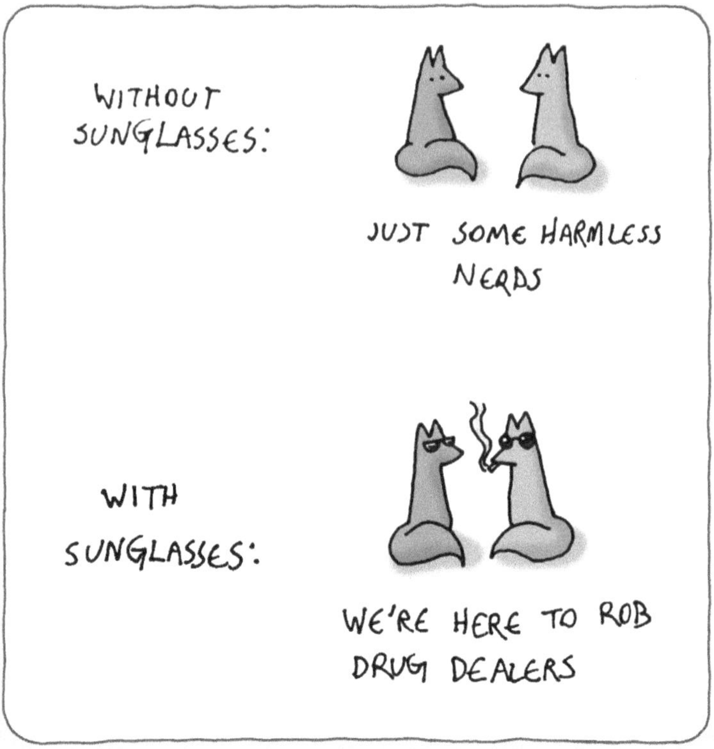
WITHOUT SUNGLASSES:
JUST SOME HARMLESS NERDS
WITH SUNGLASSES:
WE'RE HERE TO ROB DRUG DEALERS

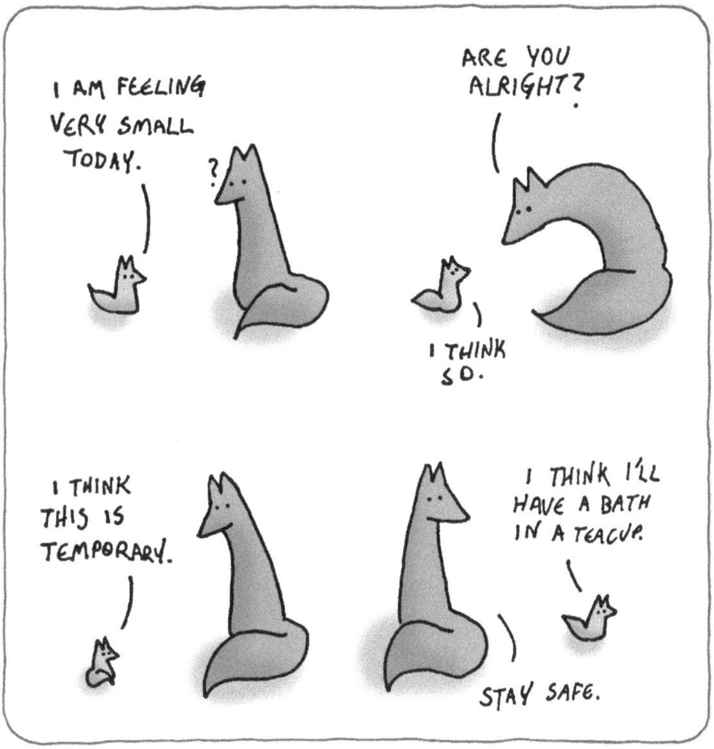
I AM FEELING VERY SMALL TODAY.
?
ARE YOU ALRIGHT?
I THINK SO.
I THINK THIS IS TEMPORARY.
I THINK I'LL HAVE A BATH IN A TEACUP.
STAY SAFE.

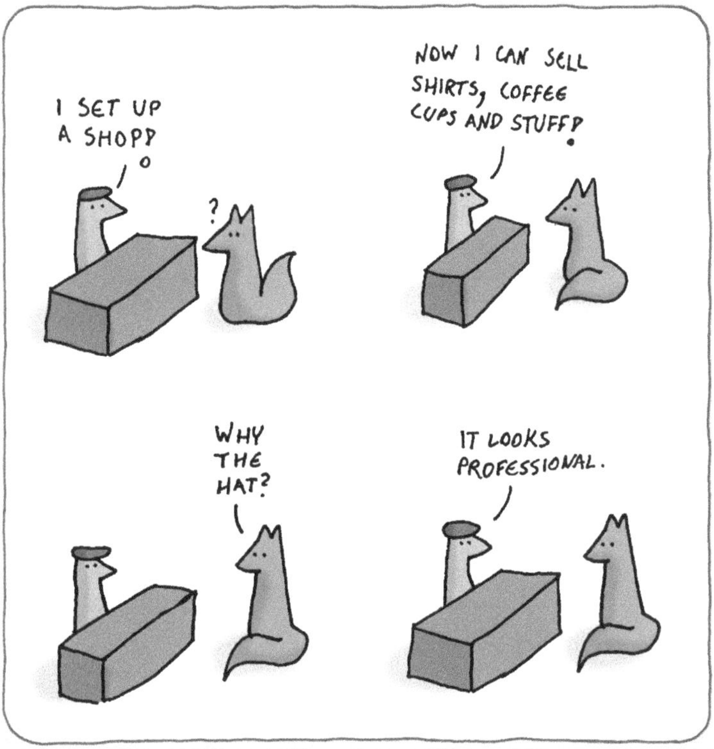
I SET UP A SHOP!
?
NOW I CAN SELL SHIRTS, COFFEE CUPS AND STUFF!
WHY THE HAT?
IT LOOKS PROFESSIONAL.

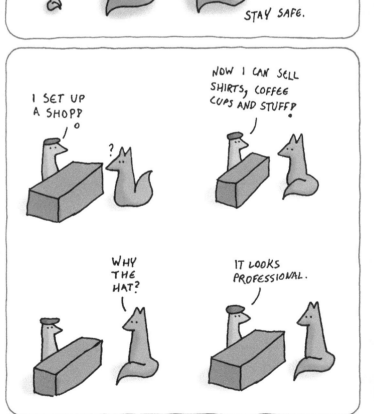

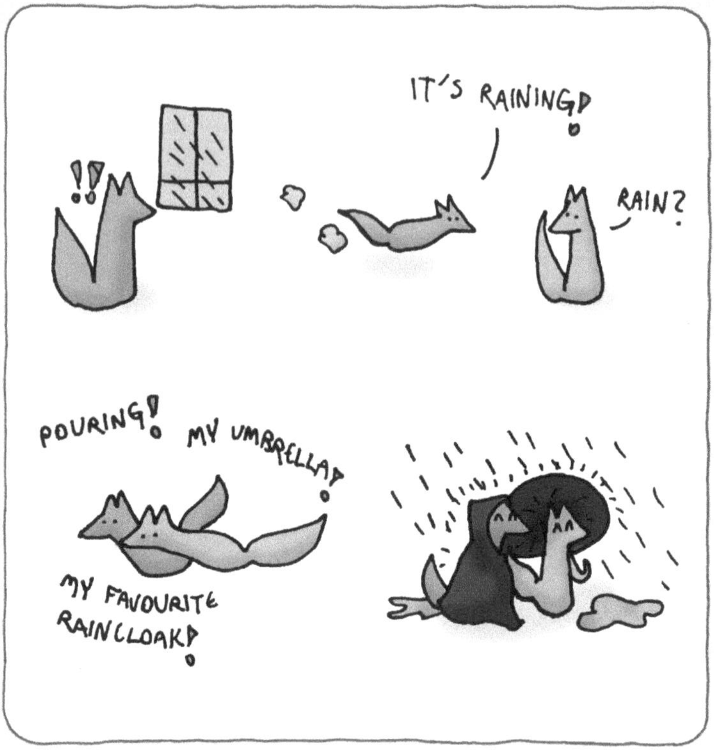
!!
IT'S RAINING!
RAIN?
POURING!
MY UMBRELLA!
MY FAVOURITE RAINCLOAK!

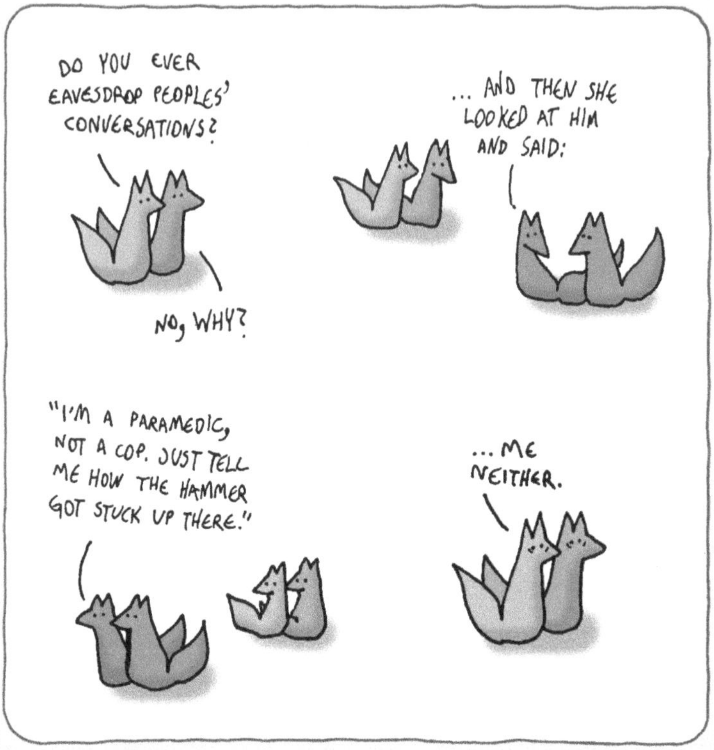
DO YOU EVER EAVESDROP PEOPLES' CONVERSATIONS?
NO, WHY?
... AND THEN SHE LOOKED AT HIM AND SAID:
"I'M A PARAMEDIC, NOT A COP. JUST TELL ME HOW THE HAMMER GOT STUCK UP THERE."
... ME NEITHER.

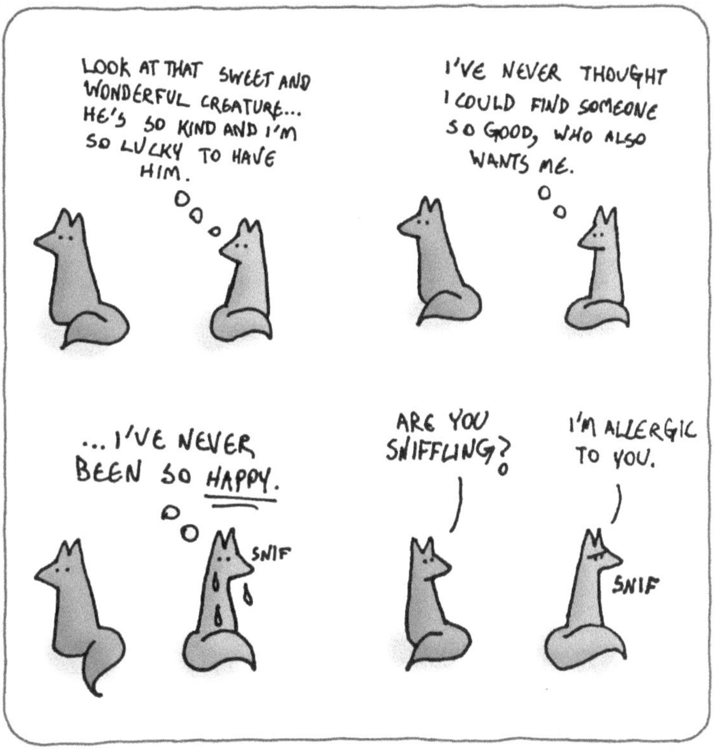
LOOK AT THAT SWEET AND WONDERFUL CREATURE... HE'S SO KIND AND I'M SO LUCKY TO HAVE HIM.
I'VE NEVER THOUGHT I COULD FIND SOMEONE SO GOOD, WHO ALSO WANTS ME.
...I'VE NEVER BEEN SO HAPPY.
SNIF
ARE YOU SNIFFLING?
I'M ALLERGIC TO YOU.
SNIF

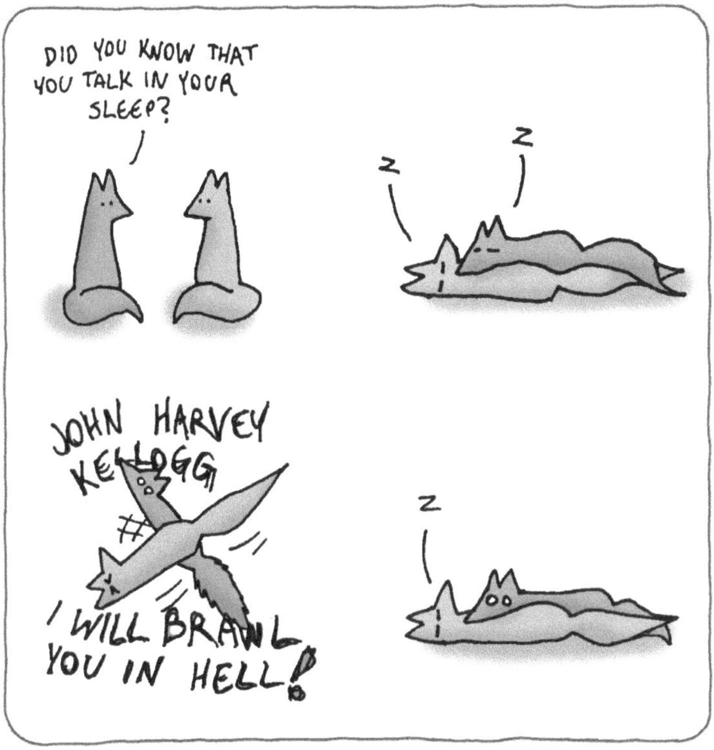
DID YOU KNOW THAT YOU TALK IN YOUR SLEEP?
Z
Z
JOHN HARVEY KELLOGG
I WILL BRAWL YOU IN HELL!
Z

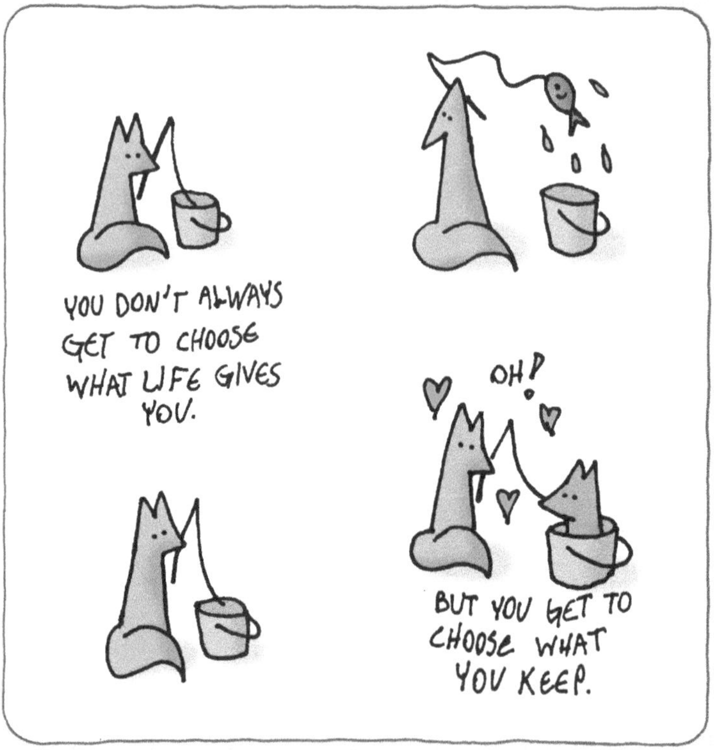
YOU DON'T ALWAYS GET TO CHOOSE WHAT LIFE GIVES YOU.
OH!
BUT YOU GET TO CHOOSE WHAT YOU KEEP.

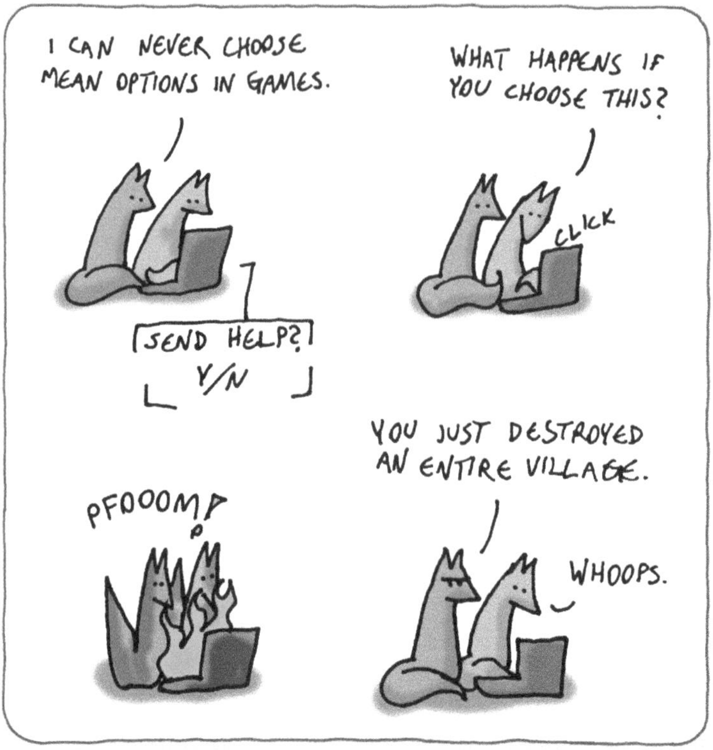
I CAN NEVER CHOOSE MEAN OPTIONS IN GAMES.
SEND HELP? Y/N
WHAT HAPPENS IF YOU CHOOSE THIS?
CLICK
PFOOOM!
YOU JUST DESTROYED AN ENTIRE VILLAGE.
WHOOPS.

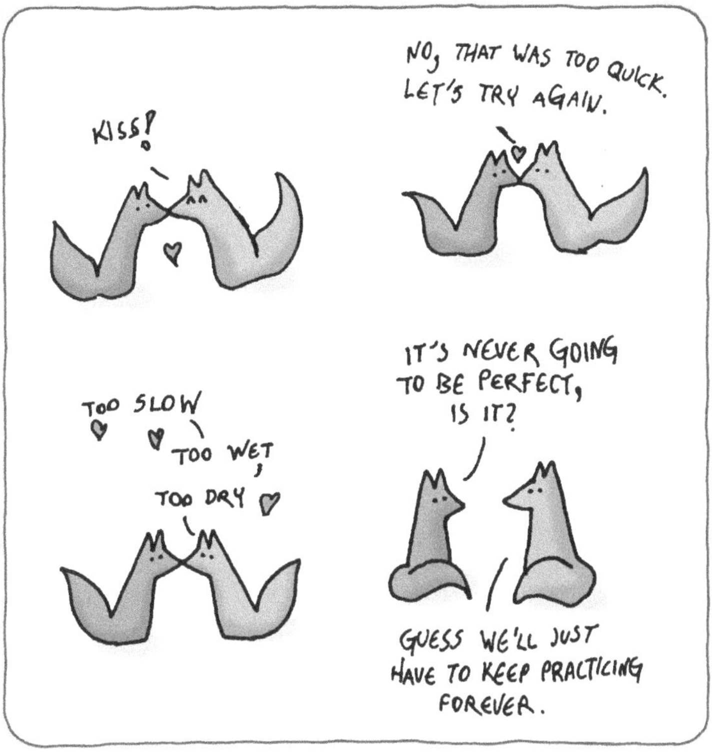
KISS!
NO, THAT WAS TOO QUICK. LET'S TRY AGAIN.
TOO SLOW
TOO WET,
TOO DRY
IT'S NEVER GOING TO BE PERFECT, IS IT?
GUESS WE'LL JUST HAVE TO KEEP PRACTICING FOREVER.

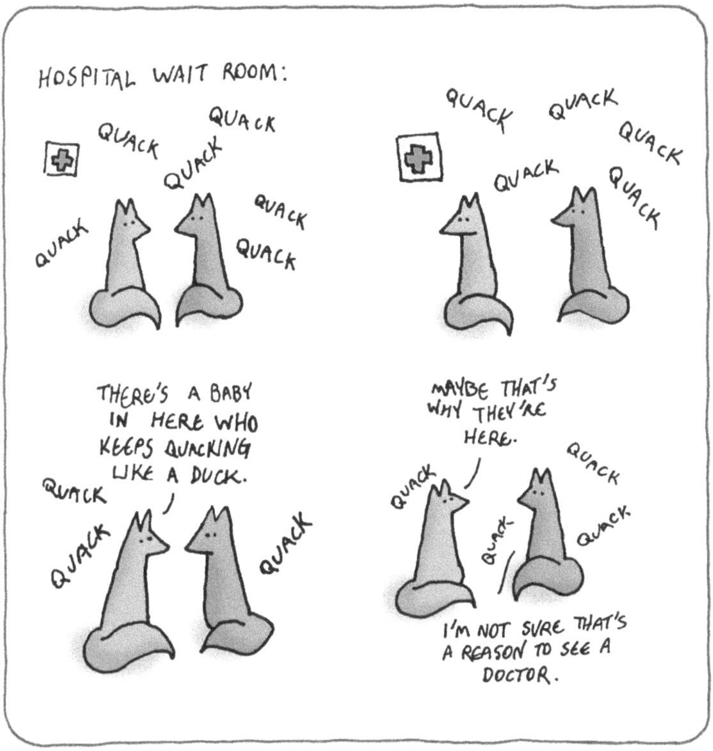
HOSPITAL WAIT ROOM:
QUACK
QUACK
QUACK
QUACK
QUACK
QUACK
QUACK
QUACK
QUACK
QUACK
QUACK
QUACK
THERE'S A BABY IN HERE WHO KEEPS QUACKING LIKE A DUCK.
QUACK
QUACK
QUACK
MAYBE THAT'S WHY THEY'RE HERE.
QUACK
QUACK
QUACK
QUACK
I'M NOT SURE THAT'S A REASON TO SEE A DOCTOR.

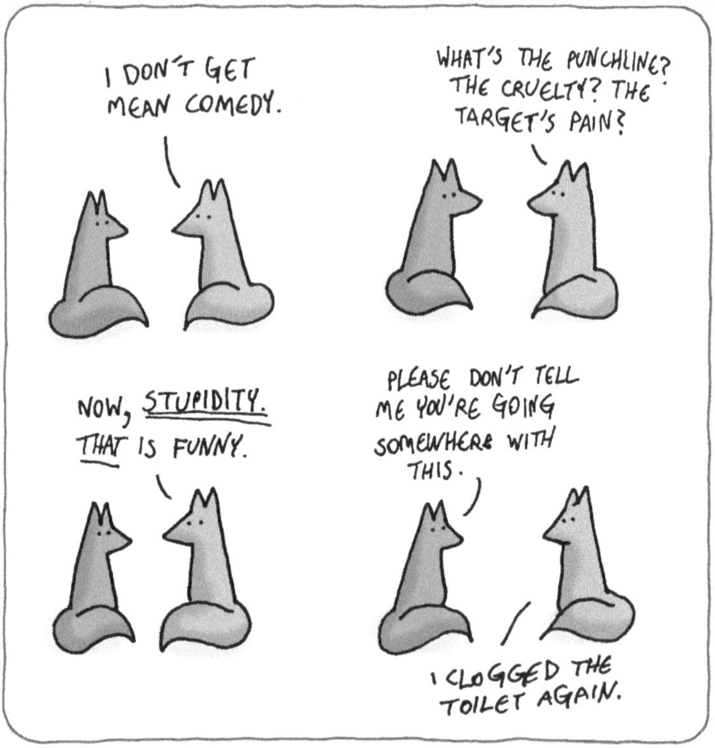
I DON'T GET MEAN COMEDY.
WHAT'S THE PUNCHLINE? THE CRUELTY? THE TARGET'S PAIN?
NOW, STUPIDITY. THAT IS FUNNY.
PLEASE DON'T TELL ME YOU'RE GOING SOMEWHERE WITH THIS.
I CLOGGED THE TOILET AGAIN.

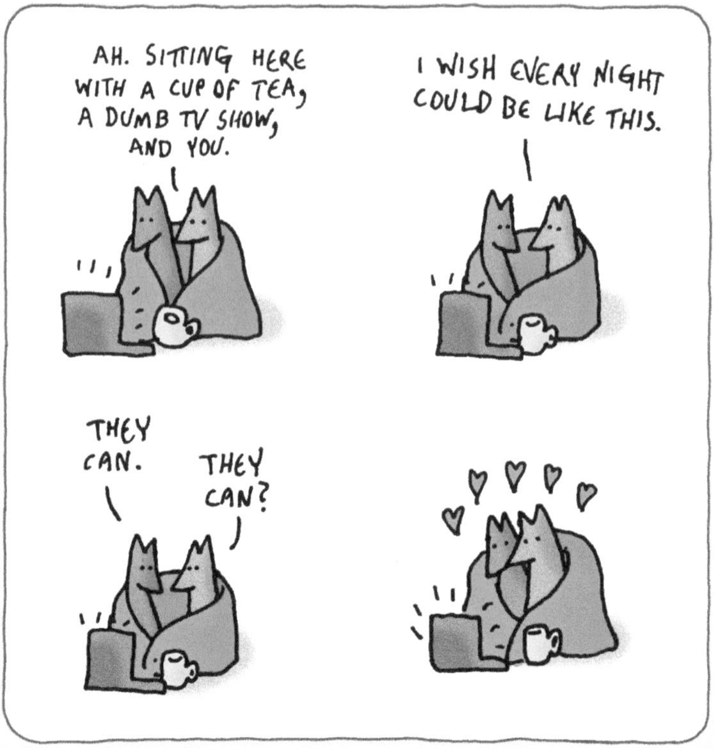
AH. SITTING HERE WITH A CUP OF TEA, A DUMB TV SHOW, AND YOU.
I WISH EVERY NIGHT COULD BE LIKE THIS.
THEY CAN.
THEY CAN?

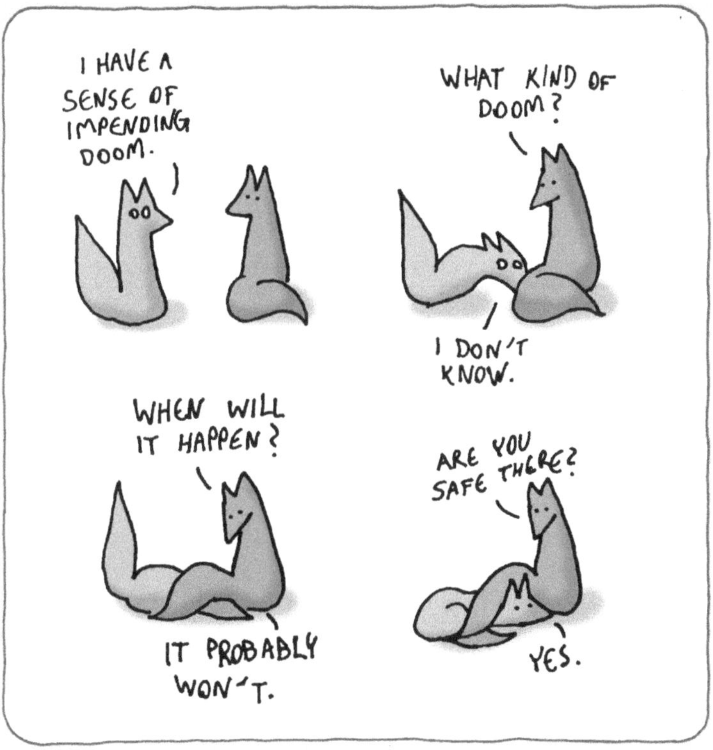
I HAVE A SENSE OF IMPENDING DOOM.
WHAT KIND OF DOOM?
I DON'T KNOW.
WHEN WILL IT HAPPEN?
IT PROBABLY WON'T.
ARE YOU SAFE THERE?
YES.

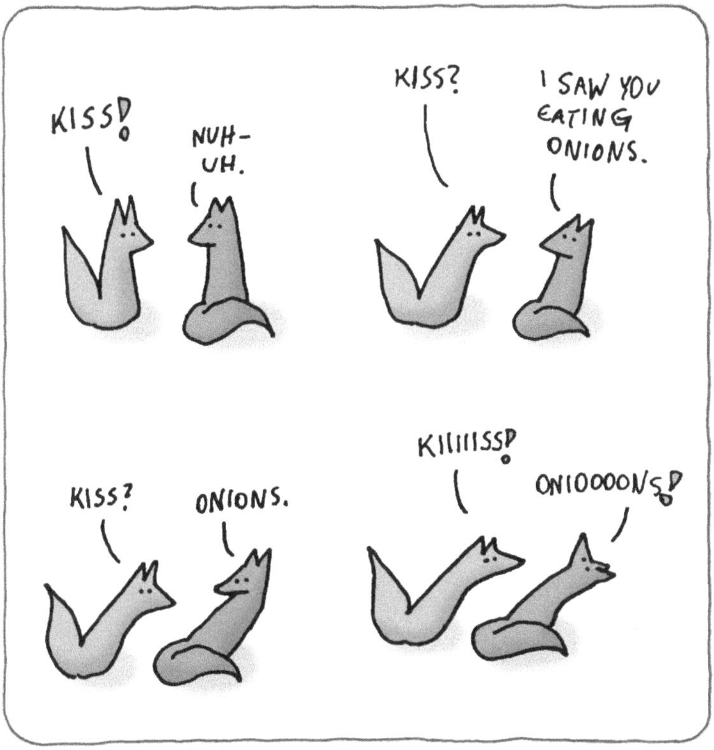
KISS!
NUH-UH.
KISS?
I SAW YOU EATING ONIONS.
KISS?
ONIONS.
KIIIIISS!
ONIOOOONS!

TOIVO KAARTINEN

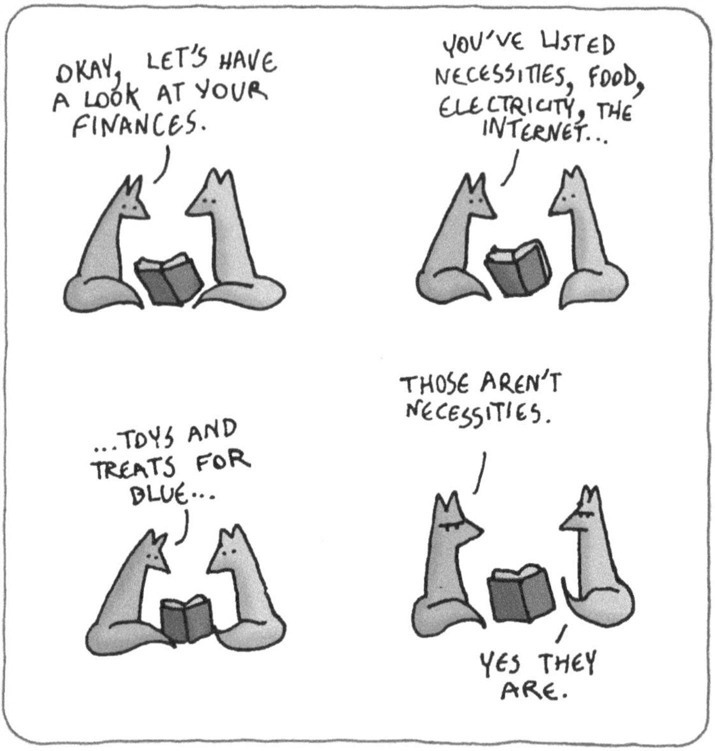
OKAY, LET'S HAVE A LOOK AT YOUR FINANCES.
YOU'VE LISTED NECESSITIES, FOOD, ELECTRICITY, THE INTERNET...
...TOYS AND TREATS FOR BLUE...
THOSE AREN'T NECESSITIES.
YES THEY ARE.

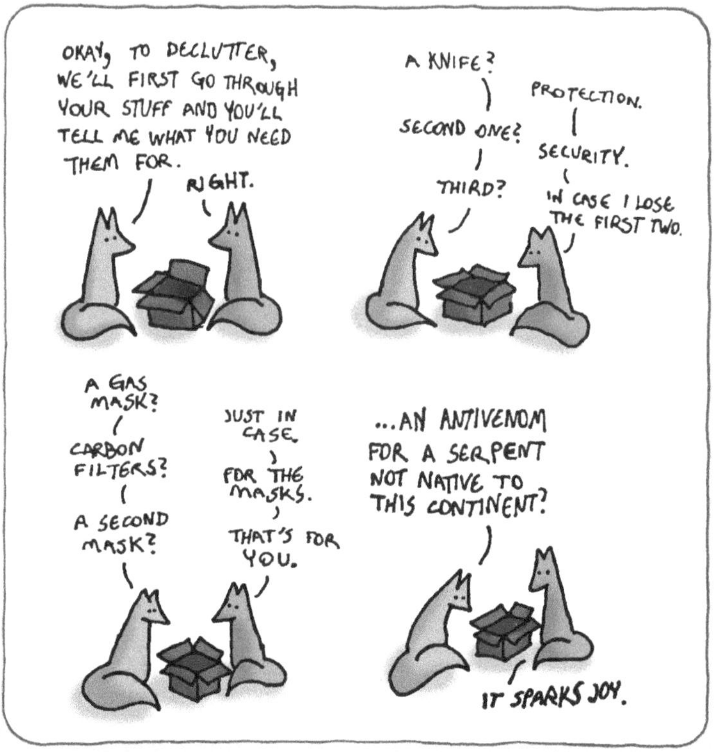
OKAY, TO DECLUTTER, WE'LL FIRST GO THROUGH YOUR STUFF AND YOU'LL TELL ME WHAT YOU NEED THEM FOR.
RIGHT.
A KNIFE?
PROTECTION.
SECOND ONE?
SECURITY.
THIRD?
IN CASE I LOSE THE FIRST TWO.
A GAS MASK?
JUST IN CASE.
CARBON FILTERS?
FOR THE MASKS.
A SECOND MASK?
THAT'S FOR YOU.
...AN ANTIVENOM FOR A SERPENT NOT NATIVE TO THIS CONTINENT?
IT SPARKS JOY.

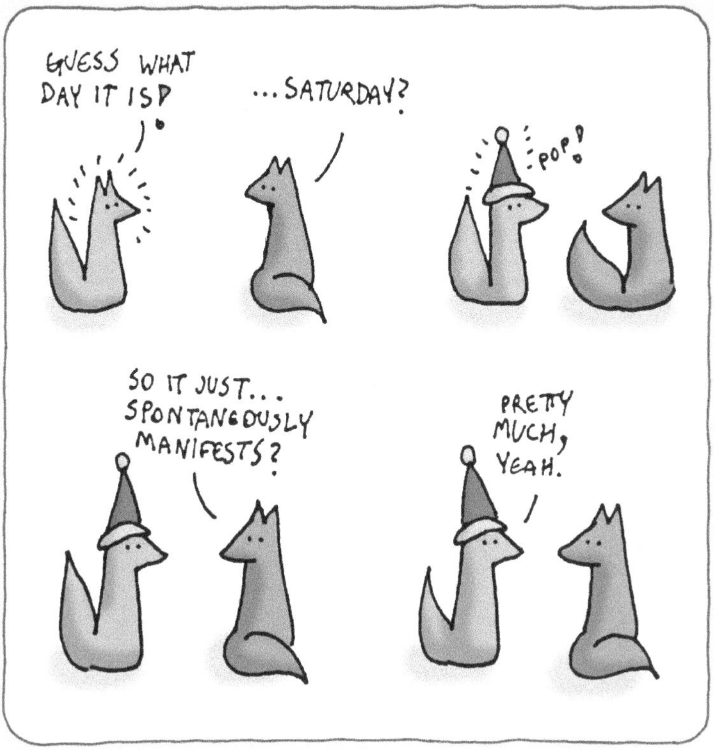
GUESS WHAT DAY IT IS?
...SATURDAY?
POP!
SO IT JUST... SPONTANEOUSLY MANIFESTS?
PRETTY MUCH, YEAH.

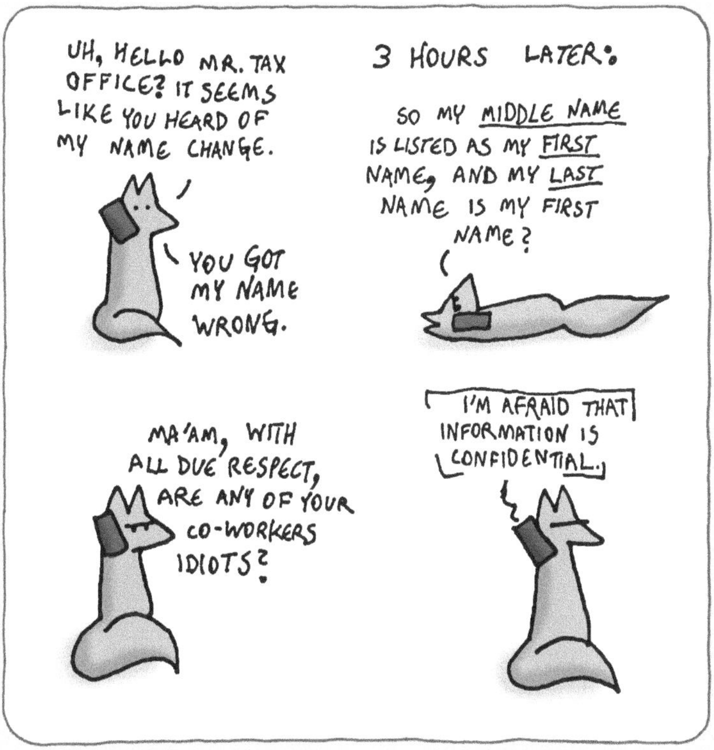
UH, HELLO MR. TAX OFFICE? IT SEEMS LIKE YOU HEARD OF MY NAME CHANGE.
YOU GOT MY NAME WRONG.
3 HOURS LATER:
SO MY MIDDLE NAME IS LISTED AS MY FIRST NAME, AND MY LAST NAME IS MY FIRST NAME?
MA'AM, WITH ALL DUE RESPECT, ARE ANY OF YOUR CO-WORKERS IDIOTS?
I'M AFRAID THAT INFORMATION IS CONFIDENTIAL.

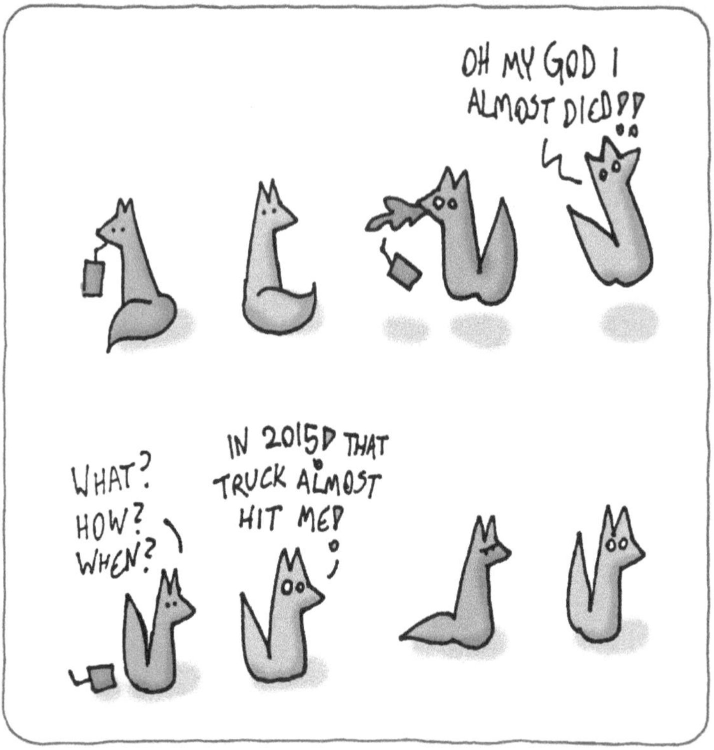
OH MY GOD I ALMOST DIED!!
WHAT? HOW? WHEN?
IN 2015! THAT TRUCK ALMOST HIT ME!

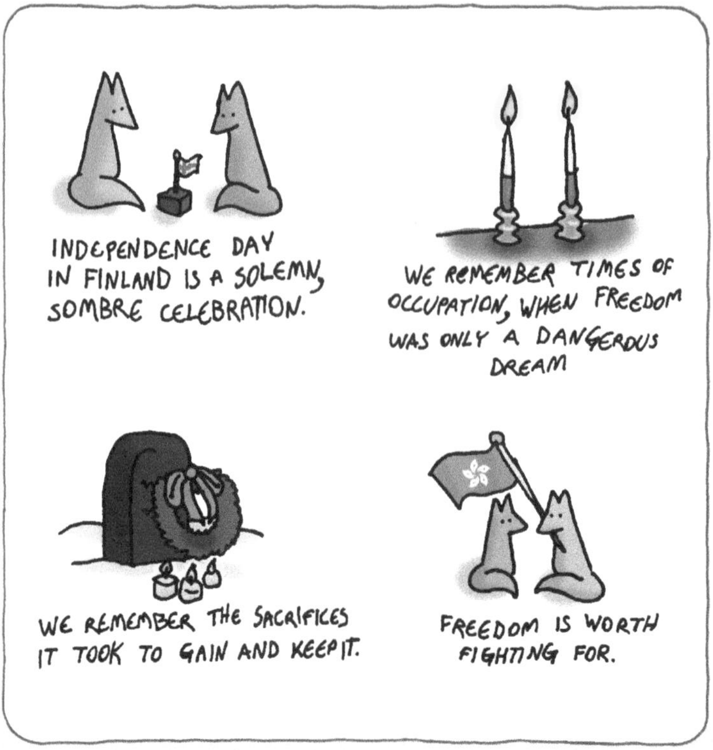
INDEPENDENCE DAY IN FINLAND IS A SOLEMN, SOMBRE CELEBRATION.
WE REMEMBER TIMES OF OCCUPATION, WHEN FREEDOM WAS ONLY A DANGEROUS DREAM
WE REMEMBER THE SACRIFICES IT TOOK TO GAIN AND KEEP IT.
FREEDOM IS WORTH FIGHTING FOR.

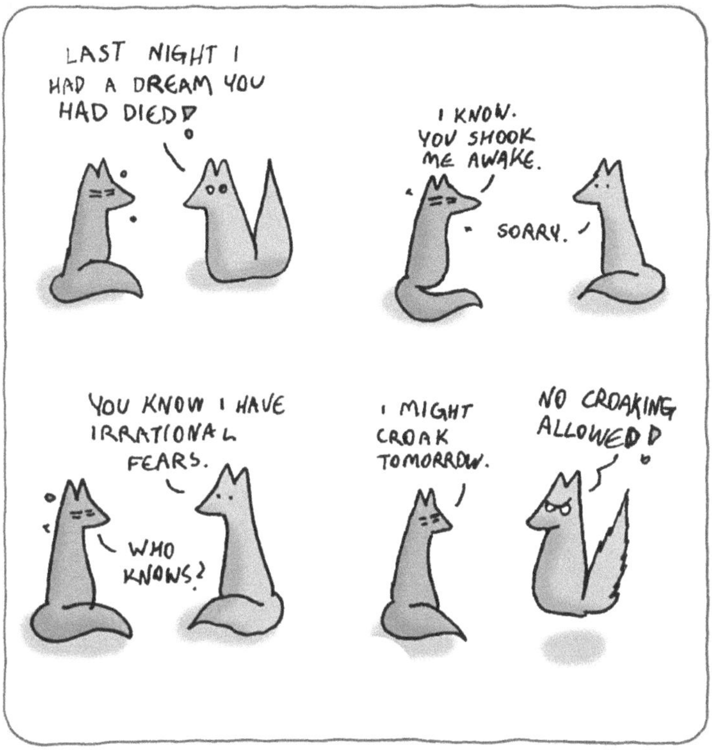
LAST NIGHT I HAD A DREAM YOU HAD DIED!
I KNOW. YOU SHOOK ME AWAKE.
SORRY.
YOU KNOW I HAVE IRRATIONAL FEARS.
WHO KNOWS?
I MIGHT CROAK TOMORROW.
NO CROAKING ALLOWED!

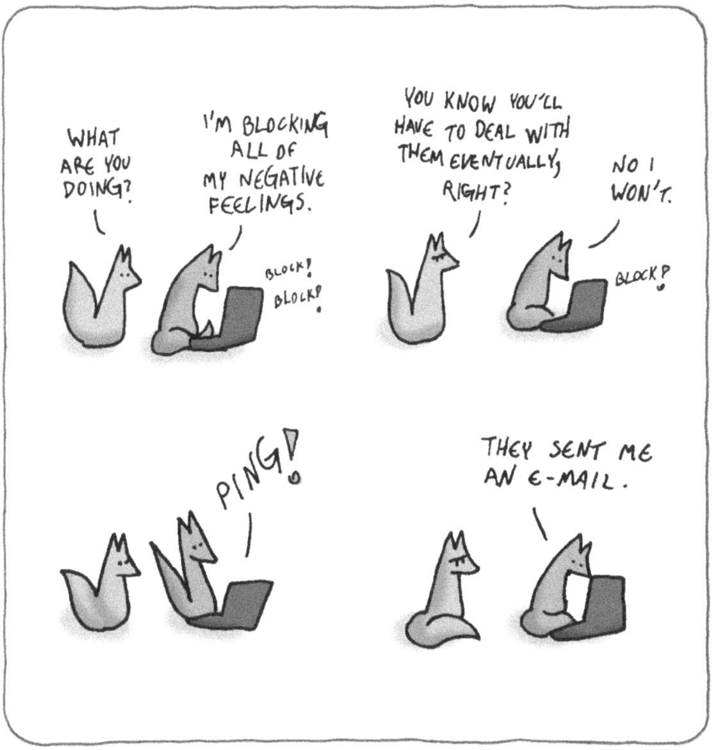
WHAT ARE YOU DOING?
I'M BLOCKING ALL OF MY NEGATIVE FEELINGS.
BLOCK!
BLOCK!
YOU KNOW YOU'LL HAVE TO DEAL WITH THEM EVENTUALLY, RIGHT?
NO I WON'T.
BLOCK!
PING!
THEY SENT ME AN E-MAIL.

TOIVO KAARTINEN

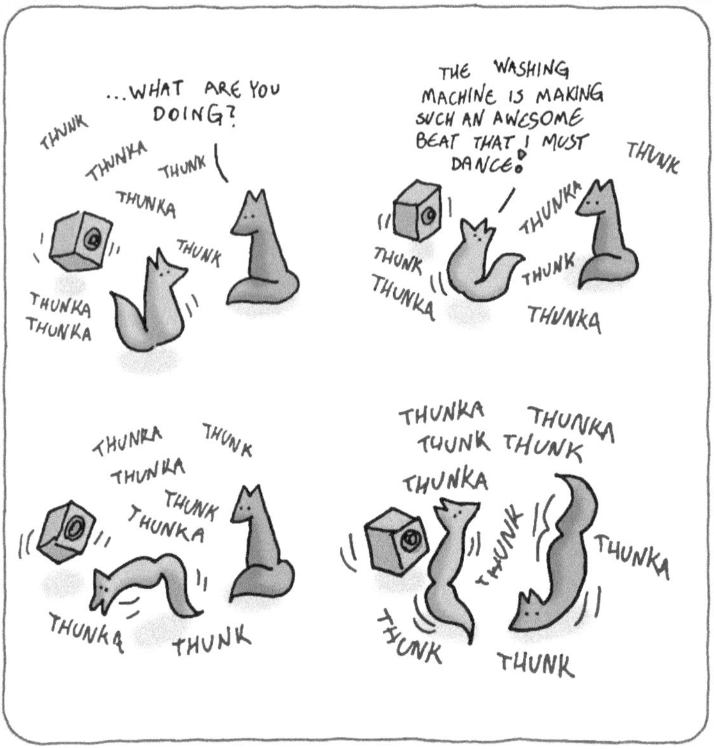
...WHAT ARE YOU DOING?
THUNK
THUNKA
THUNK
THUNKA
THUNK
THUNKA
THUNKA
THE WASHING MACHINE IS MAKING SUCH AN AWESOME BEAT THAT I MUST DANCE!
THUNK
THUNKA
THUNK
THUNKA
THUNK
THUNKA
THUNKA
THUNK
THUNKA
THUNK
THUNKA
THUNKA
THUNK
THUNKA
THUNK
THUNKA THUNK
THUNKA THUNK
THUNKA
THUNK
THUNKA
THUNK
THUNK

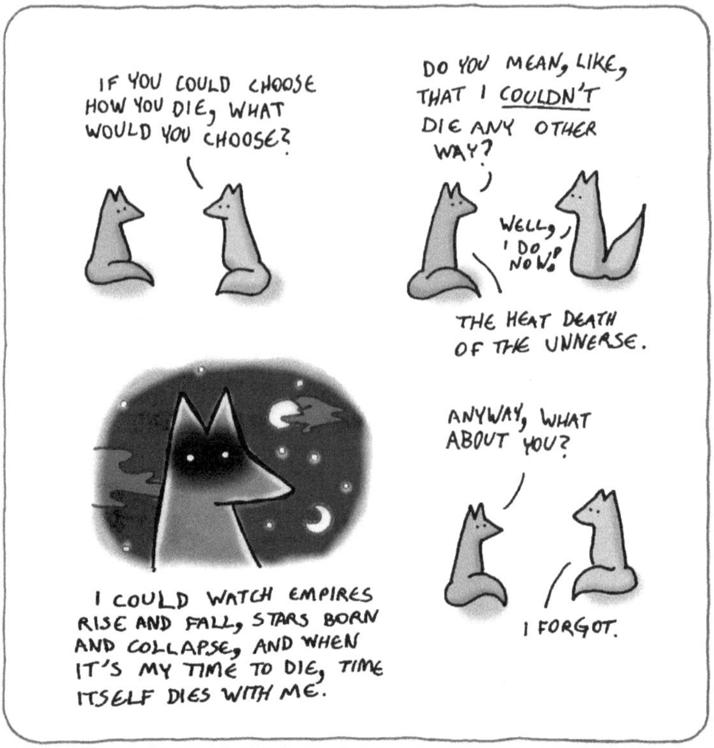
IF YOU COULD CHOOSE HOW YOU DIE, WHAT WOULD YOU CHOOSE?
DO YOU MEAN, LIKE, THAT I COULDN'T DIE ANY OTHER WAY?
WELL, I DO NOW!
THE HEAT DEATH OF THE UNIVERSE.
I COULD WATCH EMPIRES RISE AND FALL, STARS BORN AND COLLAPSE, AND WHEN IT'S MY TIME TO DIE, TIME ITSELF DIES WITH ME.
ANYWAY, WHAT ABOUT YOU?
I FORGOT.

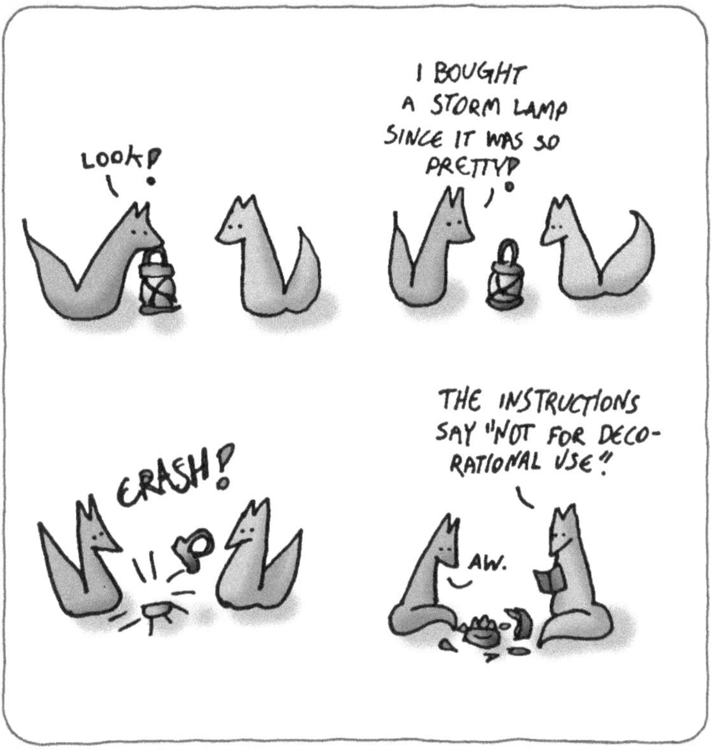
LOOK!
I BOUGHT A STORM LAMP SINCE IT WAS SO PRETTY!
CRASH!
THE INSTRUCTIONS SAY "NOT FOR DECO-RATIONAL USE"
AW.

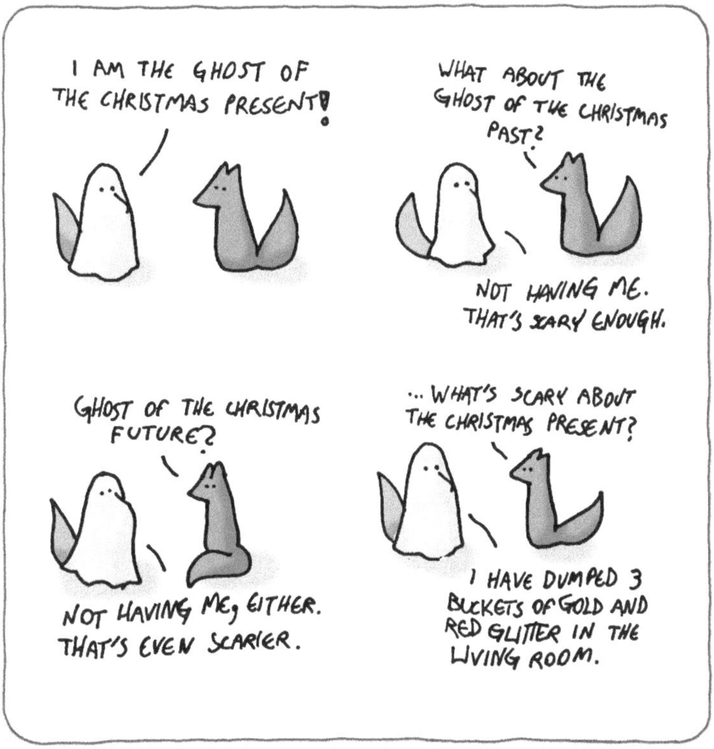
I AM THE GHOST OF THE CHRISTMAS PRESENT!
WHAT ABOUT THE GHOST OF THE CHRISTMAS PAST?
NOT HAVING ME. THAT'S SCARY ENOUGH.
GHOST OF THE CHRISTMAS FUTURE?
NOT HAVING ME, EITHER. THAT'S EVEN SCARIER.
...WHAT'S SCARY ABOUT THE CHRISTMAS PRESENT?
I HAVE DUMPED 3 BUCKETS OF GOLD AND RED GLITTER IN THE LIVING ROOM.

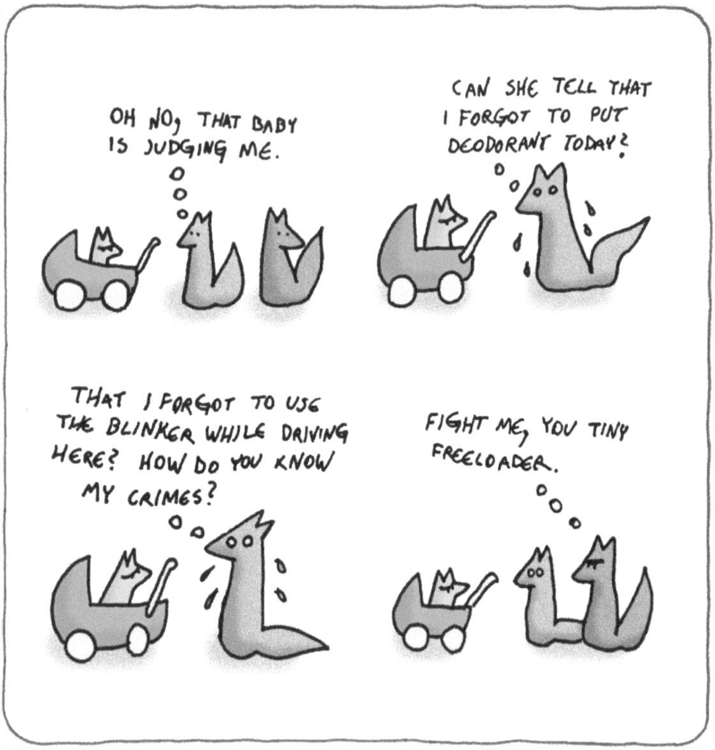
OH NO, THAT BABY IS JUDGING ME.
CAN SHE TELL THAT I FORGOT TO PUT DEODORANT TODAY?
THAT I FORGOT TO USE THE BLINKER WHILE DRIVING HERE? HOW DO YOU KNOW MY CRIMES?
FIGHT ME, YOU TINY FREELOADER.

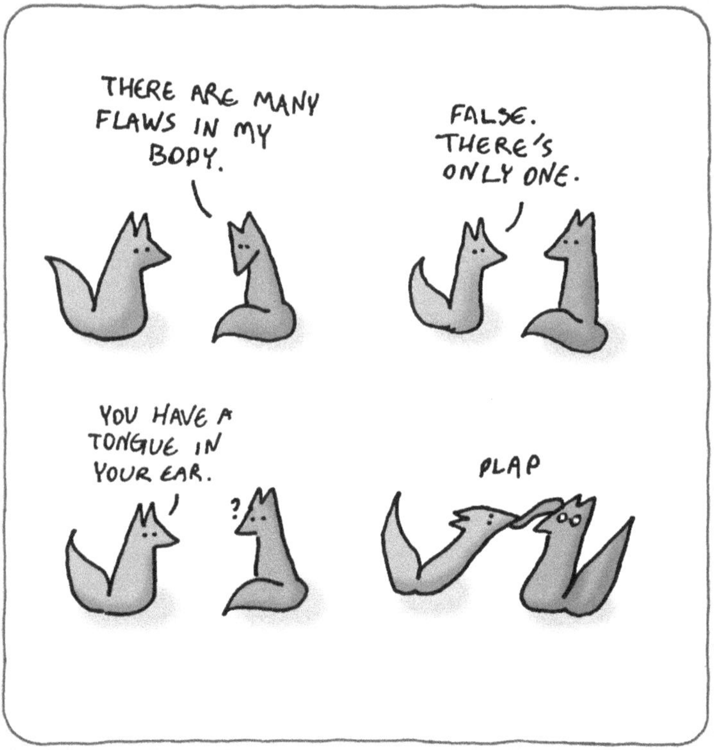
THERE ARE MANY FLAWS IN MY BODY.
FALSE. THERE'S ONLY ONE.
YOU HAVE A TONGUE IN YOUR EAR.
?
PLAP

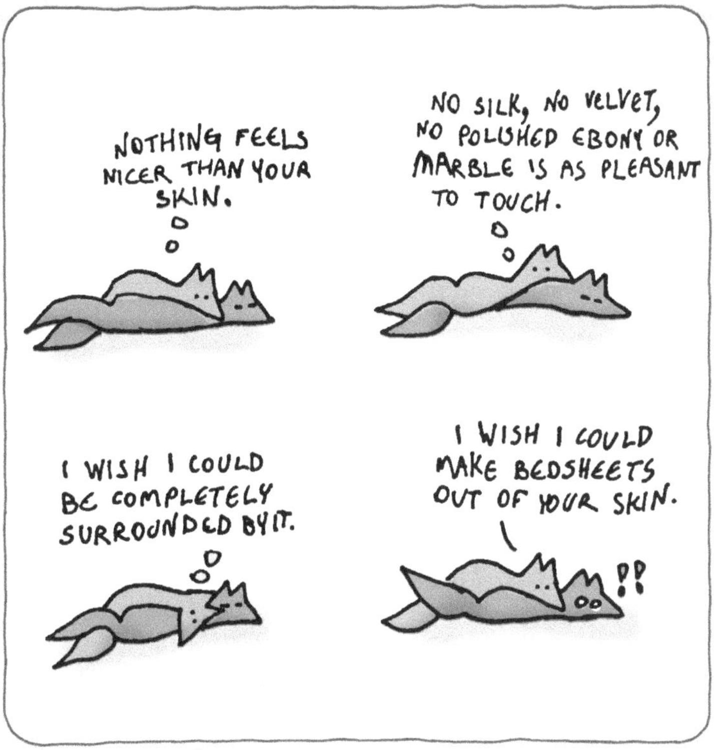
NOTHING FEELS NICER THAN YOUR SKIN.
NO SILK, NO VELVET, NO POLISHED EBONY OR MARBLE IS AS PLEASANT TO TOUCH.
I WISH I COULD BE COMPLETELY SURROUNDED BY IT.
I WISH I COULD MAKE BEDSHEETS OUT OF YOUR SKIN.
?!

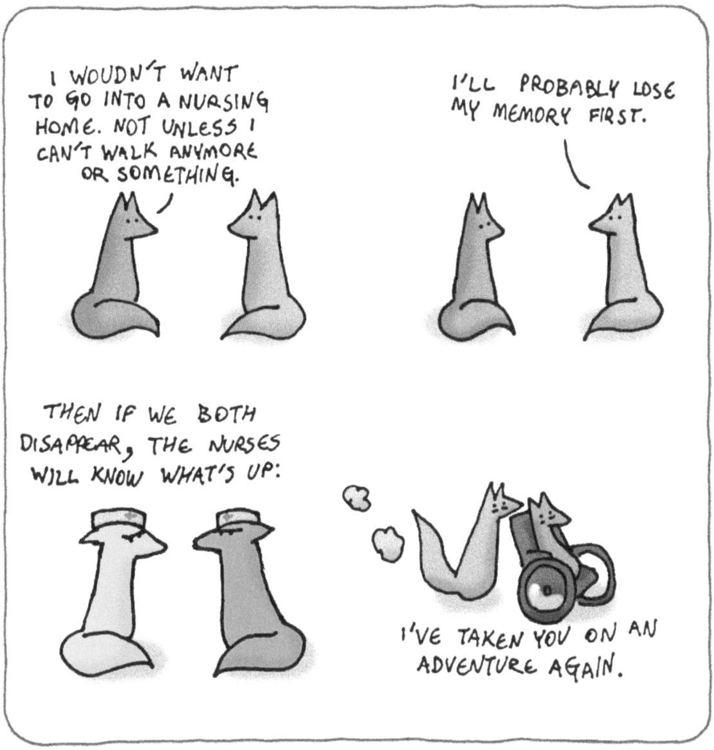
I WOUDN'T WANT TO GO INTO A NURSING HOME. NOT UNLESS I CAN'T WALK ANYMORE OR SOMETHING.
I'LL PROBABLY LOSE MY MEMORY FIRST.
THEN IF WE BOTH DISAPPEAR, THE NURSES WILL KNOW WHAT'S UP:
I'VE TAKEN YOU ON AN ADVENTURE AGAIN.

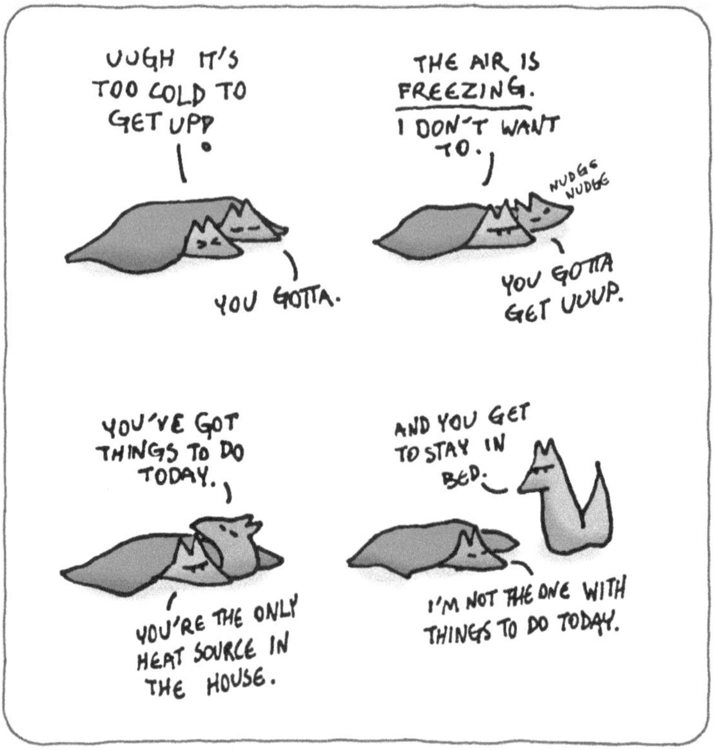
UUGH IT'S TOO COLD TO GET UPP
YOU GOTTA.
THE AIR IS FREEZING.
I DON'T WANT TO.
NUDGE NUDGE
YOU GOTTA GET UUUP.
YOU'VE GOT THINGS TO DO TODAY.
YOU'RE THE ONLY HEAT SOURCE IN THE HOUSE.
AND YOU GET TO STAY IN BED.
I'M NOT THE ONE WITH THINGS TO DO TODAY.

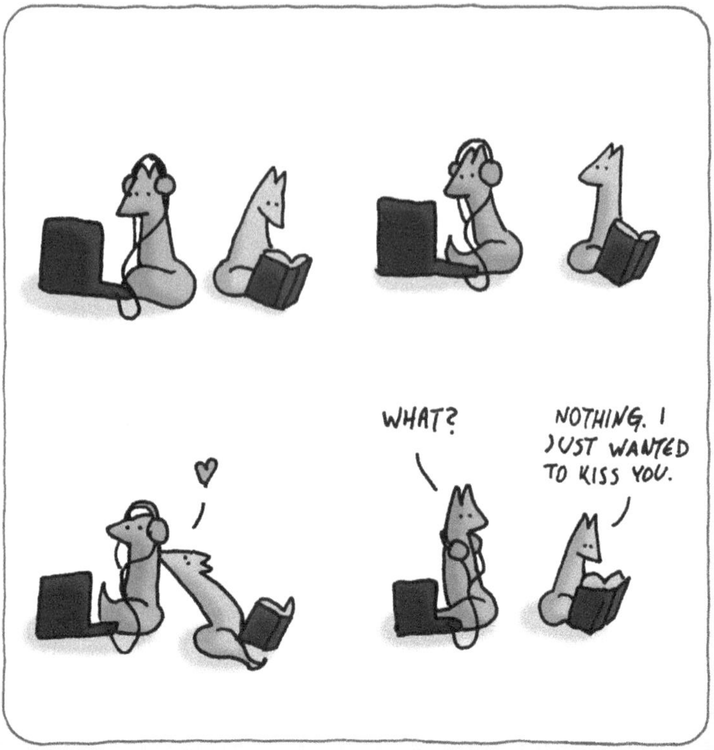
WHAT?
NOTHING. I JUST WANTED TO KISS YOU.

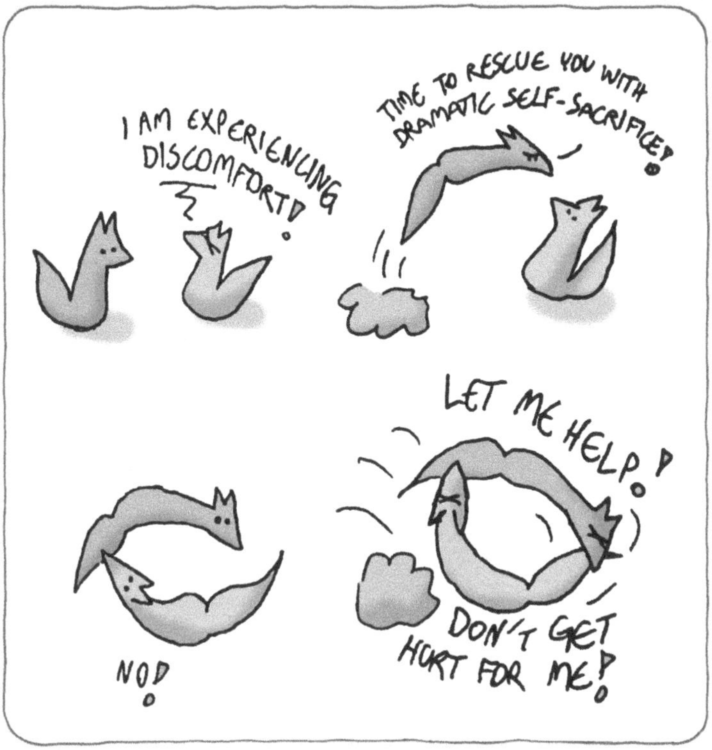
I AM EXPERIENCING DISCOMFORT!
TIME TO RESCUE YOU WITH DRAMATIC SELF-SACRIFICE!
NO!
LET ME HELP!
DON'T GET HURT FOR ME!

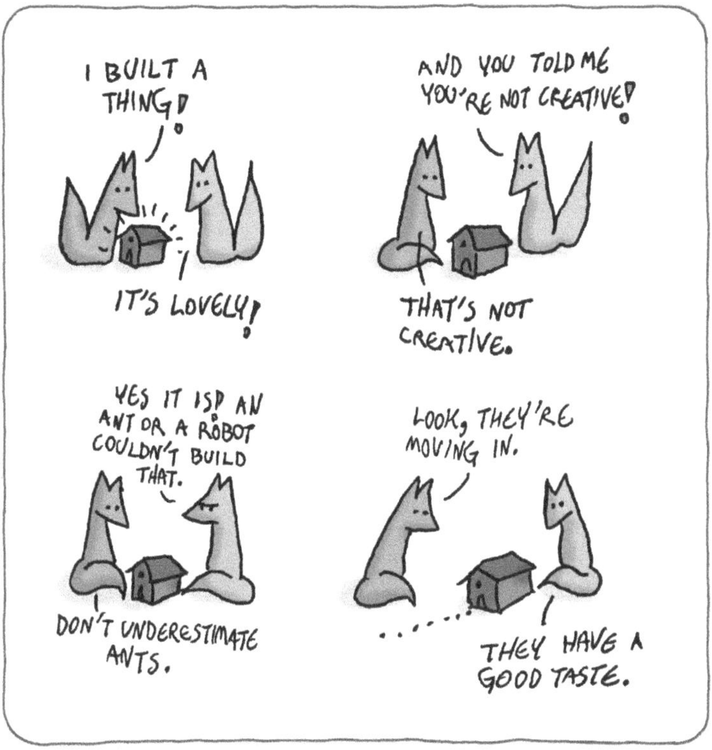
I BUILT A THING!
IT'S LOVELY!
AND YOU TOLD ME YOU'RE NOT CREATIVE!
THAT'S NOT CREATIVE.
YES IT IS! AN ANT OR A ROBOT COULDN'T BUILD THAT.
DON'T UNDERESTIMATE ANTS.
LOOK, THEY'RE MOVING IN.
THEY HAVE A GOOD TASTE.

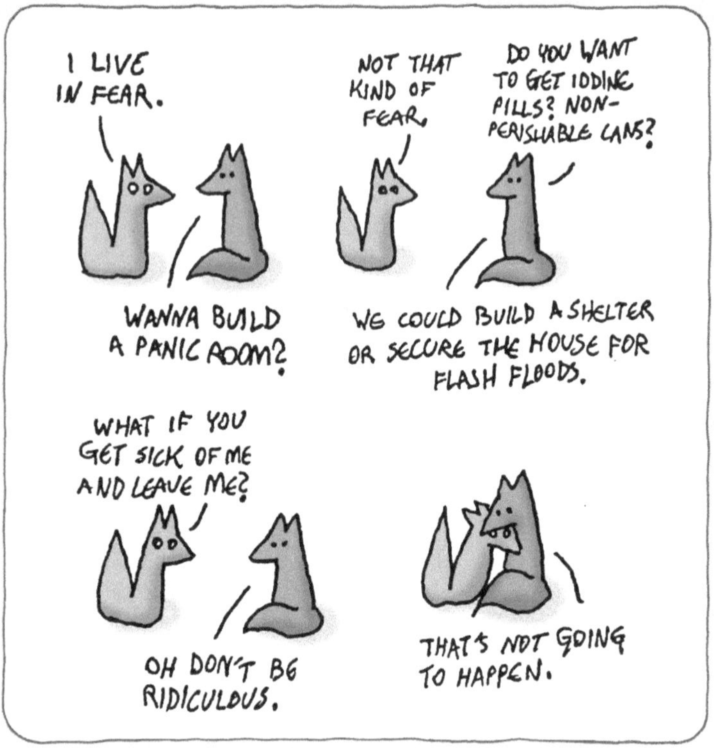
I LIVE IN FEAR.
WANNA BUILD A PANIC ROOM?
NOT THAT KIND OF FEAR.
DO YOU WANT TO GET IODINE PILLS? NON-PERISHABLE CANS?
WE COULD BUILD A SHELTER OR SECURE THE HOUSE FOR FLASH FLOODS.
WHAT IF YOU GET SICK OF ME AND LEAVE ME?
OH DON'T BE RIDICULOUS.
THAT'S NOT GOING TO HAPPEN.

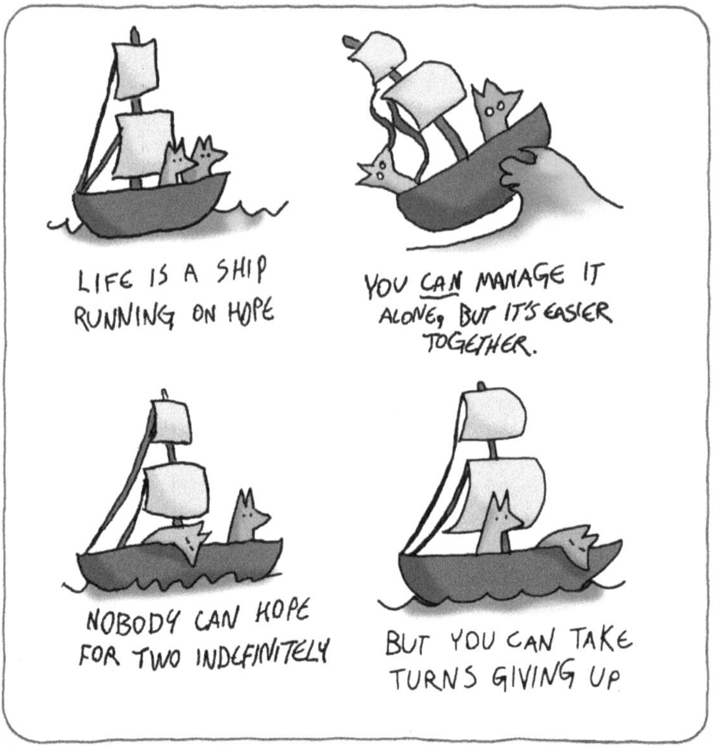
LIFE IS A SHIP RUNNING ON HOPE
YOU CAN MANAGE IT ALONE, BUT IT'S EASIER TOGETHER.
NOBODY CAN HOPE FOR TWO INDEFINITELY
BUT YOU CAN TAKE TURNS GIVING UP

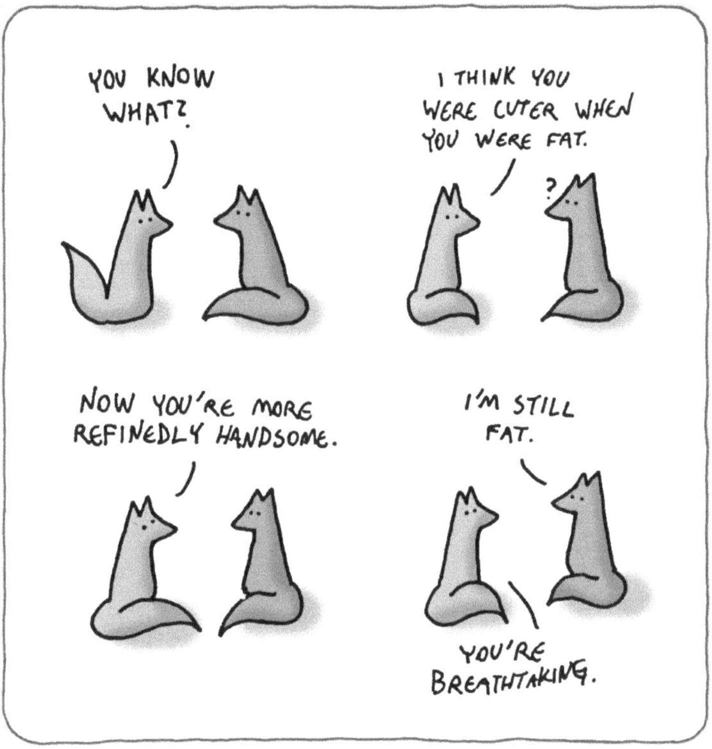
YOU KNOW WHAT?
I THINK YOU WERE CUTER WHEN YOU WERE FAT.
?
NOW YOU'RE MORE REFINEDLY HANDSOME.
I'M STILL FAT.
YOU'RE BREATHTAKING.

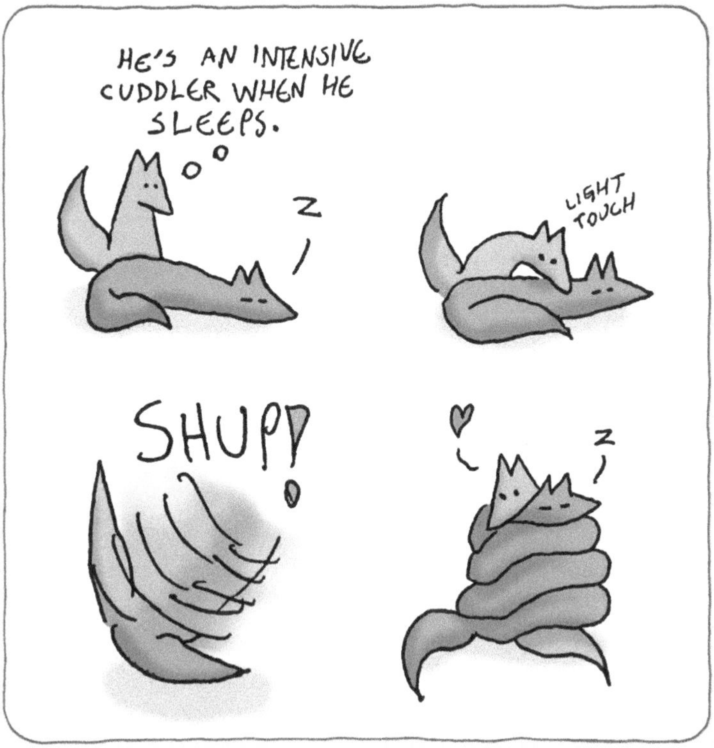
HE'S AN INTENSIVE CUDDLER WHEN HE SLEEPS.
Z
LIGHT TOUCH
SHUPP
Z

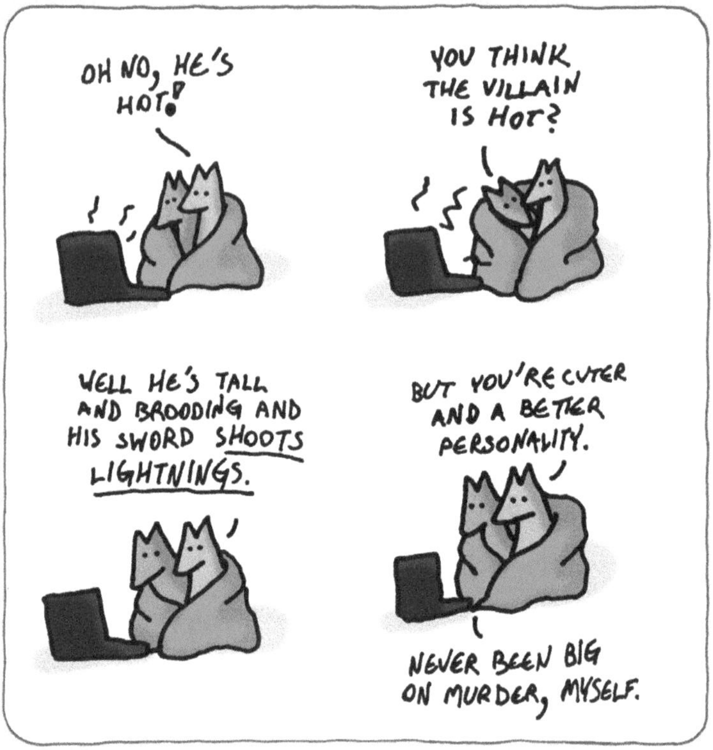
OH NO, HE'S HOT!
YOU THINK THE VILLAIN IS HOT?
WELL HE'S TALL AND BROODING AND HIS SWORD SHOOTS LIGHTNINGS.
BUT YOU'RE CUTER AND A BETTER PERSONALITY.
NEVER BEEN BIG ON MURDER, MYSELF.

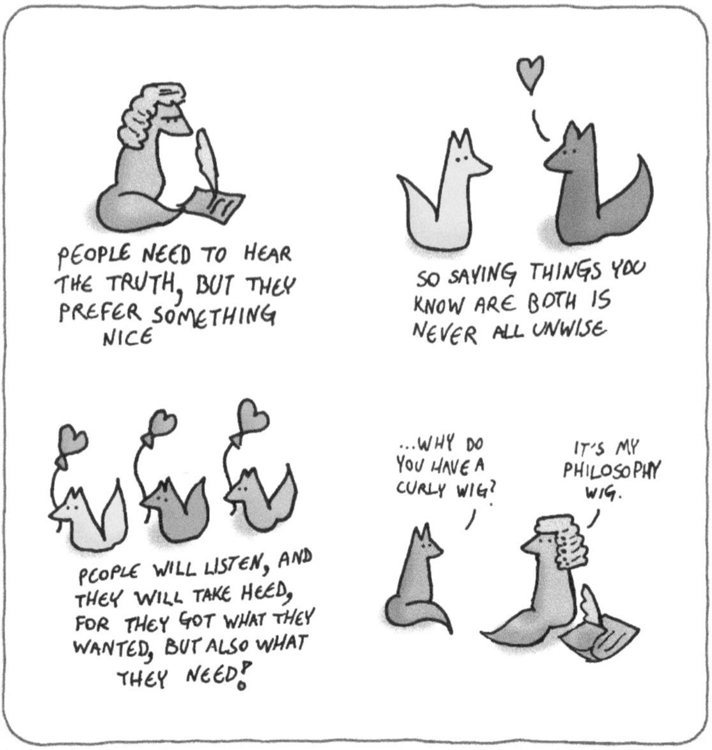
PEOPLE NEED TO HEAR THE TRUTH, BUT THEY PREFER SOMETHING NICE
SO SAYING THINGS YOU KNOW ARE BOTH IS NEVER ALL UNWISE
PEOPLE WILL LISTEN, AND THEY WILL TAKE HEED, FOR THEY GOT WHAT THEY WANTED, BUT ALSO WHAT THEY NEED!
...WHY DO YOU HAVE A CURLY WIG?
IT'S MY PHILOSOPHY WIG.

Panel 1

HEY CAN YOU HELP ME A BIT?

?

Panel 2

ONE OF THESE IS A RATIONAL FEAR. THE OTHER ONE IS IRRATIONAL.

THEY'RE THE SAME PICTURE.

Panel 3

WAIT... YOU CAN'T TELL THEM APART EITHER...?

Panel 4

MY MOM WAS SURPRISED THAT YOU'RE THE ELDEST AND NOT YOUNGEST.

WHY?

YOU'RE SO QUIET AND GENTLE.

Panel 5

IN LARGE FAMILIES THE CHILDREN ARE IN CONSTANT BATTLE FOR ATTENTION AND RESOURCES

A MERCILESS BATTLE ROYALE, THE WEAK EAT DUST AND PERISH.

Panel 6

EXCEPT FOR THE YOUNGEST, WHO IS IN MAMA'S PROTECTION, BECAUSE THAT'S HER BABY!

Panel 7

...I HAVE LITERALLY NEVER HEARD ABOUT ANYTHING LIKE THAT.

YOUR FAMILY IS WEIRD.

85

TOIVO KAARTINEN

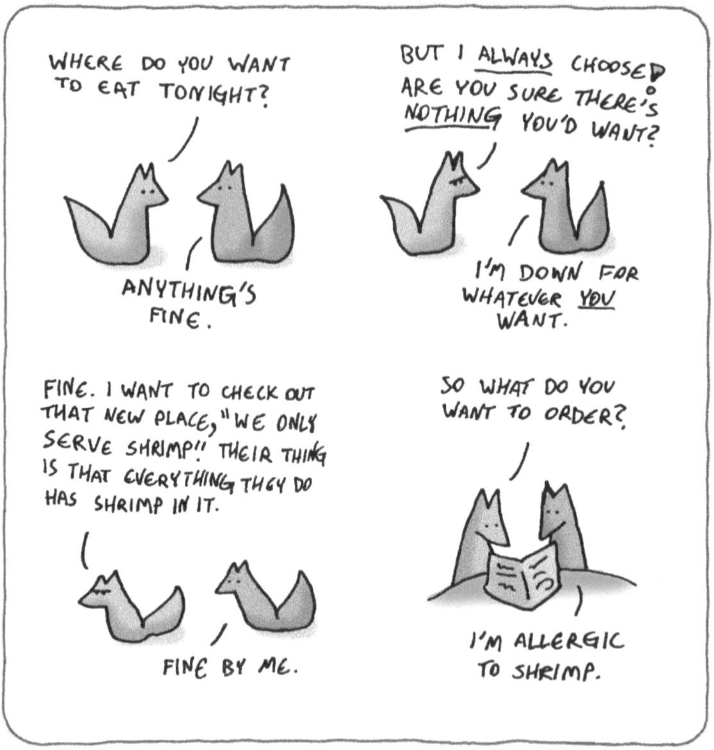
WHERE DO YOU WANT TO EAT TONIGHT?
ANYTHING'S FINE.
BUT I ALWAYS CHOOSE! ARE YOU SURE THERE'S NOTHING YOU'D WANT?
I'M DOWN FOR WHATEVER YOU WANT.
FINE. I WANT TO CHECK OUT THAT NEW PLACE, "WE ONLY SERVE SHRIMP!" THEIR THING IS THAT EVERYTHING THEY DO HAS SHRIMP IN IT.
FINE BY ME.
SO WHAT DO YOU WANT TO ORDER?
I'M ALLERGIC TO SHRIMP.

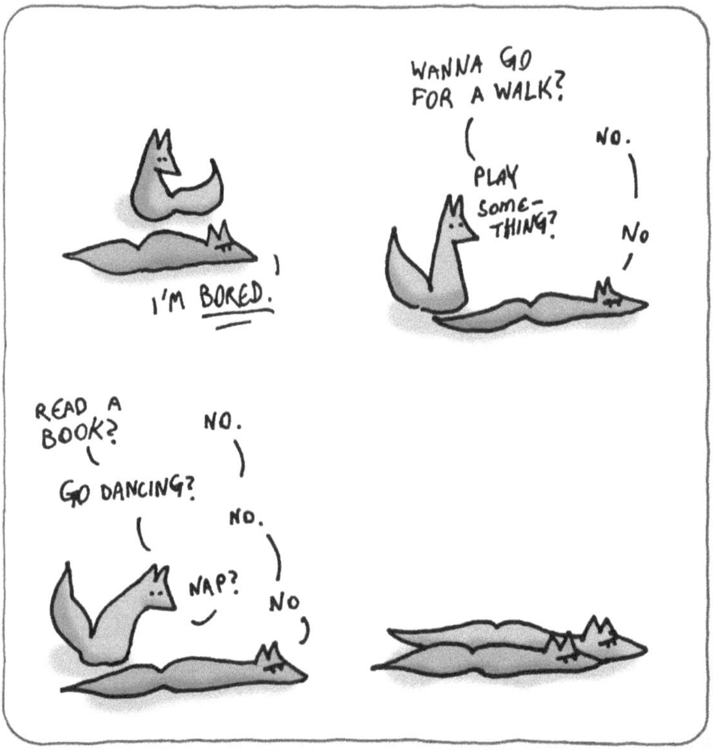
I'M BORED.
WANNA GO FOR A WALK?
NO.
PLAY SOME-THING?
NO
READ A BOOK?
NO.
GO DANCING?
NO.
NAP?
NO

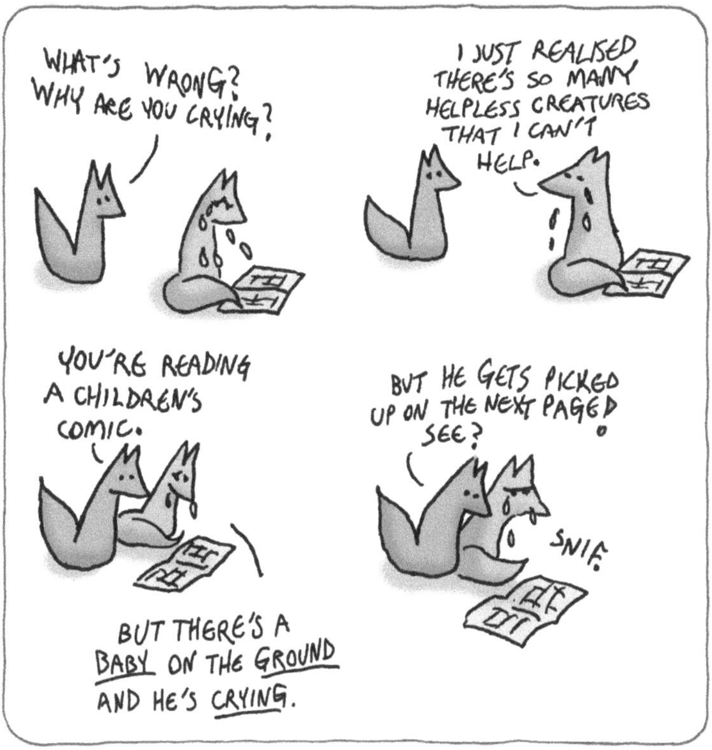
WHAT'S WRONG? WHY ARE YOU CRYING?
I JUST REALISED THERE'S SO MANY HELPLESS CREATURES THAT I CAN'T HELP.
YOU'RE READING A CHILDREN'S COMIC.
BUT THERE'S A BABY ON THE GROUND AND HE'S CRYING.
BUT HE GETS PICKED UP ON THE NEXT PAGE! SEE?
SNIF.

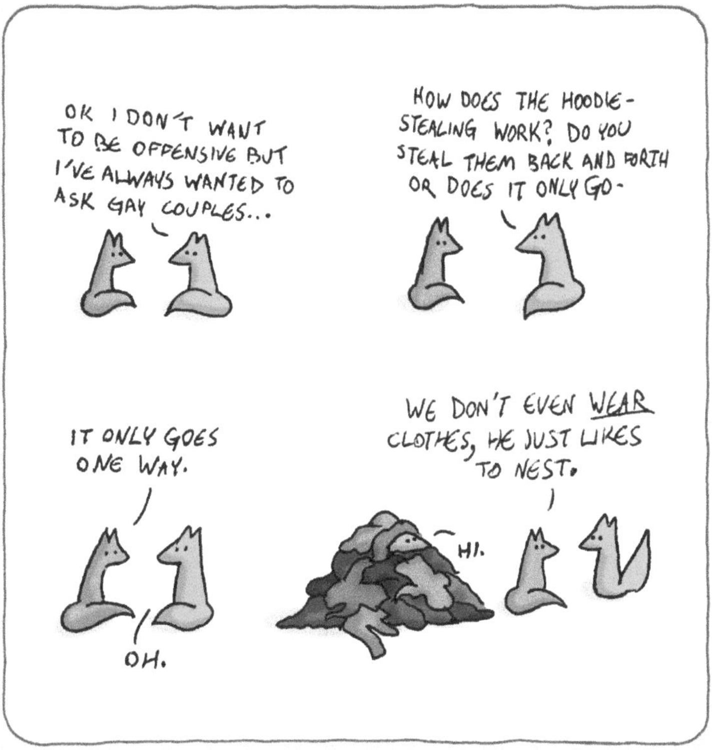
OK I DON'T WANT TO BE OFFENSIVE BUT I'VE ALWAYS WANTED TO ASK GAY COUPLES...
HOW DOES THE HOODIE-STEALING WORK? DO YOU STEAL THEM BACK AND FORTH OR DOES IT ONLY GO-
IT ONLY GOES ONE WAY.
OH.
HI.
WE DON'T EVEN WEAR CLOTHES, HE JUST LIKES TO NEST.

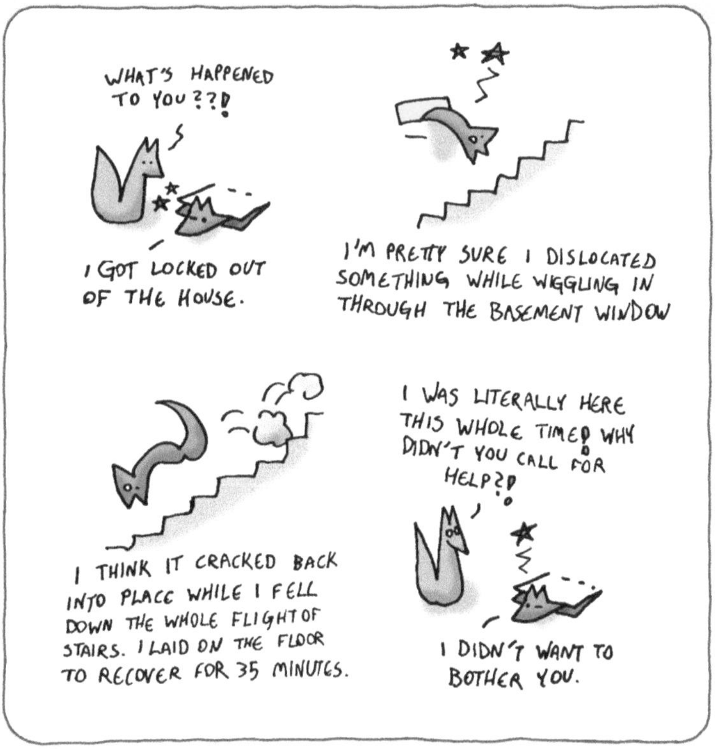
WHAT'S HAPPENED TO YOU??!
I GOT LOCKED OUT OF THE HOUSE.
I'M PRETTY SURE I DISLOCATED SOMETHING WHILE WIGGLING IN THROUGH THE BASEMENT WINDOW
I THINK IT CRACKED BACK INTO PLACE WHILE I FELL DOWN THE WHOLE FLIGHT OF STAIRS. I LAID ON THE FLOOR TO RECOVER FOR 35 MINUTES.
I WAS LITERALLY HERE THIS WHOLE TIME! WHY DIDN'T YOU CALL FOR HELP?!
I DIDN'T WANT TO BOTHER YOU.

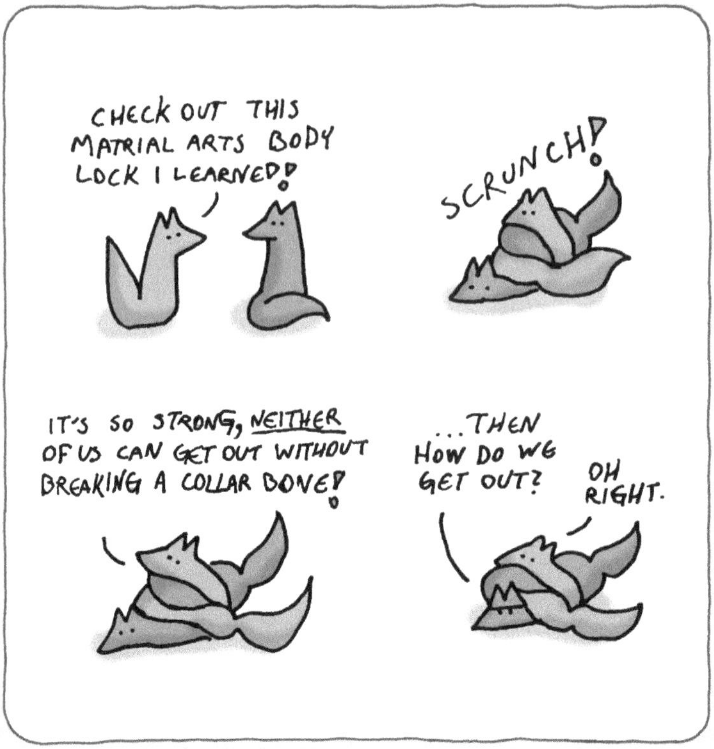
CHECK OUT THIS MATRIAL ARTS BODY LOCK I LEARNED!
SCRUNCH!
IT'S SO STRONG, NEITHER OF US CAN GET OUT WITHOUT BREAKING A COLLAR BONE!
...THEN HOW DO WE GET OUT?
OH RIGHT.

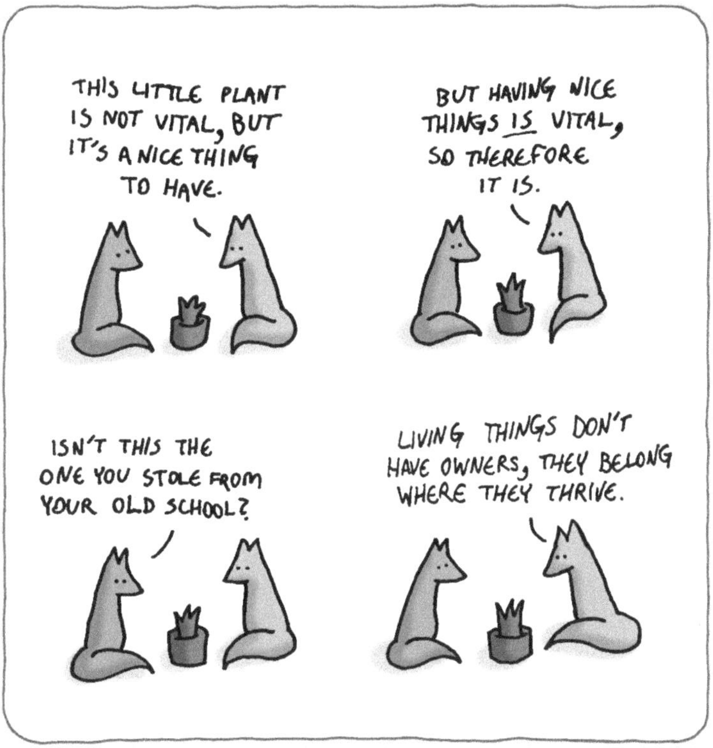
THIS LITTLE PLANT IS NOT VITAL, BUT IT'S A NICE THING TO HAVE.
BUT HAVING NICE THINGS IS VITAL, SO THEREFORE IT IS.
ISN'T THIS THE ONE YOU STOLE FROM YOUR OLD SCHOOL?
LIVING THINGS DON'T HAVE OWNERS, THEY BELONG WHERE THEY THRIVE.

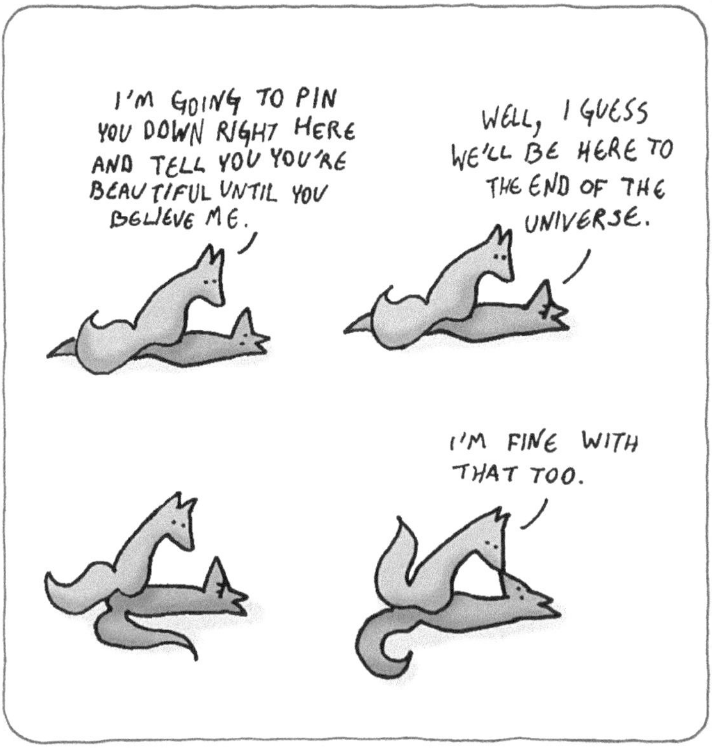
I'M GOING TO PIN YOU DOWN RIGHT HERE AND TELL YOU YOU'RE BEAUTIFUL UNTIL YOU BELIEVE ME.
WELL, I GUESS WE'LL BE HERE TO THE END OF THE UNIVERSE.
I'M FINE WITH THAT TOO.

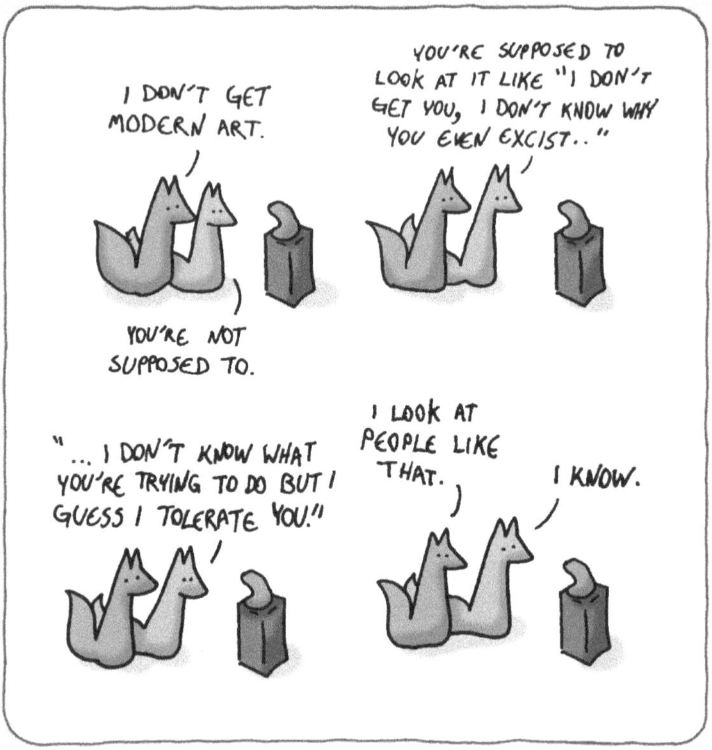
I DON'T GET MODERN ART.
YOU'RE NOT SUPPOSED TO.
YOU'RE SUPPOSED TO LOOK AT IT LIKE "I DON'T GET YOU, I DON'T KNOW WHY YOU EVEN EXCIST.."
"... I DON'T KNOW WHAT YOU'RE TRYING TO DO BUT I GUESS I TOLERATE YOU."
I LOOK AT PEOPLE LIKE THAT.
I KNOW.

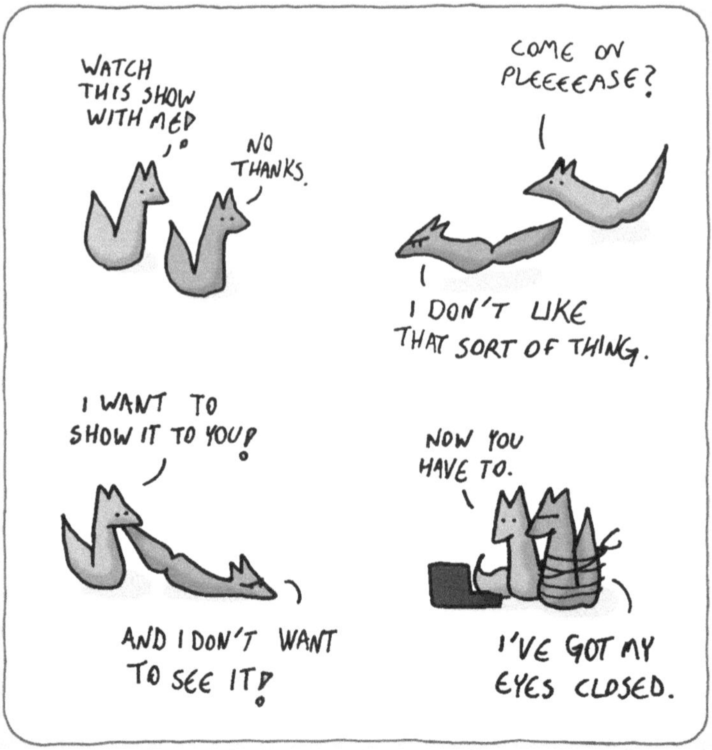
WATCH THIS SHOW WITH ME?
NO THANKS.
COME ON PLEEEEASE?
I DON'T LIKE THAT SORT OF THING.
I WANT TO SHOW IT TO YOU!
AND I DON'T WANT TO SEE IT!
NOW YOU HAVE TO.
I'VE GOT MY EYES CLOSED.

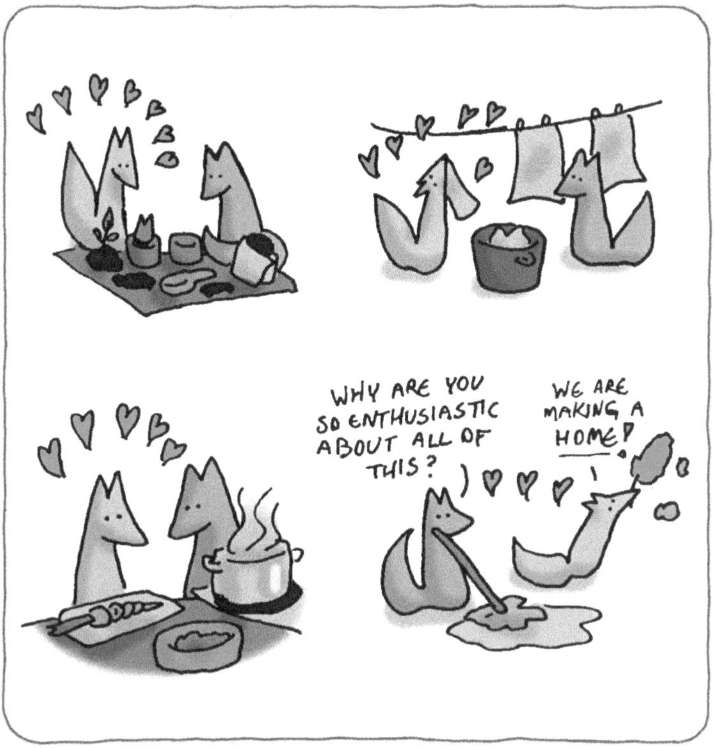
WHY ARE YOU SO ENTHUSIASTIC ABOUT ALL OF THIS?
WE ARE MAKING A HOME!

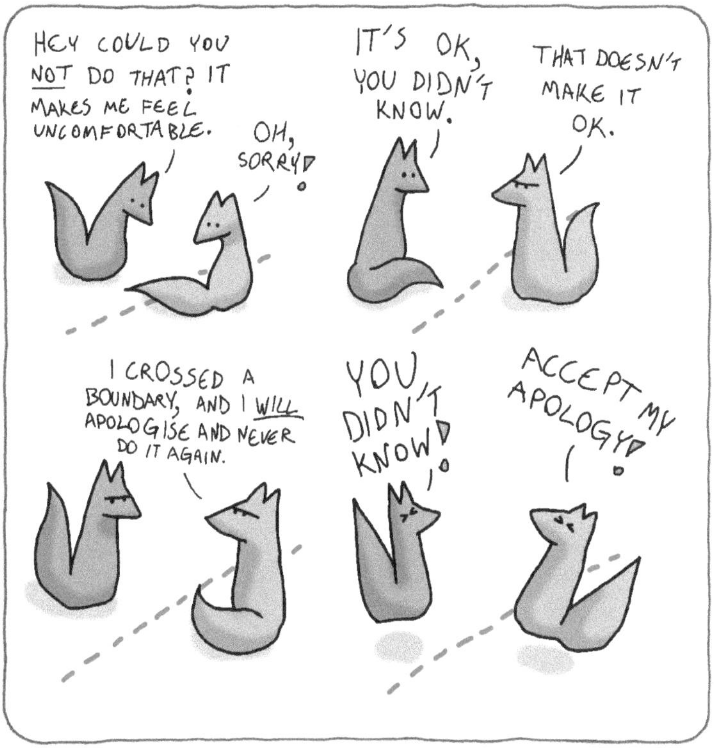
HEY COULD YOU NOT DO THAT? IT MAKES ME FEEL UNCOMFORTABLE.
OH, SORRY!
IT'S OK, YOU DIDN'T KNOW.
THAT DOESN'T MAKE IT OK.
I CROSSED A BOUNDARY, AND I WILL APOLOGISE AND NEVER DO IT AGAIN.
YOU DIDN'T KNOW!
ACCEPT MY APOLOGY!

TOIVO KAARTINEN

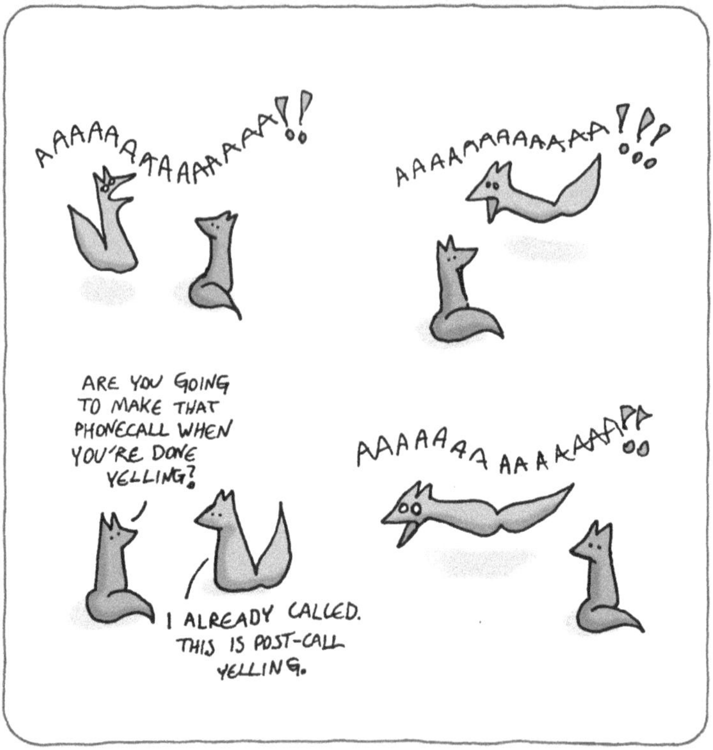

AAAAAAAAAAAAAAAA!!
AAAAAAAAAAAAA!!!
ARE YOU GOING TO MAKE THAT PHONECALL WHEN YOU'RE DONE YELLING?
I ALREADY CALLED. THIS IS POST-CALL YELLING.
AAAAAAAAAAAAAA!!

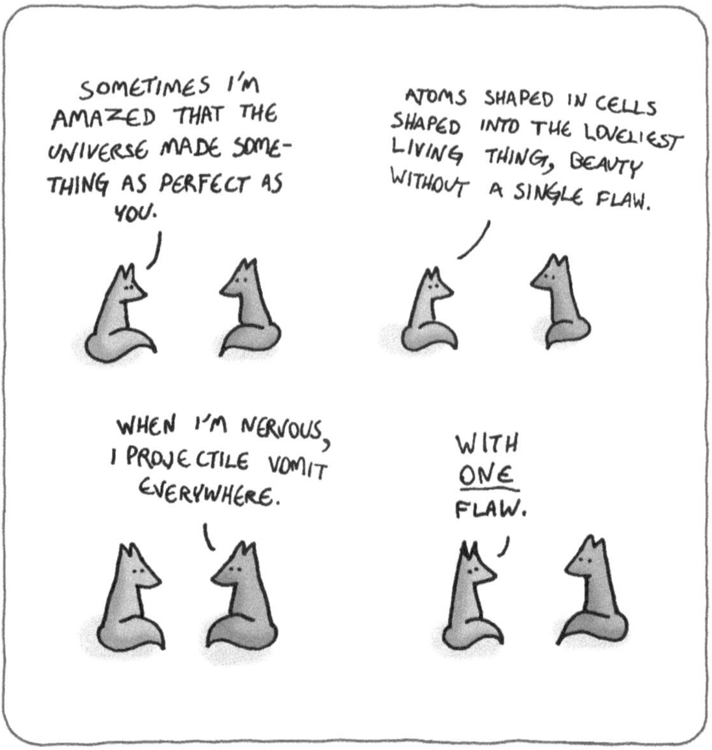

SOMETIMES I'M AMAZED THAT THE UNIVERSE MADE SOME-THING AS PERFECT AS YOU.
ATOMS SHAPED IN CELLS SHAPED INTO THE LOVELIEST LIVING THING, BEAUTY WITHOUT A SINGLE FLAW.
WHEN I'M NERVOUS, I PROJECTILE VOMIT EVERYWHERE.
WITH ONE FLAW.

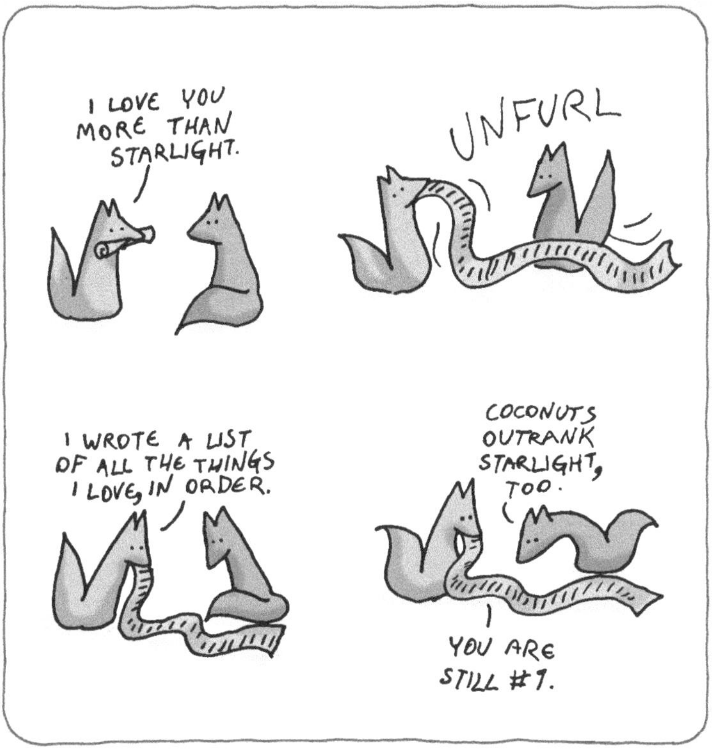
I LOVE YOU MORE THAN STARLIGHT.
UNFURL
I WROTE A LIST OF ALL THE THINGS I LOVE, IN ORDER.
COCONUTS OUTRANK STARLIGHT, TOO.
YOU ARE STILL #1.

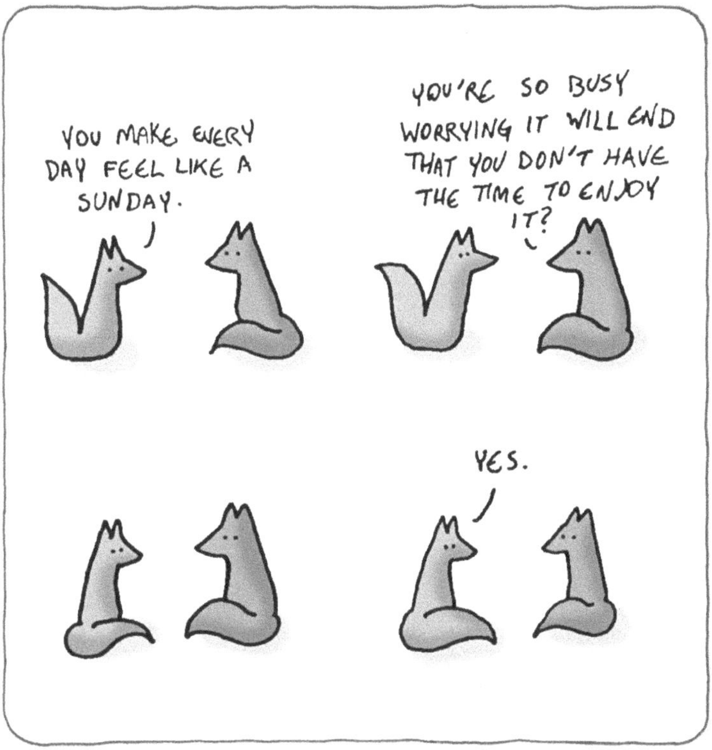
YOU MAKE EVERY DAY FEEL LIKE A SUNDAY.
YOU'RE SO BUSY WORRYING IT WILL END THAT YOU DON'T HAVE THE TIME TO ENJOY IT?
YES.

TOIVO KAARTINEN

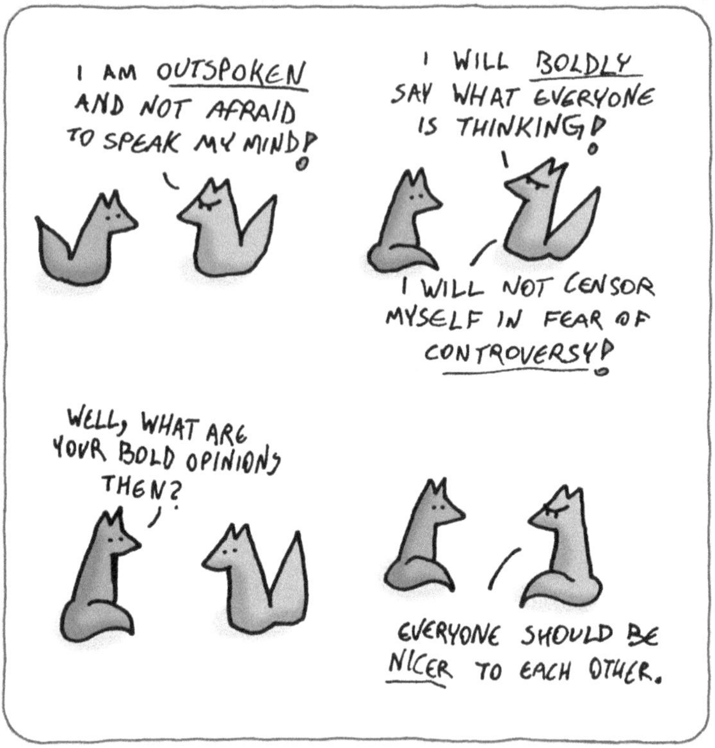
I AM OUTSPOKEN AND NOT AFRAID TO SPEAK MY MIND!
I WILL BOLDLY SAY WHAT EVERYONE IS THINKING!
I WILL NOT CENSOR MYSELF IN FEAR OF CONTROVERSY!
WELL, WHAT ARE YOUR BOLD OPINIONS THEN?
EVERYONE SHOULD BE NICER TO EACH OTHER.

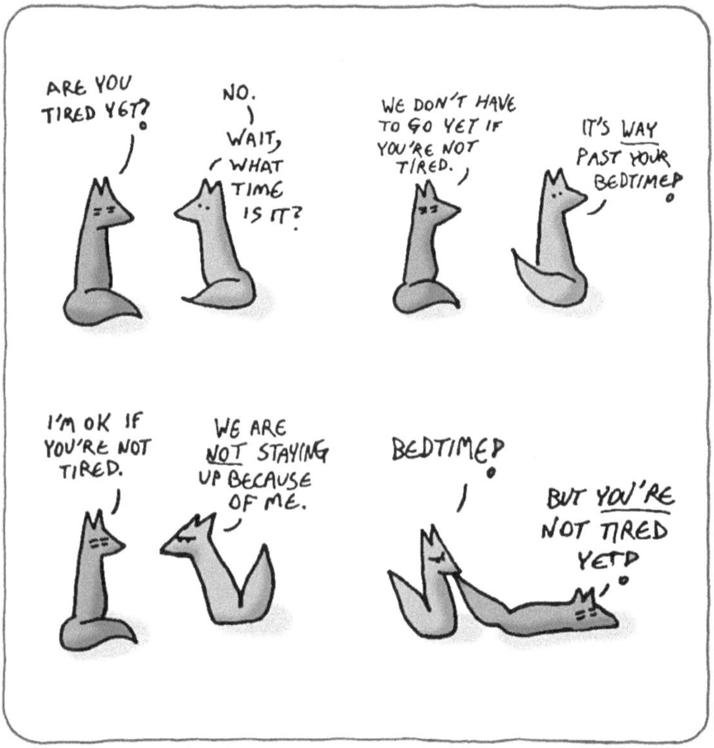
ARE YOU TIRED YET?
NO.
WAIT, WHAT TIME IS IT?
WE DON'T HAVE TO GO YET IF YOU'RE NOT TIRED.
IT'S WAY PAST YOUR BEDTIME!
I'M OK IF YOU'RE NOT TIRED.
WE ARE NOT STAYING UP BECAUSE OF ME.
BEDTIME!
BUT YOU'RE NOT TIRED YET!

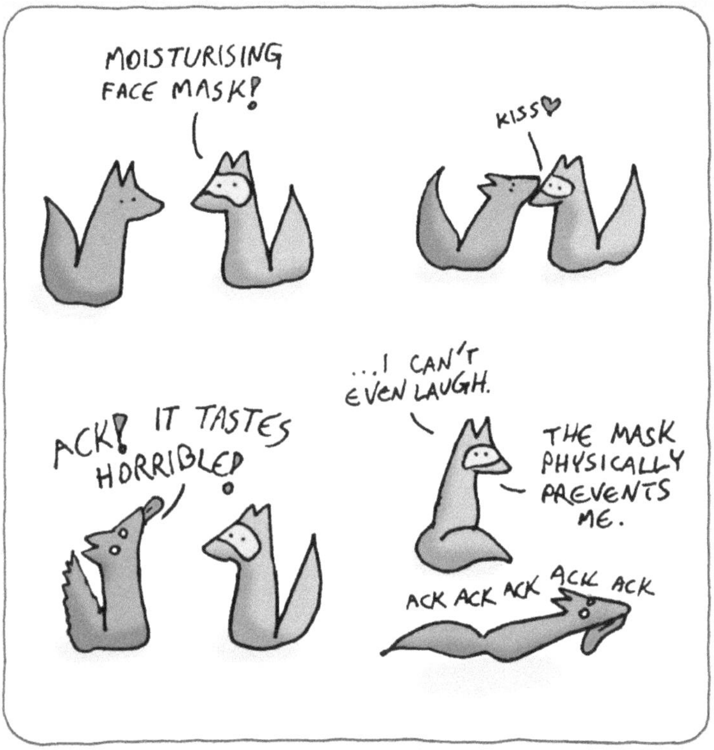
MOISTURISING FACE MASK!
KISS♥
ACK! IT TASTES HORRIBLE!
...I CAN'T EVEN LAUGH.
THE MASK PHYSICALLY PREVENTS ME.
ACK ACK ACK ACK ACK

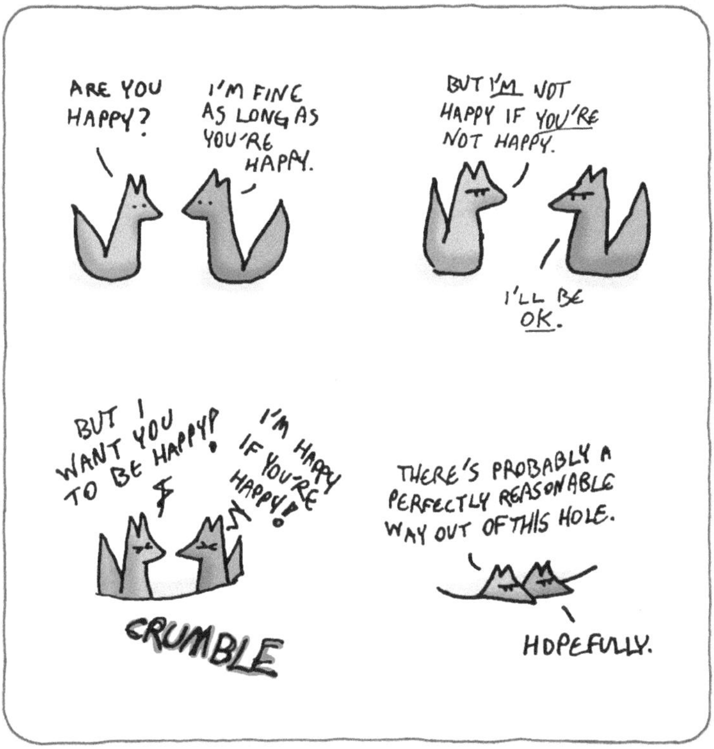
ARE YOU HAPPY?
I'M FINE AS LONG AS YOU'RE HAPPY.
BUT I'M NOT HAPPY IF YOU'RE NOT HAPPY.
I'LL BE OK.
BUT I WANT YOU TO BE HAPPY!
I'M HAPPY IF YOU'RE HAPPY!
CRUMBLE
THERE'S PROBABLY A PERFECTLY REASONABLE WAY OUT OF THIS HOLE.
HOPEFULLY.

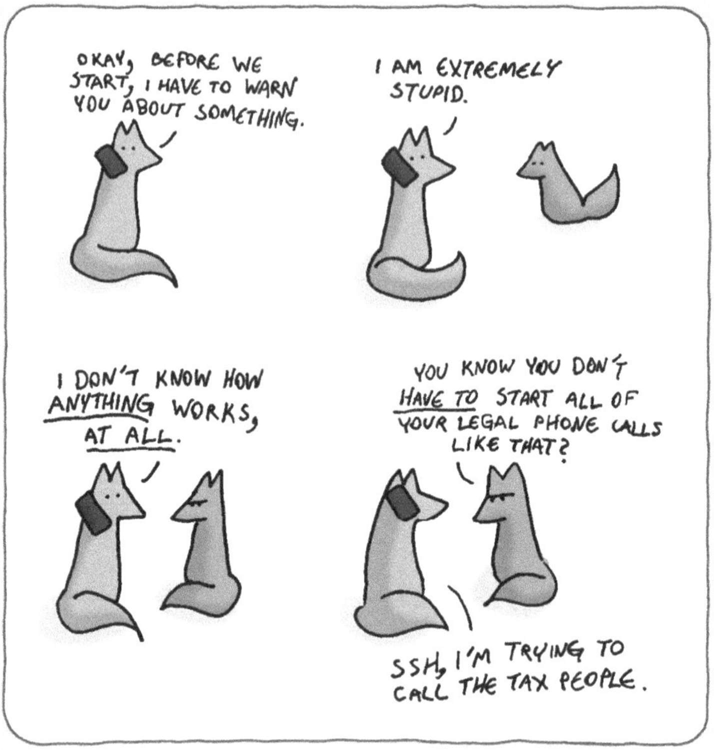
OKAY, BEFORE WE START, I HAVE TO WARN YOU ABOUT SOMETHING.
I AM EXTREMELY STUPID.
I DON'T KNOW HOW ANYTHING WORKS, AT ALL.
YOU KNOW YOU DON'T HAVE TO START ALL OF YOUR LEGAL PHONE CALLS LIKE THAT?
SSH, I'M TRYING TO CALL THE TAX PEOPLE.

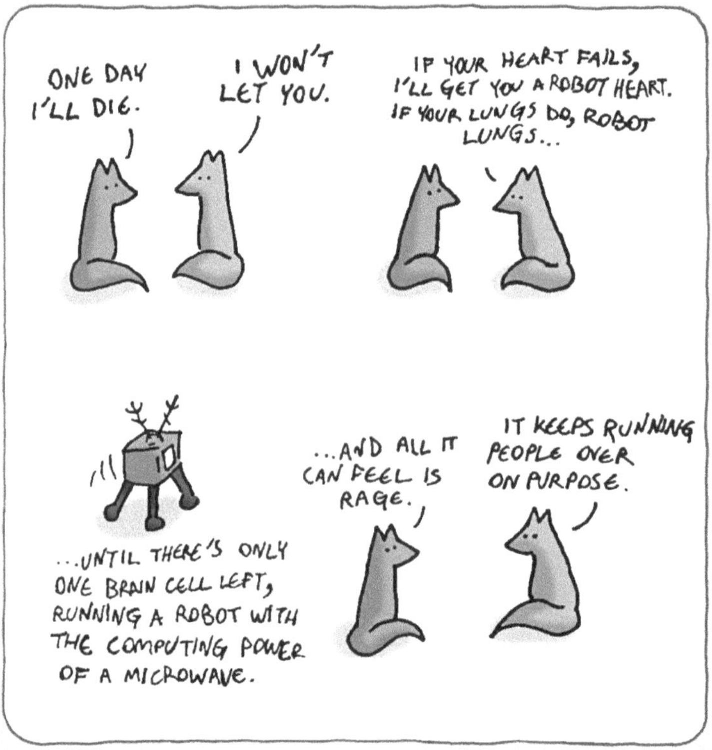
ONE DAY I'LL DIE.
I WON'T LET YOU.
IF YOUR HEART FAILS, I'LL GET YOU A ROBOT HEART. IF YOUR LUNGS DO, ROBOT LUNGS...
...UNTIL THERE'S ONLY ONE BRAIN CELL LEFT, RUNNING A ROBOT WITH THE COMPUTING POWER OF A MICROWAVE.
...AND ALL IT CAN FEEL IS RAGE.
IT KEEPS RUNNING PEOPLE OVER ON PURPOSE.

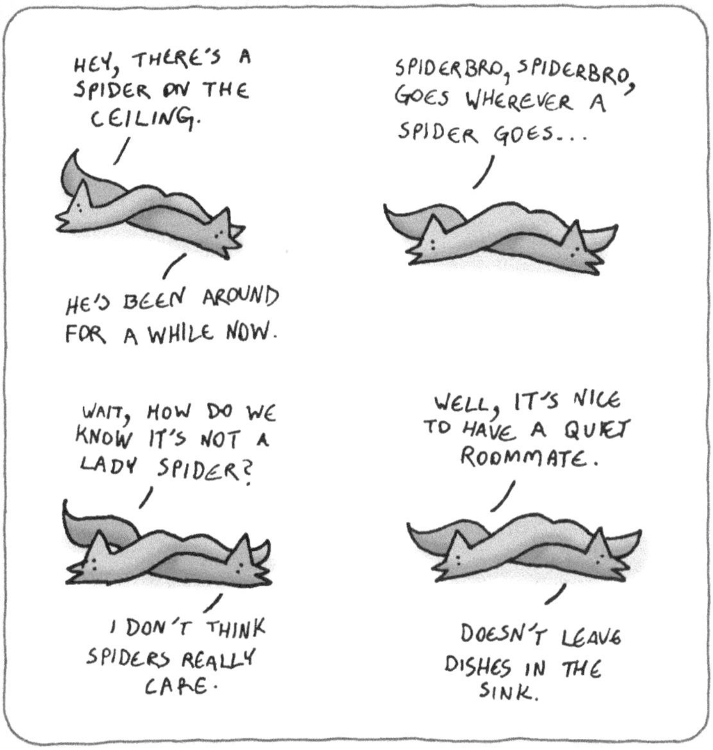
HEY, THERE'S A SPIDER ON THE CEILING.
HE'S BEEN AROUND FOR A WHILE NOW.
SPIDERBRO, SPIDERBRO, GOES WHEREVER A SPIDER GOES...
WAIT, HOW DO WE KNOW IT'S NOT A LADY SPIDER?
I DON'T THINK SPIDERS REALLY CARE.
WELL, IT'S NICE TO HAVE A QUIET ROOMMATE.
DOESN'T LEAVE DISHES IN THE SINK.

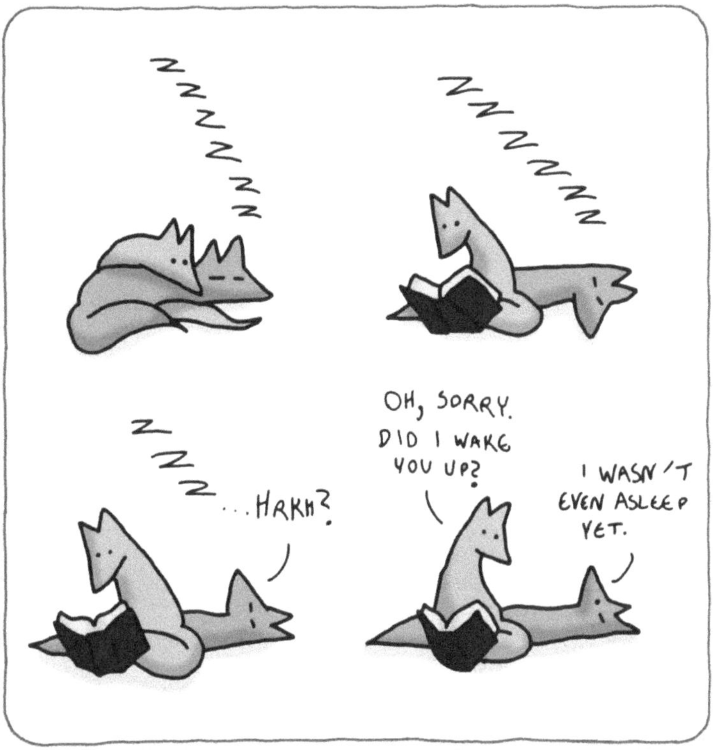
ZZZZZZZ
ZZZZZZZ
ZZZ ...HRKH?
OH, SORRY. DID I WAKE YOU UP?
I WASN'T EVEN ASLEEP YET.

TOIVO KAARTINEN

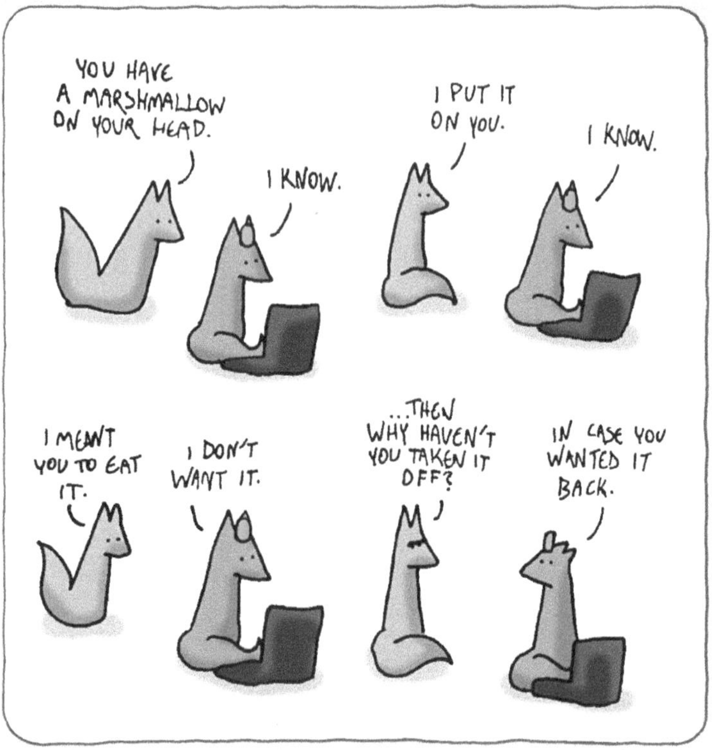
YOU HAVE A MARSHMALLOW ON YOUR HEAD.
I KNOW.
I PUT IT ON YOU.
I KNOW.
I MEANT YOU TO EAT IT.
I DON'T WANT IT.
...THEN WHY HAVEN'T YOU TAKEN IT OFF?
IN CASE YOU WANTED IT BACK.

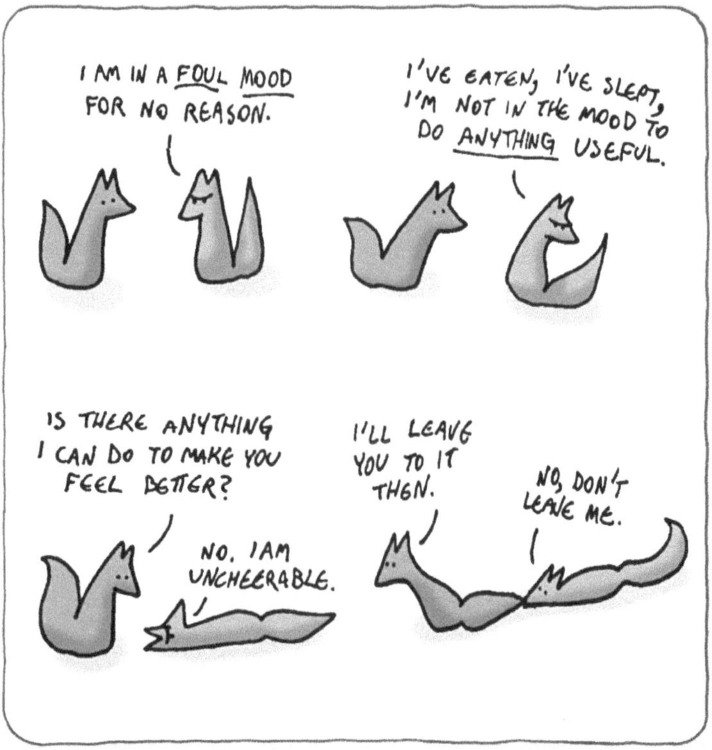
I AM IN A FOUL MOOD FOR NO REASON.
I'VE EATEN, I'VE SLEPT, I'M NOT IN THE MOOD TO DO ANYTHING USEFUL.
IS THERE ANYTHING I CAN DO TO MAKE YOU FEEL BETTER?
NO. I AM UNCHEERABLE.
I'LL LEAVE YOU TO IT THEN.
NO, DON'T LEAVE ME.

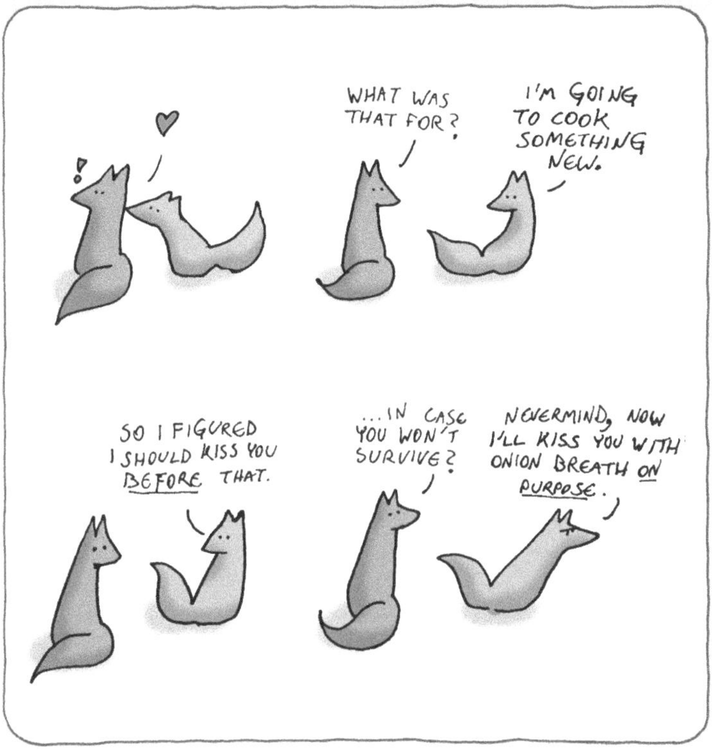
WHAT WAS THAT FOR?
I'M GOING TO COOK SOMETHING NEW.
SO I FIGURED I SHOULD KISS YOU BEFORE THAT.
...IN CASE YOU WON'T SURVIVE?
NEVERMIND, NOW I'LL KISS YOU WITH ONION BREATH ON PURPOSE.

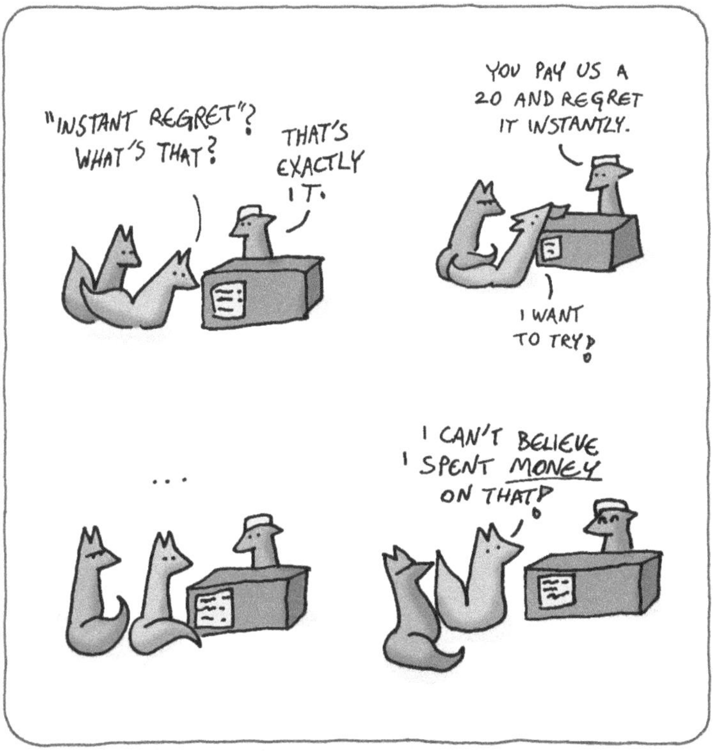
"INSTANT REGRET"? WHAT'S THAT?
THAT'S EXACTLY IT.
YOU PAY US A 20 AND REGRET IT INSTANTLY.
I WANT TO TRY!
...
I CAN'T BELIEVE I SPENT MONEY ON THAT!

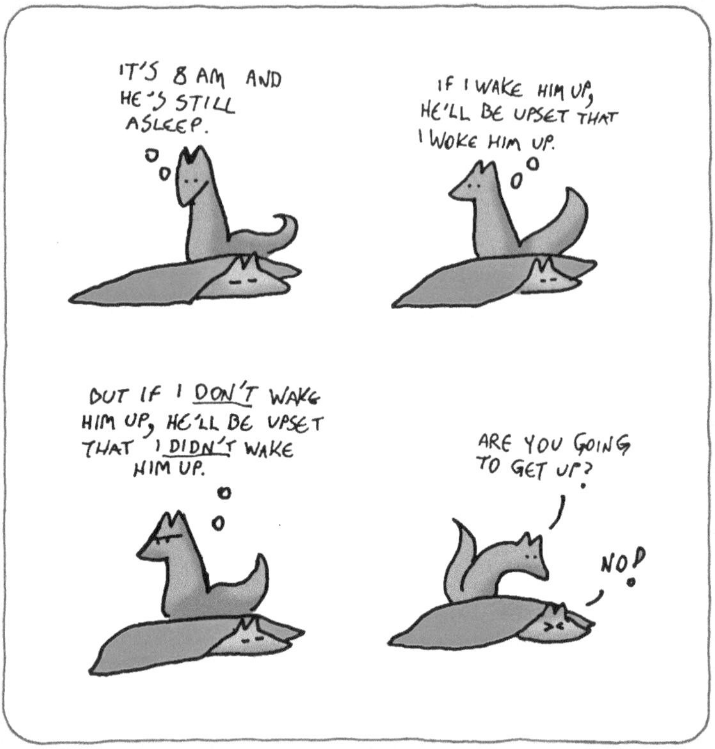
IT'S 8 AM AND HE'S STILL ASLEEP.
IF I WAKE HIM UP, HE'LL BE UPSET THAT I WOKE HIM UP.
BUT IF I DON'T WAKE HIM UP, HE'LL BE UPSET THAT I DIDN'T WAKE HIM UP.
ARE YOU GOING TO GET UP?
NO!

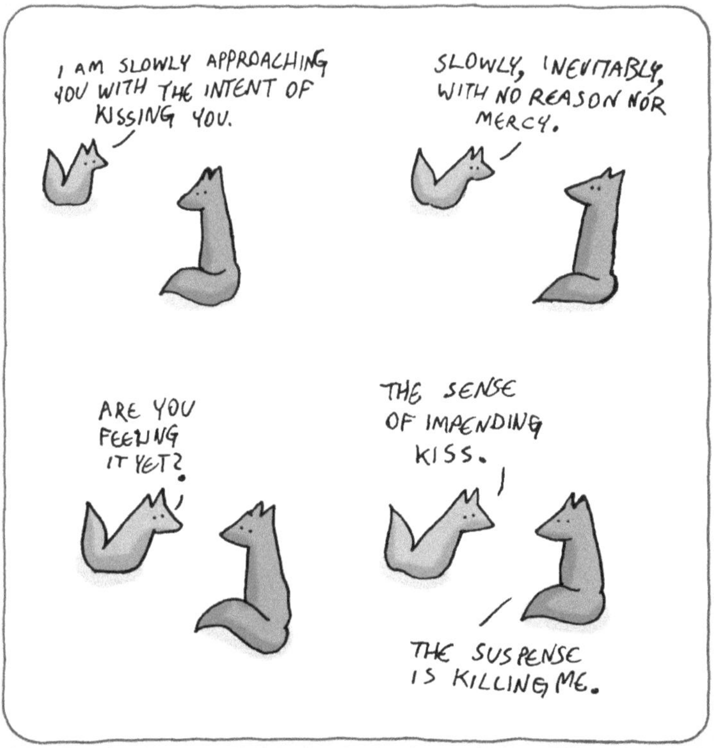
I AM SLOWLY APPROACHING YOU WITH THE INTENT OF KISSING YOU.
SLOWLY, INEVITABLY, WITH NO REASON NOR MERCY.
ARE YOU FEELING IT YET?
THE SENSE OF IMPENDING KISS.
THE SUSPENSE IS KILLING ME.

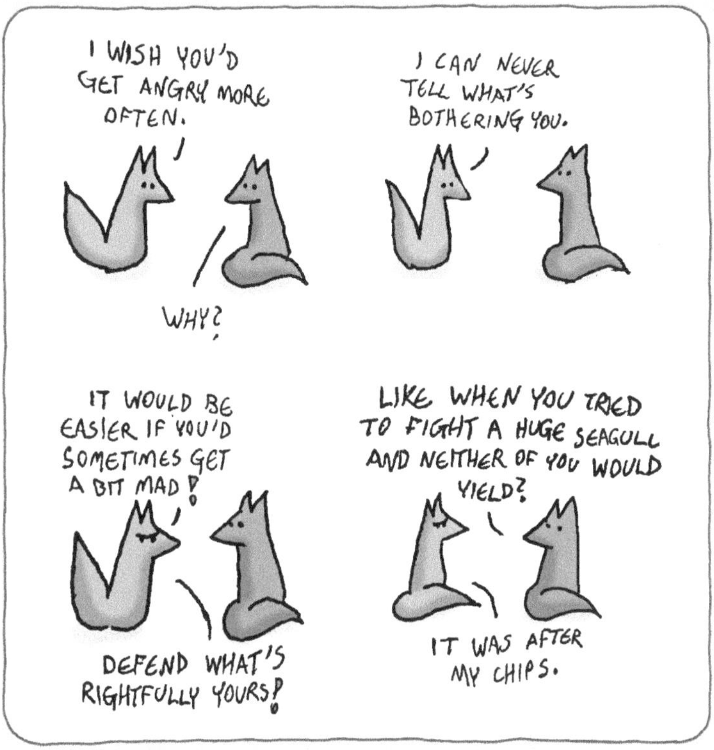
I WISH YOU'D GET ANGRY MORE OFTEN.
WHY?
I CAN NEVER TELL WHAT'S BOTHERING YOU.
IT WOULD BE EASIER IF YOU'D SOMETIMES GET A BIT MAD!
DEFEND WHAT'S RIGHTFULLY YOURS!
LIKE WHEN YOU TRIED TO FIGHT A HUGE SEAGULL AND NEITHER OF YOU WOULD YIELD?
IT WAS AFTER MY CHIPS.

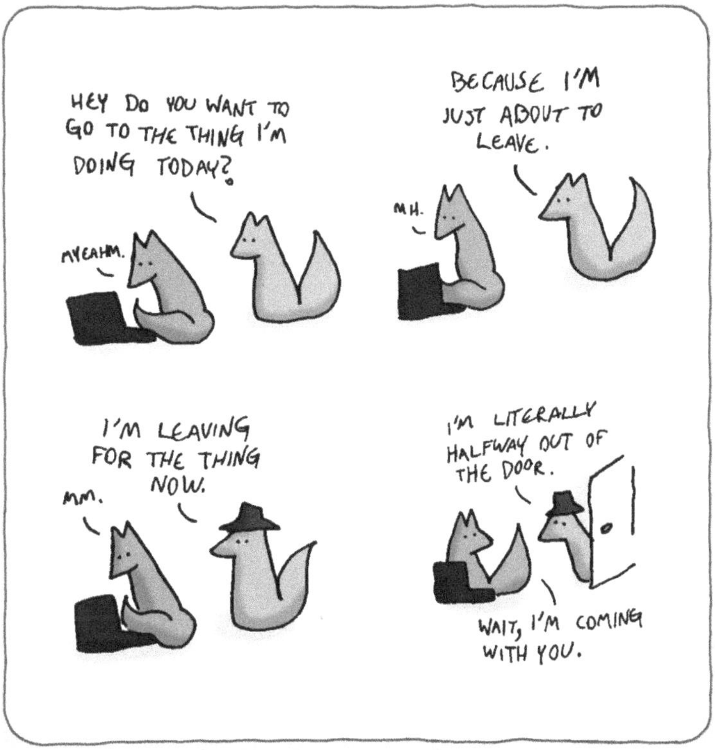
HEY DO YOU WANT TO GO TO THE THING I'M DOING TODAY?
MYEAHM.
BECAUSE I'M JUST ABOUT TO LEAVE.
MH.
I'M LEAVING FOR THE THING NOW.
MM.
I'M LITERALLY HALFWAY OUT OF THE DOOR.
WAIT, I'M COMING WITH YOU.

TOIVO KAARTINEN

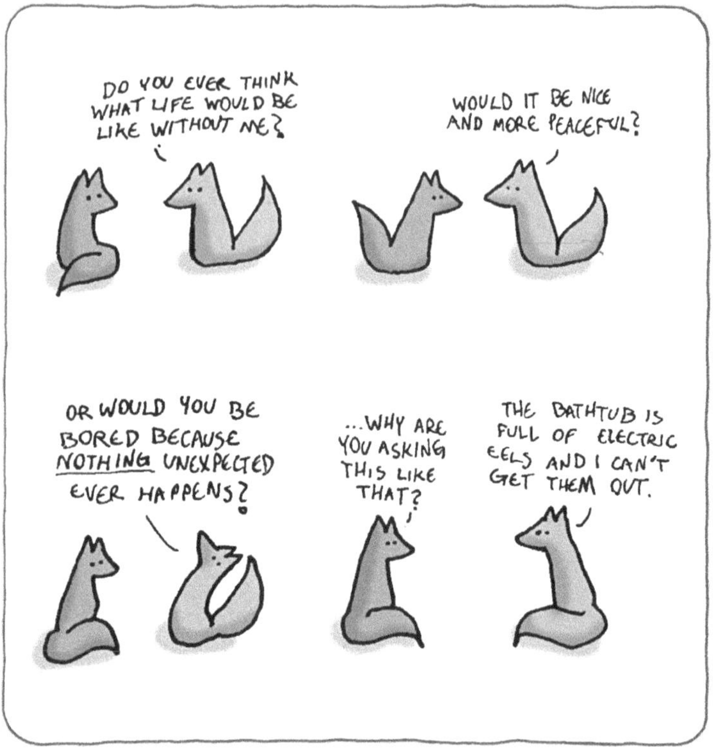

DO YOU EVER THINK WHAT LIFE WOULD BE LIKE WITHOUT ME?
WOULD IT BE NICE AND MORE PEACEFUL?
OR WOULD YOU BE BORED BECAUSE NOTHING UNEXPECTED EVER HAPPENS?
...WHY ARE YOU ASKING THIS LIKE THAT?
THE BATHTUB IS FULL OF ELECTRIC EELS AND I CAN'T GET THEM OUT.

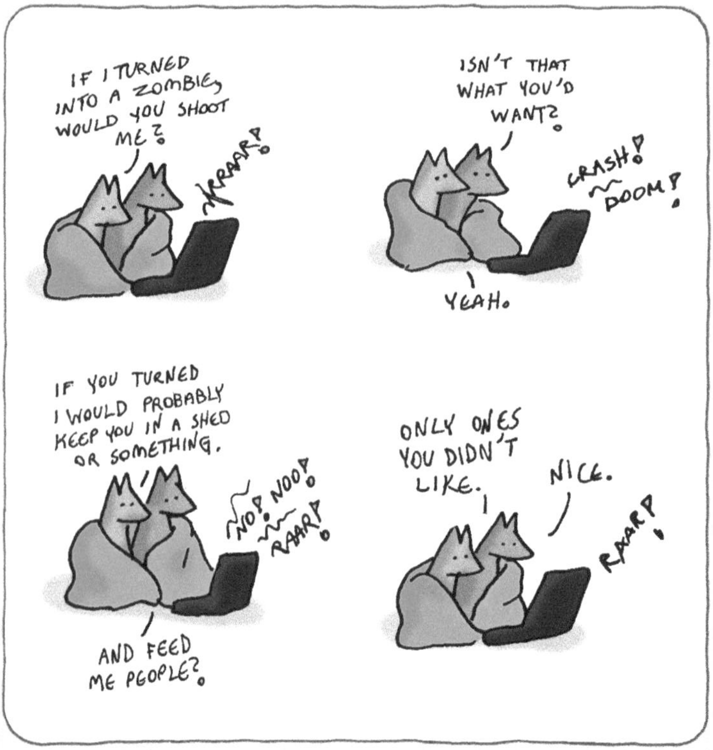

IF I TURNED INTO A ZOMBIE, WOULD YOU SHOOT ME?
RRAAR!
ISN'T THAT WHAT YOU'D WANT?
CRASH!
BOOM!
YEAH.
IF YOU TURNED I WOULD PROBABLY KEEP YOU IN A SHED OR SOMETHING.
NO! NOO!
RAAR!
AND FEED ME PEOPLE?
ONLY ONES YOU DIDN'T LIKE.
NICE.
RAAR!

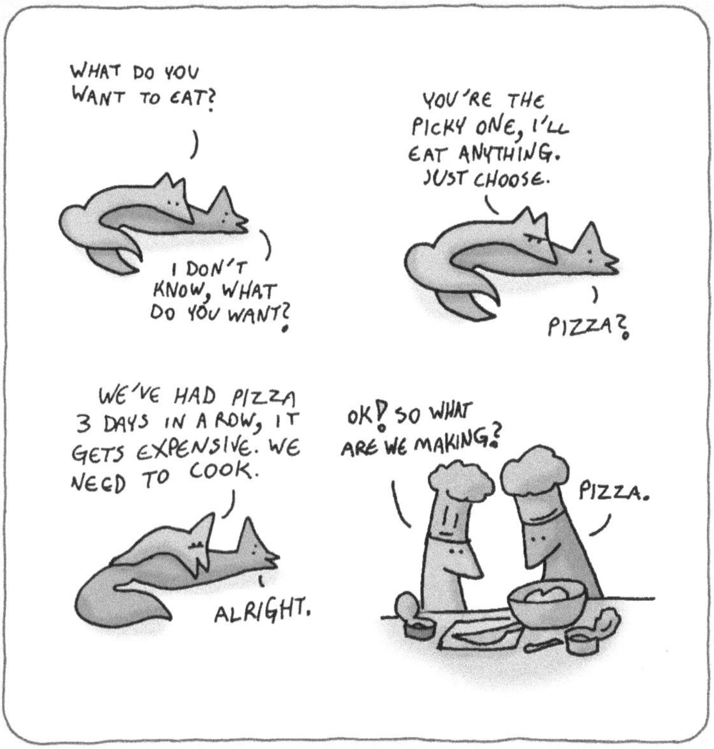
WHAT DO YOU WANT TO EAT?
I DON'T KNOW, WHAT DO YOU WANT?
YOU'RE THE PICKY ONE, I'LL EAT ANYTHING. JUST CHOOSE.
PIZZA?
WE'VE HAD PIZZA 3 DAYS IN A ROW, IT GETS EXPENSIVE. WE NEED TO COOK.
ALRIGHT.
OK! SO WHAT ARE WE MAKING?
PIZZA.

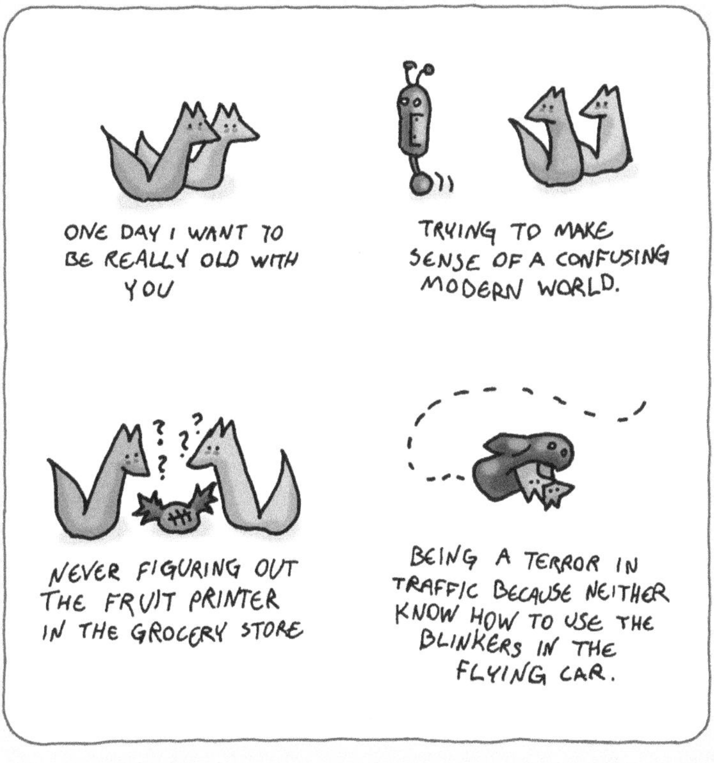
ONE DAY I WANT TO BE REALLY OLD WITH YOU
TRYING TO MAKE SENSE OF A CONFUSING MODERN WORLD.
NEVER FIGURING OUT THE FRUIT PRINTER IN THE GROCERY STORE
BEING A TERROR IN TRAFFIC BECAUSE NEITHER KNOW HOW TO USE THE BLINKERS IN THE FLYING CAR.

Lightning Source UK Ltd.
Milton Keynes UK
UKHW020807021121
393239UK00007B/164

9 780999 591642